Teaching Beyond the Diagnosis

Teaching Beyond the Diagnosis

Empowering Students with Dyslexia

Casey Harrison

JB JOSSEY-BASS™
A Wiley Brand

Published by John Wiley & Sons, Inc., Hoboken, New Jersey.
Published simultaneously in Canada.

For general information on our other products and services or for technical support, please contact our Customer Care Department within the United States at (800) 762-2974, outside the United States at (317) 572-3993 or fax (317) 572-4002.

Wiley also publishes its books in a variety of electronic formats. Some content that appears in print may not be available in electronic formats. For more information about Wiley products, visit our web site at www.wiley.com.

Library of Congress Control Number: 2024950122

ISBN 9781394196319 (paperback)
ISBN 9781394196326 (ePDF)
ISBN 9781394196333 (ePub)

Cover Design: Wiley
Cover Images: © Depiano/Shutterstock, © MARIIA VASILEVA/Getty Images
Author Photo: © Abbie Yeary

SKY10096968_012325

"We delight in the beauty of the butterfly but rarely admit the changes it has gone through to achieve that beauty." —Maya Angelou

To those students who are on this transformative journey of learning to read—your effort and determination are truly inspiring.

To those who walk the path alongside those with dyslexia—I see you, I appreciate you, and I am grateful for your support.

Contents

Preface

From a young age, I have viewed life as a journey—a series of experiences with a wide range of emotions, struggles, and successes that create opportunities to learn, grow, and shift our thinking about ourselves and the world in which we live. In part, this is due to witnessing systems at a young age in which children operating outside of the norms were left without understanding or proper support and experiencing firsthand the impact on the families fighting to be heard, leaving me with a sense of seeking to know more from different perspectives and standing up for those unable. Our experiences impact us profoundly, leaving a lasting mark on how we perceive ourselves as students, learners, and humans. I continue to carry this same sense of curiosity, wondering, and reflection on our experiences from my youth into my work as an educator and dyslexia therapist working closely with students and families.

We each have a history—a series of events that align to create our path, our journey. Speaking to children or adults with dyslexia, it is clear that the lasting threads of the impacts of dyslexia can remain, even when receiving proper academic interventions. The question then is how can we establish and promote a journey that honors the dyslexic learner and leads to the best possible outcomes?

Over the last two decades, this reality has led me to deepen my knowledge and strengthen my understanding of dyslexia, reading instruction, and the impacts that may exist outside of the narrow view of academic success. As a curious person who often asks why and seeks to understand views from different disciplines and research such as neuroscience, psychology, speech pathology, linguistics, literacy research, and more, the threads that weave together as areas of impact on learning and dyslexia became a big part of my educational journey and encompassed seeking information from these varying areas of study. I was drawn to courses and intense training, which led to specialized licenses and certifications specific to dyslexia. From my work with students, my desire to learn more about how dyslexia impacts one beyond academics and what research from other disciplines shows about learning grew, and I dug into readings, training, and research, which has allowed me to shift my approach to address the many facets experienced by those with dyslexia to address the whole child.

When approached about writing a book about dyslexia, the amount of topics to cover within dyslexia education seemed overwhelming—and I wanted to share it all with you, the reader. Yet, as this book came to be, I realized that to share with educators and interventionists a focus on how to deepen their skill set of teaching those with dyslexia while also addressing the impacts of the cascading effects of dyslexia, those areas outside of academics, through the integrated framework that I use within my work with children was needed. Therefore, this book acts as a guide and source of encouragement. It offers strategies, insights, and lessons for educators and families supporting students with dyslexia. It is not a reading program, nor does it dig into the deeper levels of academics, but instead offers a different perspective that pulls together the multiple factors (dyslexia awareness, academics and scaffolding, metacognitive awareness and strategies, self-advocacy, and success) that impact academic success for those with dyslexia and seeks to empower and encourage both student and educator.

While dyslexia awareness and the science of reading movement have created considerable momentum regarding instructional implementation in reading, much more work and awareness are needed to keep the focus on emotionally sound instruction, the whole child and for whom the instruction is addressing. The vast amount of research and information regarding evidence-based practices means that the next steps of implementation, embedding, and reflecting upon those practices that look beyond the diagnosis of dyslexia and how to bridge the research-to-implementation gap are upon us. Addressing academics in connection to preserving and developing a strong sense of self-worth and independence beyond a diagnosis of dyslexia cannot be overshadowed.

Without conversations about dyslexia, a reflection of our thinking, and shifting the narrative, a lingering sense of failure or imposter syndrome remains. Instead, we want our students to have a deeper understanding of themselves as learners and the courage to step into the arena, face struggles, and recognize their work and success—as Theodore Roosevelt said, to dare greatly.

So here I share with you the path or journey I use with my students, coming from the viewpoint of someone in the arena with the students, their families, and other educators. My integrated framework is comprehensive, incorporating the many aspects required to help those with dyslexia reach their personal potential and empower students, families, and educators. As you read this book, understand that there is no "one-size-fits-all" when working on closing the academic gaps and that, as such, educators must fully utilize and seek ways to effectively maximize their knowledge of dyslexia and evidence-based practices with multiple resources to reach as many children as possible. Regardless of the evidence-based program in use, the integrated framework can be embedded by specialists, educators, therapists, and caregivers with actionable steps and lessons from the field to empower you to teach beyond the diagnosis and, in turn, empower the students you serve.

With gratitude that you join me on this learning journey,
Casey Harrison

Introduction

Take a moment and look at this artwork titled *Dyslexia Beach* by Paddy Donnelly (see Figure 1). You see a young child sitting on the beach surrounded by letters. Notice his isolation as his peers sail away after figuring out how to put those lines and squiggles together to represent the sounds in the words that set them on their reading journey. This artwork highlights how many children with dyslexia feel. Alone and anxious about being left behind. Looking closer, you will see the little boy holding the letter Y. **Why?**

As each school year starts, parents and students head off to school excited to learn to read and write. However, year after year, the stories parents share with me contain a common thread. Parents come with heavy hearts, sharing stories of their child's struggle to read. More often than not, their child began school happy and excited about learning, and as the struggles with reading and writing became more apparent, the child's emotions were also impacted. Much like the little boy sitting on the beach, they saw their peers taking off in reading and writing, leaving them to withdraw, act out, or silently struggle—all impacting their self-esteem and confidence, leaving parents wondering what to do.

Our dyslexic students are often left behind. They are also the leading indicators of what is and isn't working. We can determine how effective our teaching approach is by observing how our struggling readers progress.

FIGURE 1 Dyslexia Beach.
Source: https://lefft.com/dyslexia-beach/. Reprinted with permission.

They are often the ones who first signal what is wrong. Yet, we may not recognize the impact of their early struggles nor reflect on why we are leaving some kids behind.

Teachers desire all children in their classrooms to achieve proficient reading and writing and also feel this lingering question of why. Why isn't this child responding to my instruction? Why wasn't I given the tools to help those with dyslexia in my teacher preparation courses? As a reading teacher and educator, I, too, held these questions of why, which led me to seek out specific knowledge and training to understand dyslexia and profoundly shifted my teaching. Two decades later, I remain steadfast in my resolve to bring awareness of dyslexia, literacy, and change to our classrooms. This is my why, because in today's society, the written word is everywhere. While reading well is something many of us take for granted, overlooking the significance of the difficulty of achieving literacy cannot occur. I hear the same questions from educators time and time again. **Why?**

- **Why** is it so hard for this child, and why can't he do what others do?
- **Why** are they struggling when they are clearly bright?
- **Why** are reading and writing so challenging for this student?
- **Why** isn't this child able to keep up with the lessons?
- **Why** isn't he progressing?
- **Why** can't I teach him?

All the while, the child also asks **why**. Why can't I do what others are doing? Why is this so hard? Why isn't this making sense? Why can't the teacher help me? Why am I so bad at reading? **Why?** Although they may not realize those exact questions, their self-esteem and confidence are shaken. Through my years of working as a dyslexia therapist and educator, I have seen the impacts that dyslexia can have on students when we fail to address academics properly, as well as the impacts students encounter in their daily lives. Students with dyslexia are often confused as to why they aren't able to do what seems to come so easily for their peers. They are confused about why the teacher or parents tell them they are bright, yet reading and writing are so hard. They may begin not to trust themselves or the adults in their lives as things feel contradictory.

When working with students, I can see that this question of why surrounds our children and impacts their academics and self-esteem. I have also seen the tremendous impact that a teacher who understands dyslexia can have on their student's learning when we reshape the teaching framework we use to one that answers the call to provide the proper support to address academic needs and a more comprehensive look at dyslexia. Through my work, an integrated framework has become the backbone of my lesson. One that intentionally weaves in proper instruction with executive function skills and metacognition, self-esteem, and agency, all to empower the student within and beyond the educational setting. This integrated framework is carefully laid out in the pages of this book to guide and empower our practice and, in turn, the students whom we serve.

Reflection:

As we move through the book and the integrated framework, remember this young boy or think of a child in your classroom or home who is left behind in the sand. Throughout the framework, return to this child and reflect on ways in which intentionally implementing the integrated framework can support academics and well-being.

What Is the Integrated Framework for Teaching and Empowering Students with Dyslexia?

The integrated framework for teaching and empowering students with dyslexia aims to connect the vital importance of the academic pursuit of teaching students with dyslexia to the whole child—the development of self-advocacy skills, accommodations, metacognitive processes, and meaningful scaffolds to help all children with dyslexia reach their potential (see Figure 2). All of these set the student up for success and self-confidence.

The integrated framework for teaching and empowering students with dyslexia encompasses the following elements, laying the foundation for our work. We begin with the big picture, a more extensive viewpoint, and an idea of where we are going along this journey and the path to success, then break down these elements throughout the book's chapters.

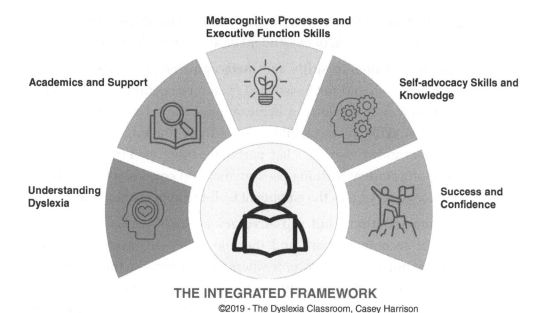

THE INTEGRATED FRAMEWORK
©2019 - The Dyslexia Classroom, Casey Harrison

FIGURE 2 The integrated framework.

The integrated framework for teaching and empowering students with dyslexia includes:

- **A deep understanding of dyslexia**—In this part of the journey, it is imperative that all learning team members (educators, students, parents, schools) understand what dyslexia is/isn't and its impacts on academics and beyond. We need to be empowered to say the word "dyslexia" to deepen our understanding and look at impacts within and beyond academics.

- **Appropriate academic instruction and support**—This part of the journey focuses on research and what this means for our instructional practices. Proper instruction, scaffolds, and support must be grounded in a deep understanding of research and evidence-based instructional practices encompassing multisensory, explicit instruction in all components of literacy development tailored to address the intensity, duration, and needs of the student based on their learning profile.

- **Executive function skills and metacognitive processes**—Dyslexia instruction should not be isolated from metacognitive processes but instead woven into lessons in meaningful ways. Fostering executive function skills, metacognition, and critical thinking skills for both teachers and students is a key part of the integrated framework that supports student learning performance and considers the academic outcomes as well as the emotional well-being of the student.

- **Accommodations and self-advocacy skills**—The knowledge and use of accommodations and the role of self-advocacy to support learner outcomes empower teachers and students on this journey. By empowering students with the tools, language, and skills that set them up for success within the classroom and beyond, they can embrace agency in their journey.

- **Success and confidence**—Our goal as we walk along this path with students is to leave them empowered with the knowledge and confidence in themselves as learners with dyslexia.

The integrated framework is the path that came from this desire to create a better system for students and to assist children in attaining the goal of preserving their self-confidence while understanding themselves as learners and their journey with dyslexia. It is not done in lock-step or isolation but becomes a tapestry of parts that enhance learning and empower students, families, and educators. I have found that the integrated framework assists children in achieving academic success while preserving or building up their self-esteem, metacognitive strategies, and self-advocacy skills. The lasting impact of this framework of instruction is apparent in the words shared by students. Through their words, they show the confidence and pride they now hold for themselves as they walk into classrooms and the world and speak to the power of the integrated framework.

"I want teachers to know that they should not put a ceiling on what I can do. Just because I'm dyslexic doesn't mean that I can only read aloud one sentence while my classmates read whole paragraphs. I can do the very same things that they do!"

—S. (student)

"My brain just processes information in a different way. It has nothing to do with how smart I am. If how you are teaching isn't working for me, just explain it to me in a different way. Break it down and give me time."

—G. (student)

Too often in education, we solely focus on the academic deficits and needs—however, without the other components, we often leave students with incomplete knowledge and awareness of their journey with dyslexia and the tools and confidence to reach their full potential.

A Call for an Integrated Framework

Teaching reading is a complex task. Teaching reading to students with dyslexia requires even more knowledge and understanding from the educator. We are encountering significant shifts in instructional approaches to teaching reading, and much information about this topic focuses on the academic components. It can be found in numerous books, courses, articles, and blogs, including mine. Many of these evidence-based practices have been in place for some time within dyslexia interventions, and we see more and more teachers and schools implementing lessons grounded in collective research called the science of reading. The science of reading is not a program or pedagogy but a vast body of research done across multiple disciplines over the last century about how we learn to read and write, much derived from the research findings in the field of dyslexia. As educators, we must understand that research is ever-evolving and uncovering new findings about how we learn to read, and therefore, the science of reading is active.

Even so, we have agreed upon research, empirical findings, and explanatory theories, or the science in the term "science of reading," to guide us in instructional practices. The research provides us with the information, while the application is the science of teaching. Current research suggests that we know a great deal about how reading works, how students learn, what to teach when, to whom, and in what dosage. How we put this into work is the art of teaching. Connecting the research to educational practices is crucial for our students, especially those at risk of reading failure or dyslexia. Failure to provide high-quality instruction and intervention at the early grades, when the brain is more malleable, can manifest as serious reading disabilities later (Stanovich 1986, 2009), and while it is never too late to intervene, with the knowledge of dyslexia and the research, we need not wait for students to experience repeated failure before addressing dyslexia. The growing knowledge and continued research is a beacon of hope for our students, especially those who are struggling with reading. This book focuses on bridging the findings of this body of work to evidence-based instructional approaches and practices grounded in research through a structured literacy approach to help serve those students with dyslexia.

> The science of reading is a vast, interdisciplinary body of scientifically-based research about reading and issues related to reading and writing. This research has been conducted over the last five decades across the world, and it is derived from thousands of studies conducted in multiple languages. The science of reading has culminated in a preponderance of evidence to inform how proficient reading and writing develop; why some have difficulty; and how we can most effectively assess and teach and, therefore, improve student outcomes through prevention of and intervention for reading difficulties. (The Reading League, Science of Reading: Definition Guide)

The good news is that we know so much about how to help our students with foundational reading skills to become proficient readers and writers. Decades of evidence and research support the use of explicit, systematic instruction of the five pillars of literacy (phonemic awareness, phonics, fluency, vocabulary, comprehension) identified by the National Reading Panel, which should be at the core of every effective reading instruction program (2000). These large pillars of reading include a vast amount of instructional components under each pillar or band, all of which are necessary for ensuring student success in reading acquisition. While this report was written over 20 years ago, the research remains the foundation for building reading instruction today. Using decades of research, the National Reading Panel Report (2000) identified five critical areas at the core of every effective reading instruction program. The report also determined that systematic and explicit instruction was the most reliable approach to teaching these elements. While the five pillars are necessary for all educators to understand, I have added the domains of language under the pillars, as language provides the foundation for literacy instruction and should be included in our instructional practices as everything we do in education is rooted in language (see Figure 3). Language is the vehicle for learning, and in turn, literacy is the language of opportunity.

The five pillars for foundational reading instruction (NRP):

- Phonemic awareness (phoneme awareness)—Awareness of the smallest units of sound in speech, and the ability to isolate, segment, blend, or manipulate the individual phonemes (sounds) in words.

- Phonics—Phonics is the paired association between sounds and letter representations (phoneme-grapheme correspondences); explicit instruction to teaching reading and spelling that emphasizes sound-symbol relationships.

- Fluency—The ability to read words at an adequate rate, with a high level of accuracy, appropriate expression (prosody), and understanding.

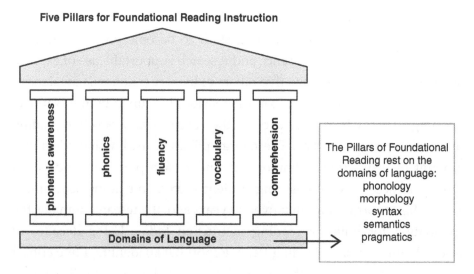

Five Pillars for Foundational Reading Instruction

phonemic awareness

phonics

fluency

vocabulary

comprehension

The Pillars of Foundational Reading rest on the domains of language:
phonology
morphology
syntax
semantics
pragmatics

Domains of Language

FIGURE 3 Elements of Foundational Reading Instruction.

- Vocabulary—The large storage of words recognized and/or used by a person in their oral and written language for comprehension and communication.

- Comprehension—Making sense of and interpreting what is read, heard, or discussed. It is a complex neurological process that rests on the solid foundations of instruction (phonemic awareness, phonics, fluency, and vocabulary).

A structured approach to literacy brings these pillars to life within lessons through explicit and systematic instruction, which is essential for students with learning differences, such as dyslexia, or who struggle to read and write. There is a general scientific consensus about the components of effective instruction and intervention, including highly explicit, systematic instruction of foundational skills and literacy, as only a small percentage of children learn to read with little support.

This understanding of research and evidence-based practices is becoming part of the culture of teaching reading, which means the next steps of implementation, embedding, and reflecting upon practices that look beyond the diagnosis are upon us. While the academic focus is of the utmost concern, teacher knowledge of how to implement these components with appropriate differentiation and scaffolds to move students' learning, in addition to the significant secondary and emotional impacts of dyslexia, continue to be a topic of conversation with the teachers, specialists, and parents that I work with. Addressing academics in connection to preserving and developing a strong sense of self-worth and independence from dyslexia cannot be overshadowed. In other words, we need to possess the knowledge and know-how to teach beyond the diagnosis of dyslexia.

The Path Forward

Dyslexia is a journey for every student. The paths we forge as educators of dyslexic learners have similarities and differences, but the core components and guiding principles remain the same.

My children love to go for walks, and along the way, they pick up little stones—reminders of our places and points in our journey in this life and place them in their pockets. Each of these memories, experiences, and understanding of their world lays the foundation of their journey—their path—forever changed and moving forward. Our students' and their families' journey with dyslexia operates similarly. Along a student's academic experiences, they pick up little knowledge nuggets and experiences, both positive and negative, that lay the foundation and set the trajectory for academic success and lasting impacts on the student's emotional well-being and future outcomes. These experiences, or stepping stones, shift their path and send them further along their journey either in a negative or positive way. Parents and educators also walk alongside the students, collecting stones and guiding them on this path. A journey will have highs and lows, curves, and unforeseen obstacles, but when guided and supported correctly, it can lead to discoveries, learning, and self-achievement. As educators, it is our immense responsibility to provide access to the proper stepping stones for our students to build a path that serves them on their academic journey and develops their self-advocacy skills.

This book is designed as a path and journey, and I share with you those pivotal stepping stones to aid in determining the path for your students. What you take and pick up to place in your pocket is based on your journey into shifting practices to best meet the needs of dyslexic learners. And just as my children fill their pockets with rocks along the way, at some point, they need to release some of those stones to make room for new ones—much like we do with instructional beliefs that no longer serve our work and scaffolds that need to be released as students become independent in their learning. Those stones we use to create our path are reminders of continually releasing and gathering instructional tools, strategies, understanding, and connections laid down to make this path for learning. As we progress in our journey, we keep those stones in our hearts and minds, knowing they have forever altered our path. This occurs as we make meaningful shifts in our work with students and realize the crucial role that these foundational stepping stones to learning play in our instructional delivery, knowledge, and, ultimately, the progress of our students. Simultaneously, our students are collecting their stones and creating their path to understanding their dyslexia, knowledge about themselves, and potential as learners.

I will share these stepping stones that guide our work in creating these necessary guideposts with practical strategies to serve students through the integrated framework of teaching and empowering students with dyslexia. This book will focus on key aspects linked to how we implement, embed, and reflect on instruction within dyslexia education, including the latest academic research and reflections from my experiences. It is my hope to bring something new to the table surrounding how we teach and guide students with dyslexia to find autonomy and agency in their learning journey. I am well aware that readers will come with varying degrees of knowledge surrounding dyslexia, and I hope to address this within the pages of this book. I wrote as if I were the reader seeking ways to improve my practice and grow my confidence in teaching students with dyslexia.

As educators walking this path with students, we ask ourselves many questions, and we must have the foundational pieces, or these stepping stones, in place to ensure we understand our student's needs and provide them with the tools and guidance to move forward and find their path to reaching their potential. Throughout the book, there will be reflection questions for you to pause and think about and where you and your students are on their journey.

Some big questions we may ask ourselves include:
  What evidence-based instructional practices need to be in place?
  How do we ensure we are meeting the needs of students?
  What do we know about dyslexia?
  What role do empathy and understanding play in supporting success and self-confidence for our students?
  How does the environment support success?
  What role do metacognitive practices play?
  How can we build self-advocacy skills, and what is the role of the educator within this framework?

Conclusion

This book is primarily written for reading teachers, educators, dyslexia specialists, and therapists who have the immense responsibility of walking alongside students with dyslexia in providing academic services and a path to empower them.

This book is also for educators, administrators, and professionals who support our students in many different ways. Its goal is for all parties to better understand the impacts of dyslexia within and beyond the classroom, enabling collaboration and a team approach on a larger scale to support students with dyslexia.

Finally, this book is for parents, caregivers, community members, and students who seek to expand their understanding of dyslexia and the impacts that can exist beyond the diagnosis.

This book provides a perspective for understanding dyslexia within and beyond the academic diagnosis through the larger picture. As integration is the framework's name, when writing, it became highlighted even more just how interconnected each piece is. As you read, you will see mention of the different areas of the framework, and while I did my best to pull the elements out into chapters, the way in which they are woven together made it impossible to isolate them completely. As you move through the book, look at how the connections between the components are woven together and integrated. You may wish to pause and turn to that chapter when noted or revisit parts as you read and begin to see the clearer picture of this integrated framework. The integrated framework can be embedded regardless of your evidence-based Structured Literacy/Orton-Gillingham program. I firmly believe this is the support that our teachers need and our students with dyslexia deserve.

Welcome to the journey!

Throughout the book, you will find mini-lessons and resources you can use with students.

These downloadable resources can be located at www.thedyslexiaclassroom. com/teachingbeyondthediagnosis

---

Key Takeaways

- Every teacher has had or will have students with dyslexia in their classrooms.

- Students and educators create a more comprehensive understanding and approach to dyslexia when we embed and integrate all of the parts and pieces from the integrated framework.

- The integrated model honors students on their journey with dyslexia.

- There is no age limit for teaching someone to read or improve reading.

- Both teacher knowledge and research-based instructional approaches are needed for effective literacy instruction

- Dyslexia impacts beyond the academic diagnosis.

Simplify your path to practice. What did you put in your pocket?
What stepping stones, or nuggets of knowledge, are you taking from this chapter?

Understanding Dyslexia

"In dyslexia, there is an abundance of high-quality scientific knowledge, so we have not a knowledge gap but an action gap."

—Dr. Sally Shaywitz, speaking at a Congressional Hearing

Integrated Framework Component: Understanding Dyslexia

In this part of the journey, it is imperative that all learning team members (educators, students, parents, and school) understand and differentiate between dyslexia facts and myths, and be able to speak to and spread awareness of dyslexia (see Figure 1.1).

For many students, upon receiving a diagnosis of dyslexia comes a moment of relief that the struggles they have endured have a name, a reason. A student stated, "With my diagnosis, I felt lighter, as though I was no longer confined in my own mind or belief that I was dumb, but instead free to view my dyslexia as one part of myself and not all-encompassing ...." Statements like these are all too familiar to the students and families I work with. The overwhelming sense of self-doubt, negative self-talk, and impact on self-worth that comes with repeated failure in a system that doesn't understand or, at times, recognize dyslexia

FIGURE 1.1 The integrated framework—understanding dyslexia.

have lasting impacts on our students and their families. The lasting impacts of dyslexia on our children are real, and yet a teacher or school with an understanding of dyslexia can provide a lifeline to our students and ensure that they are seen and provided with the instruction and tools to take flight. In education, we can be slow to recognize the depth or seriousness of this often-lasting connection between the academic impacts of dyslexia, such as reading acquisition and comprehension and writing skills, and emotional well-being. Yet, research indicates that early identification and remediation have been found to increase both academic success and emotional well-being of those with dyslexia and perhaps even prevent reading difficulties (Al Otaiba et al. 2009; Mathes et al. 2005)

While the research surrounding dyslexia is extensive and noted as a specific learning disability commonly characterized by to have, difficulty in accurate or fluent word recognition and spelling (Fletcher et al. 2019; International Dyslexia Association 2002), the understanding of dyslexia continues to be wrapped in misunderstandings and limited knowledge of the impacts on students sitting in our classrooms. Teachers provide the first line of defense and play a vital role in identifying early indicators of dyslexia, supporting and teaching students with, or suspected to have, dyslexia within general classroom instruction anchored in evidence-based practices. Every educator will have or has encountered students with dyslexia in their classrooms, whether identified or not, and therefore, this warrants the need for deeper understanding.

What Is Dyslexia?

At its most straightforward meaning, dyslexia is difficulty reading and spelling words, yet it is much more. When discussing dyslexia with parents, educators, or the community, it's crucial to remember that it's the most common learning difference. Specific Learning Disabilities (SLD) refers to the term used within the educational setting for neurodevelopmental disorders characterized by a persistent impairment in at least one of three major areas: reading, written expression, and/or math (American Psychiatric Association, APA). Dyslexia falls under the broader term of Specific Learning Disability (SLD) as individuals with dyslexia often struggle with acquiring and processing language, leading to reading, spelling, and writing difficulties. Dyslexia significantly impacts reading, particularly in decoding and accurate and/or fluent word recognition and spelling. These challenges at the word reading level can impact the acquisition and/or development of reading, fluency and reading, comprehension capabilities, and/or skills. For those with dyslexia, the hurdles can be more than just one SLD, affecting various aspects of functioning, including language, communication, social-emotional development, and behavior. Moreover, some students may also have co-existing disorders such as Attention Deficit Hyperactivity Disorder (ADHD), Developmental Language Disability (DLD), or anxiety. These difficulties can manifest at any stage of a child's development, underscoring the need for understanding and support.

You will see me using the term "learning difference" throughout this book in place of "disability," especially when speaking with my students about their difficulties. The term "learning difference" is used to emphasize that individuals with dyslexia and other neurodivergent conditions have unique ways of learning, rather than using the word "disability" when discussing dyslexia with students. This term has gained traction as we see shifts in the narrative and awareness surrounding neurodivergent learners and dyslexia.

Neurodiversity is a concept that encourages us to view the natural variation in the ways that humans perceive, interact, and experience the world as a positive aspect of our society. Dyslexia, and other learning differences are part of this neurodiversity umbrella due to the neurobiological variations.

Despite the extensive research on dyslexia, the understanding of dyslexia can be clouded by misunderstandings and limited knowledge of its impacts on students. Every educator will have or has encountered students with dyslexia in their classrooms, whether identified or not. This commonality should provide a sense of preparedness by the teacher and a reminder that students are not alone in this journey. It also underscores the need for a deeper, more comprehensive understanding, which we will explore in this book. In addition, there are cascading secondary impacts that are often long-lasting. Regarding educational research on dyslexia, decades of research, data, and instructional implications, indicate that "research conducted across many disciplines and many decades has now provided a clearer understanding of the complexities that are inherent to dyslexia" (Hasbrouck 2020, 2024) highlighting the need for educators, parents, and students to deepen their understanding of all that dyslexia entails. While there are ongoing conversations surrounding the definition of dyslexia, The International Dyslexia Association's current definition of dyslexia is as follows:

> Dyslexia is a specific learning disability that is neurobiological in origin. It is characterized by difficulties with accurate and/or fluent word recognition and by poor spelling and decoding abilities. These difficulties typically result from a deficit in the phonological component of language that is often unexpected in relation to other cognitive abilities and the provision of effective classroom instruction. Secondary consequences may include problems in reading comprehension and reduced reading experience that can impede the growth of vocabulary and background knowledge. (International Dyslexia Association 2002)

For parents and teachers in classrooms or intervention settings, several questions might be asked, such as "What is dyslexia?", "What should I look for in my students?", and "Where do I access the research?" In addition, "There is so much research and information available; what should I trust or refer to?" Rest assured, a wealth of trusted research and resources is available to guide you as we deepen our understanding of dyslexia through the integrated framework.

As we move through this chapter, I encourage you to reflect on how you describe dyslexia and develop some speaking points to bring up when talking about dyslexia to others.

Common Questions, Comments, and Answers About Dyslexia

Is Dyslexia Real? Yes, Dyslexia is Very Real

The first line of the IDA definition is of importance, as "neurobiological in origin" means dyslexia is a variation of the brain system from birth. It is generally agreed upon that there are variations in the brain processing systems that involve difficulty connecting the sounds that make up words with the letters that represent those sounds. Studies have discovered that these brain differences exist *before* formal instruction and likely reflect the cause of dyslexia. Researchers have also identified distinct neural networks associated with the specific factors of dyslexia (Norton 2015) and may also underlie the differences in activation and connectivity noted in functional imaging studies (Norton and Wolf 2012; Pugh et al. 2000; Shaywitz 2003, 2020). These differences make learning to read more challenging for students with dyslexia than that of their neurotypical peers, and therefore, we should not think of dyslexia as a developmental reading delay, or what may be called "late bloomers." For this reason, it is imperative that students with dyslexia not be delayed in receiving appropriate interventions. Without intervention, children who are poor readers at the end of first grade seldom acquire average-level reading skills by the end of elementary school (Francis et al. 1996; Juel 1988; Shaywitz et al. 1998; Torgesen & Burgess 1998) highlighting the need for early intervention as the brain's plasticity decreases through childhood. It should also be noted that appropriate interventions at any age are beneficial, though the duration and intensity for older students may require a longer stint to close the reading gap. This understanding of neurobiological origin helps anchor our understanding that dyslexia is not anyone's fault or that parents or students must try harder.

How Common is Dyslexia? Is it Rare?

Dyslexia is the most common learning difference, affecting a significant percentage of the population. Different studies show a range in the percentage of people with dyslexia, in part because of how dyslexia is identified across our school systems. However, an estimated 5–15% of school-age children struggle with a learning disability, of which the most common is dyslexia (American Psychiatric Association, *Diagnostic and Statistical Manual of Mental Disorders*, 5th ed. (DSM-5) 2013). The variance in distribution or percentages of those with identified dyslexia ranges across studies from as low as 3% to as high as 20%, partly due to the testing processes and the fact that there is currently no universal definition of dyslexia. However, it is believed that some form of dyslexia impacts 20% of the population (Shaywitz et al. 2021). This means that, as a teacher, every year, you will have dyslexic students in your classroom.

In addition, dyslexia has been shown to have a familial clustering, which can have a significant impact on families. Researchers believe that dyslexia is genetically passed through families, and therefore, as educators, we need to consider this possible family history of dyslexia. "Dyslexia is strongly heritable, occurring in up to 50% of individuals who have a first-degree relative with dyslexia" (Gaab 2017) and other researchers noting a possible 70% heritability of dyslexia (Erbeli et al. 2021). Somewhere between 25–60% of parents whose children struggle with reading also show signs of challenges (Fletcher et al. 2019) when screening and testing students. For families to open up about a history of reading difficulties or dyslexia, we must build strong relationships in which trust and respect are the foundation and lead with a deeper understanding of dyslexia and the academic and emotional implications.

Can Those With Dyslexia Learn to Read and Spell?

Yes! While dyslexia is characterized by difficulties with accurate and/or fluent word recognition, and by poor reading and spelling abilities (IDA 2002), with the proper instruction, students with dyslexia **can** learn to be proficient readers and spellers. Among researchers, there is compelling evidence that the majority of students, approximately 95% of all students, can achieve literacy skills at or approaching grade level (Goldberg et al. 2022; Vaughn et al. 2020; Kilpatrick 2015; Moats 2020; Lyon 2002; Rashotte et al. 2001). Students with dyslexia require intensive instruction over time, provided in small groups or a one-to-one setting that addresses the critical elements of reading through explicit, systematic instruction and abundant opportunities for practice and feedback (Vaugh et al. 2014). It is important for educators to hold a deep knowledge of these components to provide a comprehensive approach, as the research indicates that when provided with appropriate and sufficiently intense instruction, reading difficulties can be overcome in many children (Simos et al. 2002). In other words, how teachers implement instruction is of key importance for those with dyslexia.

The question "Isn't dyslexia seeing and writing words and letters backward?" is one of the most common misunderstandings surrounding dyslexia. It's crucial to understand that dyslexia is not a problem with vision. The difficulties with dyslexia typically result from a deficit in phonological processing or the ability to hold, manipulate, and connect sounds to letter representations. Word reversals and skipping words, which are often seen in those with dyslexia, have been shown to be a result of linguistic deficits (Vellutino et al. 2004) and not due to vision processes. The eyes of all readers track print through small eye movements called fixations and saccades, where the reader's eyes fixate or take in a word for a short duration and rapidly scan to the right of the word before jumping to the next fixation point (Rayner et al. 2011). Studies of these eye movements have shown that those with dyslexia show normal saccadic eye movement when the reading content is at their reading level but similar to beginning readers when the content is above reading ability in which reading speed is impacted due to less proficient lexical processing resulting in longer reading times and increased fixation times (Justino & Kolinsky 2023). In addition, reading is achieved with letter-by-letter processing of the word (Rayner et al. 2001), allowing the reader to quickly recognize the differences between *saw* and *was, advice* and *advise*, and *compliment* and *complacent*. The visual input of objects in the world around us remains constant regardless of orientation; letters and words require a consistent and set orientation associated with the sounds or words we read. Letter reversal is a product of mirror invariance, which is the innate ability of our visual system to consider mirrored images as corresponding to the same object. When students begin to learn letters, they must unlearn this mechanism to distinguish between letters with mirror symmetry, like b/d, p/q, and m/w (see Figure 1.2). Explicit instruction in integrating letter names, sound representation, and letter formation is necessary to help students solidify letter orientation (National Reading Panel et al. 2000).

One of the most detrimental misunderstandings about dyslexia is the belief that those with dyslexia lack the intelligence to read. This is one of the most damaging myths surrounding dyslexia. Dyslexia is not linked to intellect. Our society and culture are deeply woven with the thought that reading equates to intelligence, yet intelligence is not lacking in those with dyslexia. Dyslexia is not a thinking problem. It is a specific learning disability in which the ability to connect sounds to letters and decode/ read and spell fluently is impacted. The apparent brightness of many students with dyslexia tends to stump parents and educators, resulting in their struggles perplexing those trying to help, and may inadvertently and falsely lead people into thinking that a child with dyslexia needs more time or to try harder or can't learn. It should be noted that students with dyslexia are working incredibly hard throughout the day. Their

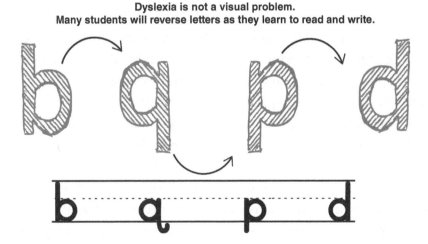

Dyslexia is not a visual problem.
Many students will reverse letters as they learn to read and write.

FIGURE 1.2 Reversals.

difficulties with reading are not due to laziness or stupidity, and promoting that idea is dangerous to a child's self-esteem. With the understanding that a child with dyslexia needs appropriate and targeted instruction, parents and educators can feel empowered and capable of providing the necessary support.

Do All Students Acquiring Reading Need a Structured Literacy Approach?

While many educators and parents assume that because each child is unique, foundational instruction will greatly vary, however, Dr. Stanislas Dehaene, notes that, "It is simply not true that there are hundreds of ways to learn to read … when it comes to reading, we all have roughly the same brain that imposes the same constraints and the same learning sequence" (Dehaene 2009). Therefore, using a structured literacy approach is beneficial to all but *essential* to those with dyslexia. The brain processing systems show that learning to read and spell occurs roughly the same way for all, indicating that for reading to be acquired, all readers must build a new reading circuit. Students must be proficient in sound-letter associations to help them develop the skills needed for accurate and fluent reading. This includes letter-sound knowledge and spelling patterns. When students read or spell words based on the sound symbols explicitly taught, they engage in the orthographic mapping process, the mental process of linking speech sounds to their written representations, which is essential for reading and writing. This is done over time with a systematic scope and sequence that builds in difficulty. Understanding the relationship of the sounds in our language to the letter or letter representations helps students unlock the reading code. Students with dyslexia need more intensive instruction through the Orton-Gillingham/structured literacy approach and all of the components as the ease with which they may acquire reading and writing skills varies. So, while we all create a reading circuitry in the brain, the path to unlocking reading and writing may look different in intensity, pacing, and delivery.

Does Dyslexia Impact Everyone in the Same Way?

While there is a profile for dyslexia, no two dyslexics present precisely the same way. Dyslexia exists on a continuum where the impacts vary from person to person. While the characteristic markers of dyslexia remain consistent, the range in which they impact an individual differs in severity. While decoding may be a struggle for one student with dyslexia, for another, spelling is the primary obstacle; for others, fluent reading and writing pose a struggle, and for some, there are many areas of need. Some students struggle with identifying and linking sounds to print, others struggle with quick word recognition and decoding, and others' spelling is significantly impacted.

Severe Difficulties	Range of Difficulties ↔	Mild Difficulties
Most Intensive Needs Requires: • Explicit and systematic instruction • Higher intensity • Longer duration • Intentional increase in repetition and retrieval practices • Small group or individualized		Less Intensive Needs Requires: • Explicit and systematic instruction • Retrieval practices • May respond quicker
Explicit and systematic structured literacy approach focused on integrating language, reading, and writing instruction that supports automaticity, fluency, and reading proficiency (IDA 2024)		
Students may have a wide range of oral language skills.		

Each student has a unique learning profile, which educators and parents must understand. This leads us to the necessity of understanding the dyslexic profile better so that we may determine which instructional path will best serve the student. It allows us to be diagnostic in our approach to working with students. It makes us think beyond the curriculum and address individual needs to help students reach their potential. As stated by Margaret Rawson, past president of the International Dyslexia Association, "The differences are personal. The diagnosis is clinical. The treatment is educational. The understanding is scientific."

Doesn't Dyslexia Only Impact Reading and Spelling? Other Academics?

This is another big question surrounding dyslexia that beckons us to dig deeper as dyslexia often has secondary consequences, which may include problems in reading comprehension and reduced reading experience that can impede the growth of vocabulary and background knowledge (IDA 2002), in addition to including behavior, self-esteem, life-long economic outcomes, and more. Students who struggle with reading often dislike reading and writing; as a result, they read less than their classmates who are stronger readers, negatively impacting their access and growth in vocabulary development, background knowledge, written expression, and higher reading concepts and comprehension. In the education setting, this is called the Matthew Effect; the idea that the rich get richer and the poor get poorer, so that students who are not yet strong readers read less which increases the gap in multiple areas of literacy and language development leaving those students struggling further and further behind. Academic support is crucial to success in closing this gap.

Other academics can be impacted by dyslexia due to literacy being woven into all aspects of learning, from the reading in chemistry to the writing in history classes, or the written assessment in physical education; the threads of dyslexia impact learning within and beyond the academic setting, stressing why all those who work with students need to understand dyslexia. We also know that those with dyslexia may have feelings of shame, unacceptance, anxiety, and low self-esteem and students with dyslexia show an increased incidence of depressive symptomatology and internalized anxiety (Mugnaini et al. 2009). A child's ability to read effectively will have a long-lasting impact on multiple aspects of their lives. Reading affects everything you do, and therefore, educators and parents need to understand the impact of dyslexia on the student within and outside of academics, recognize the child holistically, and respond through patient and persistent teaching and understanding.

Many people mistakenly believe dyslexia is a learning difference that only affects English speakers. However, this is not the case. Dyslexia is a global issue that can impact individuals across all languages, races, socio-economic statuses, and genders. While the prevalence rates for dyslexia may vary somewhat across writing systems, core deficits appear to exist across writing systems in the area of phonological deficits (Goswami 2011). In English, we may see the impacts primarily in the area of accurate word reading, decoding, and spelling, and in other languages with more consistent orthographies or spelling systems, fluency appears as the primary difficulty (Ziegler and Goswami 2005). It's important to note that longitudinal studies show no difference in dyslexia impacting boys vs. girls (Shaywitz et al. 1998, 2003). However, boys may have more identification within schools, and there are possible reasons that need further research to determine why.

Definitions of dyslexia exist across the globe. The following all have definitions of dyslexia: British Dyslexia Association (BDA), Dyslexia Association of Ireland, European Dyslexia Association, Dyslexia Association of Singapore, Australian Dyslexia Association, Maharashtra Dyslexia Association, Dyslexia Association of Hong Kong.

Currently, in our school systems, we tend to wait until students have experienced reading failure before we intervene and identify students with dyslexia or at risk for dyslexia under the misguided belief that dyslexia can't be recognized until at least the third grade, causing a delay in intensive intervention services during the prime learning window in kindergarten and first grade (Wanzek and Vaughn 2007). However, early indicators and characteristics of dyslexia can be observed in young children in the early ages of school, as oral language competence underpins the development of reading skills. Language and early literacy development in preschool and kindergarten is rooted in language, phonological awareness, and letter knowledge, areas many dyslexic learners find challenging, and sets the stage for broader literacy skills. Schools may have an early reading screening to identify the most at-risk students; however, without high-quality instruction and intervention, these early reading problems become profound reading disabilities later (Stanovich 1986). Early identification and intervention are best, and with the right support, these students can succeed. Yet this does not mean that older students should be without identification or services. In addition, even with early intervention, some students may need continued services and support. While new conversations exist about beginning early intervention and identification, the best bet for our students with identified dyslexia, or characteristics of dyslexia, is to provide appropriate intervention from the start and not rely on a "wait to fail" model as this can have lasting impacts on students' educational and emotional standing.

Can We Say the *D* Word? Dyslexia?

In the United States, the Department of Education issued a letter in 2015 to all schools clarifying that there is nothing in the Individuals with Disabilities Education Act (IDEA) that prohibits the use of the terms dyslexia, dysgraphia, or dyscalculia in an IDEA evaluation, eligibility determination, or Individualized Education Plan (IEP). Students with dyslexia are entitled to protections under the IDEA. This federal law requires public schools to provide free, appropriate education to children with disabilities, including dyslexia. The laws established within the United States are designed to protect the rights of those with disabilities and learning differences. Students with a suspected area of disability are entitled to an assessment, regardless of whether they are in a public, private, or charter school. Dyslexia is a complex neurodevelopmental condition. For that reason, experts generally recommend comprehensive dyslexia evaluation conducted by a multidisciplinary team (Mather & Schneider 2023). Saying the word dyslexia can provide a name for struggles and deepen our understanding of dyslexia. The laws and path to diagnosis differ from the laws of other countries. However, conversations about dyslexia continue to be worldwide, and safeguarding the education of children with dyslexia remains a topic of priority.

Reflection time:

How would you describe dyslexia to a colleague? A parent? A student?

Taking time to write down or practice how you explain dyslexia is helpful and provides you with the language and understanding to communicate with others with consistency. How we speak to dyslexia matters, and how we advocate for our children and students as we spread awareness matters. In turn, we want our children with dyslexia to have the language to speak to what dyslexia is and isn't, and this exercise can also benefit them.

*Tip for teachers, parents, and students—create talking points to share about dyslexia. Download one-page talking points at www.thedyslexiaclassroom.com/teachingbeyondthediagnosis

---

Conclusion

Expanding our understanding of dyslexia, dispelling myths and misunderstandings, and acknowledging that reading is a complex cognitive process that does not develop naturally is critical. It is vital that educators and parents are clear about what dyslexia is and is not and the instructional and emotional impacts that this has on our lessons and students. Our dyslexic learners, and all students, deserve instruction rooted in what the collective science says about how the brain learns to read. The ability to read well can no longer be accepted as something unattainable for specific groups. The complexity of dyslexia should cause us to reflect on how dyslexia is viewed by all parties—educators, families, students, and the community. Part of this means that students themselves determine how they wish to speak to dyslexia, as well as advocate for themselves, all part of the integrated framework for empowering students on this journey. I encourage educators to move to a more comprehensive approach to dyslexia instruction that shifts the narrative to focus on the remediation of skills and the amplification of strengths and doesn't view dyslexia through rose-colored glasses, but rather one that honors the challenges and strengths that all humans hold.

Key Takeaways

- Dyslexia is the most common learning difference.
- Early intervention is the best practice, but intervening is never too late.
- Dyslexia is a Specific Learning Disability.
- Dyslexia is a worldwide conversation.
- Create talking points to share facts about dyslexia.

> Simplify your path to practice. What did you put in your pocket?
> What stepping stones, or nuggets of knowledge, are you taking from this chapter?

CHAPTER TWO

Characteristics and Contradictory Signs of Dyslexia

"The five-year-old who can't quite learn his letters becomes the six-year-old who can't match sounds to letters and the fourteen-year-old who reads excruciatingly slowly. The threads persist throughout a person's life. But, with early intervention, this scenario doesn't need to happen."

—Dr. Sally Shaywitz, The Yale Center for Dyslexia and Creativity

Integrated Framework Component: Understanding Dyslexia

In this part of the journey, we deepen our understanding of dyslexia and its characteristics across ages and grades as well as contradictory signs.

A young elementary student sat in the classroom day after day, struggling with reading and writing. Despite his clear intelligence, he was not making the expected gains. In classroom discussions, he demonstrated a deep understanding of the concepts being taught. However, when it came to reading or writing, he would sit at his desk, seemingly unfamiliar with the work, and engage in off-task behaviors. His learning difficulties were broad and complex, affecting both word reading and language comprehension, particularly in written expression. He consistently grappled with writing letters, recalling letter names and sounds, and painfully sounding out the same word repeatedly. Despite the teacher working with this child in whole group and small group reading sessions applying systematic and explicit instruction, the child wasn't making gains, instead was frustrated, and the teacher, too, felt lost, not knowing where the breakdown was occurring or how to help this student. This scenario is common, and I know this because this is what sent me on my own learning journey all those years ago to seek more knowledge of dyslexia. I felt lost and knew that some students were being left behind, just like the little boy on the beach. The impact of dyslexia on his educational journey was profound, and it was a journey that could have been different with the right knowledge and support. Teachers with knowledge of dyslexia and its characteristics can change students' lives. Parents and early educators are at the forefront of identifying dyslexia and ensuring that evidence-based practices are utilized. The more we as educators understand dyslexia, how the brain learns, how to implement an Orton-Gillingham/Structured Literacy approach with proper intensity and duration, and the research behind best practices for students with dyslexia, the better we can serve our students. A teacher with knowledge of dyslexia and its characteristics can make a world of difference in a student's educational journey.

Understanding Dyslexia in the Classroom—Characteristics of Dyslexia

Across the United States, there is legislation in most states for administering early reading screeners to provide interventions and, when applicable, early identification. These screeners serve as a safety net to identify students at risk for reading failure. However, while these screeners are a crucial tool, they don't specifically address the characteristics of dyslexia and are usually administered within our elementary schools, requiring educators, professionals, and parents to be aware of the wide range of characteristics of dyslexia across the grades so as not to miss students in lower or upper grades who present with characteristics of dyslexia.

The goal of these screeners is to better identify students at the start of struggles in hopes of preventing many students from falling through the net, offering them a more hopeful and optimistic educational journey. Parents and educators play a crucial and valued role in this process, and their efforts are integral to ensuring that identification and evidence-based practices and interventions are utilized. Holding knowledge of the characteristics of dyslexia is a first step in helping students, underscoring the importance of their role in this journey.

Starting With the Language Literacy Link

Everything we do in education is rooted in language. Language is the comprehension and use of spoken and written language through receptive (listening, reading, watching) and expressive (speaking, writing) components, which act as a vehicle for learning. Students' use of language provides them with opportunities to share thoughts, ideas, conceptual understanding, beliefs and opinions, etc. While oral language development is considered a natural learning progression, where implicitly students learn the rules of the (native) language (grammatical usage, word order, etc.); reading and writing require explicit and systematic instruction. Children with spoken language difficulties often struggle to read and write, and children with reading and writing challenges can struggle with spoken language, primarily related to higher-order spoken language skills (Scott & Windsor 2000) or the awareness of how language and communication work. This may be evident when students have difficulty making inferences, monitoring their comprehension, or understanding text structure. Teachers may note that students have big ideas or knowledge of the concepts yet need help expressing themselves comprehensively. On the contrary, some students may exquisitely express their thoughts orally, displaying their higher-level thinking, but need help to connect that same thinking to print. Understanding how language impacts learning and possible challenges students may encounter is essential for delivering appropriate instruction and meeting student needs. This underscores the complexity of dyslexia and the need for comprehensive solutions.

Researchers agree that reading is a language-based skill and that the relationship between oral language and reading is reciprocal, with each influencing the other (see Figure 2.1). According to the American Speech-Language-Hearing Association (ASHA), the five language domains are phonology, morphology, syntax, semantics, and pragmatics, and while they contribute to language in different ways, together they form a dynamic integrative whole (Berko Gleason 2005). The five language domains are often grouped under three major components—form, context, and usage—and link directly to a structured approach to literacy. Form encompasses the rules that govern phonology (structure, distribution, and sequencing of speech sounds), morphology (change in meaning at the word level), and syntax (grammar, word order, organization, and

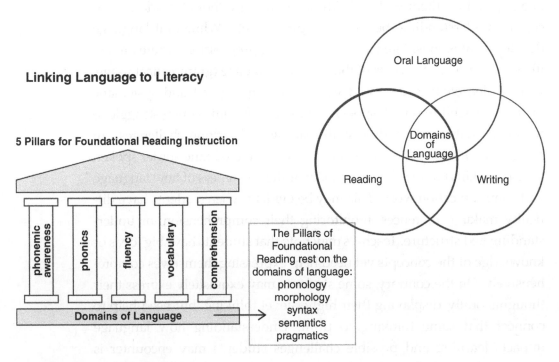

FIGURE 2.1 Linking language to literacy.

variety of sentences). Content is the meaning component of language including recognizing, understanding, and using words in meaningful ways (semantics). Usage, often called pragmatics, involves rules that dictate communication behavior in our language intentions, reasons, and discourse. All of these contribute to higher-order language skills such as verbal reasoning, inference, advanced vocabulary, and word relationships, interpreting language and use of text structure, comprehension, etc., which are critical to academic and social success.

This link of language to literacy is reflected consistently in research indicating that students with stronger language skills are better equipped for reading and writing success (Burns et al. 1999; National Center for Family Literacy 2009). We may see language impacting our students' ability to use vocabulary within content areas, or the ability to interpret or understand lectures and the delivery of lessons. Other students may struggle with instructions and directions and understanding the academic language in oral and written form. At the same time, others may struggle to derive meaning and inferences from unspoken, spoken, and written language. Since dyslexia falls under Language-Based Learning Disability (LBLD), which refers to a spectrum of difficulties related to understanding and using spoken and written language, we may encounter challenges for some students in terms of language acquisition, and educators need to be acutely aware of the impacts and possible indicators that language can provide regarding early signs of dyslexia.

Underlying Causes of Dyslexia: Phonological Processing

While impacts on language on a broader scale may occur, for those with dyslexia, phonological processing is typically a core deficit (Nelson 2014; Nelson et al. 2015; IDA 2012), and the identification of these challenges has helped explain the discrepancy between the ease with which most children acquire spoken language and the difficulty many of these same children have in learning to read (Brady & Shankweiler 1991; Goswami & Bryant 1990; Liberman & Shankweiler 1985; Wagner & Torgesen 1987).

The phonological component of language, how we use and manipulate sounds in the language in connection to letter representations, is of primary concern and focus when working with dyslexic learners. Early indicators for possible at-risk reading difficulties can exist before explicit instruction in reading begins. Current studies at the University of Helsinki are indicating "that stronger neural responses measured in the brain in infancy to changes in speech sounds were associated with better pre-reading skills, such as rapid naming," which we understand as key skills in the area of literacy development (Navarrete Arroy et al. 2024). Other researchers, such as Dr. Nadine Gaab's lab, focus on pinpointing when dyslexia manifests, to find students and intervene in response before students struggle. Their current study has found that some atypical brain characteristics involving white matter (where information and communication is exchanged), connectivity patterns, and other measurements found in older children are already present as early as infancy (Rojas 2024). Studies like these will continue to give us insights into the importance of early intervention and instruction for students at-risk for reading difficulties so we may respond in a preventative instead of reactive manner, and many of the early indicators for dyslexia are rooted in language.

These phonological deficits can often be seen in preschool and kindergarten, for example, when a child says "hangabur" for hamburger or "restanot" for restaurant or has difficulty learning nursery rhymes. As students progress in the grades, phonological difficulties can persist beyond kindergarten, and some students are aware of these challenges and will utilize their knowledge of language to compensate for phonological deficits. A bright student of mine struggled with pronouncing certain sounds and would substitute with words she could pronounce in their place, such as her inability to say *specific*, which she consistently pronounced as "pacific," would be substituted with "particular." This highlighted her brightness and knowledge of the language, as she used a word with a similar meaning and masked her instructional needs within the classroom and at home, specifically in phoneme and phonological awareness. Phonological awareness, the ability to recognize and manipulate the sounds of language, is a critical skill for early reading and writing.

Early Indicators of Reading Difficulties/Dyslexia: Preschool

Because children in these early grades have yet to be exposed to formal reading and writing instruction, understanding how language and phonological awareness may indicate dyslexia or reading difficulties is important knowledge for educators and parents. Early indicators for at-risk reading difficulties or dyslexia do not identify dyslexia but give us an early clue to student development in the areas necessary for future reading acquisition. When identified early, these underpinnings can be directly addressed within reading and language instruction and monitored for progress, providing educators and families with the knowledge and insight into early appropriate intervention and identification when needed. This proactive approach empowers educators and parents to make a significant impact on the future reading success of their students.

In preschool, a student may have some or all of the characteristics noted below. Early intervention and targeted instruction are key. At this early stage, the focus is on oral language development, letter knowledge, and early literacy skills to set students up for success. Students in preschool may have some or all of these characteristics:

- Delayed speech or persistent "baby talk"
- Mispronunciation of words ("hang-buger" for hamburger, "psgetti" for spaghetti)
- Substitution of words

- Difficulty learning and remembering the letter names in the alphabet
- Difficulty learning nursery rhymes
- Likes listening to stories but shows little interest in letters or words
- Confusion between directional words (up/down, atop/below)
- Poor auditory discrimination
- Difficulty with two or more instructions given at one time, but does fine when tasks are presented in smaller chunks
- Difficulty pronouncing words by targeted age
- Difficulty recognizing own name and letters in name
- Difficulty identifying rhyming words
- Difficulty recalling names of friends, objects, etc.
- Family history of dyslexia
- Students with speech or developmental language delays should be monitored for reading difficulties as they move into formal instruction.

These characteristics highlight the impact of language on literacy development and how this impacts students with dyslexia. One of the biggest takeaways for educators and parents is that early indicators for possible at-risk reading difficulties can exist before explicit instruction in reading. Oral language should continue to be developed in the preschool years and beyond as a part of dyslexia instruction and intervention. The three- and four-year-old classrooms are prime environments for capitalizing on the explosive language development acquired at this learning time. For educators and parents of young children, focusing on language acquisition in knowledge-rich environments where instruction is grounded in science and social studies topics, read-alouds across multiple genres, and informational text aids in literacy and knowledge development to shape lifelong learning habits and acceleration of literacy and language.

These experiences are crucial for students at risk of reading disabilities as they build their knowledge and vocabulary, which aids them in reading and writing later on. When we hold knowledge about a topic and have the content-rich language associated with that topic in our oral language, such as the pronunciation of the word and use of the word in our oral language, the easier it is to access when we later read and spell with that word because students have built knowledge networks and schemas, or conceptual frameworks around that topic. Literacy-language instruction in these classrooms should include playful interactions with language, such as nursery rhymes, playing with syllables in words, playing with language, and lots of conversational turns to develop students' meta-phonological awareness or get students to intentionally think about the structures of how words work within our language, which is a key aspect and critical skill for later literacy development as students move to phoneme awareness and connecting speech to print. Early reading instruction should be rooted in language and phonological awareness, an area many dyslexic learners find challenging.

Early Indicators of Reading Difficulties/Dyslexia: Kindergarten to Second Grade

Formal education around the alphabetic principle, the concept that letters and letter patterns represent the sounds of spoken language, traditionally begins in kindergarten when students enter the school system. In kindergarten, students' literacy education focuses on letters, sounds, beginning reading, and language development. There is a varying degree of ease at which students acquire understanding and mastery of letters and sounds, and therefore, teachers in these early grades can be on the lookout for early characteristics or markers of dyslexia or reading difficulties. With more shifts to evidence-based instruction in kindergarten, early identification can help schools move away from the "wait to fail model" in which identification and appropriate intervention and accommodations are delayed as students move through the primary grades, often leaving students with low self-esteem and feelings of shame.

As students progress to first grade, a continuation of mastering and applying their knowledge of sound-symbol correspondences, knowledge of high-frequency words, segmenting, blending, and decoding strategies continues to build. Students on target for acquiring these foundational reading skills should finish the second grade having learned some of the more advanced phonics patterns and applications in reading and spelling. This knowledge continues to grow as students progress through the grades. For some students, the ease with which they acquire these word reading skills is slower and needs targeted early and strategic instruction. However, for many students with dyslexia, this trajectory may vary in the instructional time needed to acquire these skills. Educators with an understanding of the trajectory of these skills, awareness of characteristics of dyslexia, and knowledge of how to address these for students act as first responders and can provide appropriate early intervention proven to benefit students best.

In kindergarten, first grade, and second grade, a student may have some or all of these characteristics:

- History of language delays (see preschool indicators)
- Difficulty with phoneme segmentation tasks
- Limited letter knowledge
- Difficulty with sound-symbol correspondence
- Reading errors (omission, substitution, guessing of words/sounds)
- Difficulty sounding out simple words
- Choppy, disfluent reading at the word, sentence, or text level
- Difficulty recognizing familiar words
- Avoidance behaviors when asked to read or write
- Uses unusual sequencing of letters or words in written work

- Spells a word several different ways in one piece of writing
- Difficulty recalling sequential order (days of the week, months, numbers, etc.)
- Family history of dyslexia

Just as we look for areas of need, we must recognize the areas of strength. Like all humans, our students hold varying strengths such as curiosity, oral language, large oral vocabulary, knowledge of the world, quick-to-solve puzzles, comprehension of stories read aloud, quick to pick up concepts taught, seeing the big picture, etc. It is crucial that educators focus their observations on identifying what a student needs and looks for and identify strengths while targeting areas of need. This approach empowers us to bring students into a metacognitive awareness of their strengths and needs, enlightening us about the unique abilities each student possesses.

Characteristics of Dyslexia in Upper Elementary to High School

As students progress through the upper elementary grades and into high school, we may see many of the indicators carry over from the earlier grades, as well as some or all of these characteristics:

- Slow, awkward reading
- Omits, repeats, or adds words when reading
- Difficulty recalling specific words in oral language resulting in vague language such as "thing," "umm," "stuff," etc., in place of particular words
- Difficulty reading unknown words—may guess at words
- Difficulty with pronunciation of words and/or grammar
- Limited decoding strategies
- Difficult time taking notes in class

- May write very little but orally has a lot to say about topic
- May write a great deal but lose the main point
- May avoid reading aloud
- Difficulty in pinpointing the main idea
- Confuses directions
- Difficulty in processing information quickly
- Difficulty holding a sequence, list, or directions to memory
- Is often tired due to the amount of concentration and effort required
- Family history of dyslexia
- Confuses words that sound alike (for example, conscience/conscious)
- Reading and writing avoidance behaviors

As humans, we all have unique strengths that should be celebrated, especially in students with dyslexia. These strengths, which may not be related to reading or writing, can include sophisticated oral language and vocabulary use as well as thinking skills, excelling in areas unrelated to reading and writing, out-of-the-box thinking and problem-solving, gathering the big picture or "gist" of things, a high level of understanding of what is read aloud or heard (lectures, podcasts, audiobooks, etc.) to name a few.

Characteristics of Dyslexia in Adults

Quite often in my work with students, once a child has been diagnosed with dyslexia or characteristics of dyslexia, a family member often will seek out further understanding of their learning journey and find out they, too, have dyslexia. Some of the characteristics that adults may connect with regarding their journey in reading and writing challenges may include:

- History of reading and spelling difficulties
- Limited reading or limited reading for pleasure
- Slow reading rate
- May avoid reading aloud

- May mispronounce names or trip over parts of words

- May avoid writing in a public space which is visible to others

Just as with children, areas of strength can also exist for adults, such as out-of-the-box thinking, spatial reasoning, creative thinking, interpersonal skills, empathy, higher-order thinking, high articulation when expressing ideas, etc.

While there is some discussion about specific traits for those with dyslexia, I think the importance lies in developing awareness of each individual's areas of need and strength as human beings. As we continue to see narrative shifts about dyslexia, more and more adults are stepping forward and sharing their journey, struggles, and successes. Dyslexia transcends words and is a complex condition that must be defined because it manifests in various forms and degrees. In this regard, remember that while many people with dyslexia have one or more of these strengths, it is important to be mindful in discussions and not generalize, as this may create expectations for students that don't align with their learning path. Instead, reinforce to students that all people have areas of strength and areas they are developing within and outside of academics.

Contradictory Signs of Dyslexia

As we lean into understanding dyslexia, some components tend to confuse and may impact or hinder providing what is appropriate to students. Sometimes, dyslexia can feel contradictory, but we must understand the learning profile and that it isn't stagnant or secure. Our students are unique. Human. Beautiful. They deserve to have all aspects of themself be recognized and celebrated—therefore, we must have awareness so as not to pigeonhole students into a deficit model but rather recognize the unique strengths that each may hold. This comes to light, especially with those contradictory signs that we may see in our dyslexic learners. Per the definition of dyslexia, it is characterized by difficulty in reading accurately and/or fluently and poor spelling and decoding abilities. While it is often unexpected in relation to one's intellectual abilities, it is important to note that dyslexia can exist across all ranges of intellect. In education, we often hear about the deficits of dyslexia, and it's important to understand and highlight areas of strength and know how these strengths may impact academics.

Figure 2.2 shows some contradictory pieces you may see in your students with dyslexia or suspected dyslexia. This is not an all-encompassing list. However, it does highlight the common areas seen with dyslexia and shines a light on why we may inadvertently delay testing or remove the necessary supports, in turn negatively impacting our students. A comment that comes up often in IEP meetings or when discussing student progress with parents and teachers is that the child is getting good grades, so they no longer need accommodations. This is false. Chapter 13 is dedicated to understanding the importance and impact of accommodations—but understanding that the accommodations provide the necessary support and tools for students to access learning while removing the

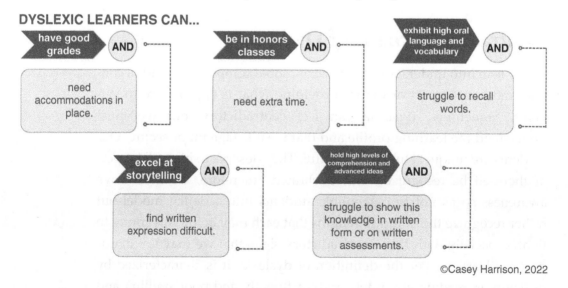

FIGURE 2.2 Contradictory parts of dyslexia.

barrier due to their learning difference is crucial. So, it may feel contradictory that the child is getting good grades **and** needs accommodations. Students with dyslexia can be in honors or Advanced Placement classes **and** need extra time. This may mean extra time for processing, completing assignments, and extended time on assessments—but it does not mean they don't need or deserve to be in the advanced classes.

You may also see that some students have a high level of oral language use and vocabulary; however, they struggle to get those words out and may substitute "umm" and "that thing" or less targeted words in speaking or writing even though they know the academic language and vocabulary their retrieval of those words can be inhibited. Another common contradictory piece I hear from parents and teachers, as well as observe, is that the student is a wonderful storyteller, yet they find it difficult to express the same story in written form. This can inadvertently lead people to think the child is lazy or needs to try harder when, in fact, their dyslexia is impacting this disconnect between their oral and written language. In the dyslexia community, it is frequently shared and noted that our students are "out-of-the-box thinkers" who often have a high level of understanding and advanced ideas about a concept. However, that understanding does not transfer to traditional assignments or assessments. Again, this can feel quite contradictory and reinforce some of the misunderstandings of dyslexia if we are unaware that these contradictory pieces exist. As educators and parents, understanding that there can be contradictory aspects of dyslexia must be considered to ensure that intervention and testing are not delayed and that appropriate supports are provided.

Conclusion

This chapter discussed expanding our understanding of dyslexia, to include characteristics across grade levels as well as the impact of language on reading development providing educators with the knowledge to be proactive instead of reactive in their early identification of needs and response to helping struggling students. We also looked at what may be perceived as contradictory aspects of dyslexia, highlighting the complexity. Broadening our understanding of dyslexia to include these aspects enhances our abilities for early intervention, proper response, and moving to a more comprehensive understanding of dyslexia. In addition, each learner is unique and, therefore, as a human being, will hold areas of strength and need, and dyslexia instruction should be comprehensive in terms of academics as well as emotionally sound.

Download Characteristics of Dyslexia checklists at www.thedyslexiaclassroom. com/teachingbeyondthediagnosis

---

Key Takeaways

- Teachers and parents knowledgeable about dyslexia and its characteristics can change the trajectory of instruction for students with or at risk of dyslexia.

- There can be contradictory aspects of dyslexia, which must be considered to ensure that intervention and testing are not delayed and that appropriate supports are provided.

- A deeper understanding of dyslexia is necessary for all educators.

- Dyslexia instruction should be comprehensive in terms of academics and the student's social and emotional well-being.

> Simplify your path to practice. What did you put in your pocket?
> What stepping stones, or nuggets of knowledge, are you taking from this chapter?

CHAPTER THREE

The Dyslexia Iceberg and Cascading Effects of Dyslexia

"It's easy to look at people and make quick judgments about them, their present and their past, but you'd be amazed at the pain and tears a single smile hides. What a person shows to the world is only one tiny facet of the iceberg hidden from sight. And more often than not, it's lined with cracks and scars that go all the way to the foundation of their soul."

—Sherrilyn Kenyon

Integrated Framework Component: Understanding Dyslexia

In this part of the journey, we deepen our understanding of dyslexia with a look at The Dyslexia Iceberg and the secondary consequences, or cascading effects of dyslexia.

Many people don't realize the impact that dyslexia has on students. Children may go to school or come to lessons with smiles. But often, the invisible load of dyslexia is heavy. As humans, we tend to focus on what is visible and judge others and ourselves without pausing or reflecting on what may lie underneath the outside facade. As Sherrilyn Kenyon states, "more often than not, it's lined with cracks and scars that go all the way to the foundation of their soul."

Whenever I hear the word iceberg, I instantly think of the Titanic and how something not fully visible could rip through a ship designed as the top-of-the-line in travel with dire consequences. Dyslexia is much like that iceberg, and our education system is the ship designed to deliver students from not knowing how to read to literate students. And here, the dyslexia iceberg sits. Floating in this sea of life and educational opportunity, and for some students, ripping a hole in their learning ship. In some ways, dyslexia is visible if we know what to look for. Above the surface are the academic components, the visible side of dyslexia. The primary characteristics of dyslexia in the classroom sit above the iceberg. The tip of the iceberg implies that we only see a small part of a larger issue or problem impacting students. What we see is often only a fractional part of what is.

A Deeper Look at Dyslexia

In academics and schooling, the primary focus is on the academic components, especially in reading and writing. Educators and parents often hyper-focus on the educational components surrounding reading and writing performance, especially for those struggling with reading acquisition or those diagnosed with dyslexia. With good reason! Literacy is not just a school requirement; it is a societal necessity. Our society is deeply rooted in literacy, and it affects one's ability to participate and contribute to the world around them entirely. A strong correlation exists between literacy, future employment opportunities, higher income, health outcomes, and economic well-being. As a result, literacy is of primary concern across our nation and schools. This societal importance of literacy underscores the urgency of addressing dyslexia and its impacts.

As educators and parents, we see the academic pieces as we encounter schools and educational expectations in the primary characteristics such as decoding and word reading, fluent and accurate reading, spelling errors, and writing difficulties, which become more visible in the classroom as students enter the school setting (see Figure 3.1).

The primary underlying causes of dyslexia include phonological processing skills, particularly phonological awareness skills (such as difficulty with segmenting, blending, and manipulating sounds in words) as well as possible impacts on phonological memory (holding sounds in memory for reading and spelling, remembering words in sentences, etc.), rapid naming (quick recall of letters, sounds, items), and orthographic knowledge (spelling patterns) become visible to educators, parents, and students as they navigate classroom academic expectations. Often the most visible in the classroom are word reading difficulties in decoding applications at the word level and dysfluent and inaccurate reading of words, sentences, and texts.

A DEEPER LOOK AT DYSLEXIA

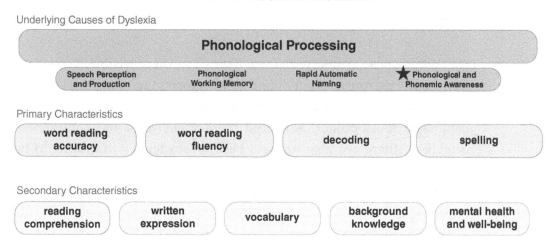

FIGURE 3.1 A deeper look at dyslexia.

We often see:

- Word reading difficulties
- Difficulty decoding words
- Difficulty with phonemic awareness tasks
- Difficulty comprehending what was read
- Spelling difficulties
- Difficulty with written expression
- Difficulty with accurate and fluent reading
- Difficulty in word or sound retrieval

Reflection:

What are some visible aspects of dyslexia within the classroom or school setting? What are some visible aspects of dyslexia within the home setting that parents may mention?

While these primary characteristics are more visible, secondary consequences can occur. While many factors play into the academic impact of these, such as reduced reading impacting vocabulary and language development, advanced literary elements and comprehension, etc., there are also impacts beyond academics that need to be addressed. For many students, reading comprehension is impacted by dyslexia as fluency and language deficits may impede learning the meaning of words and comprehending academic language. Students who find reading a frustrating experience will most likely avoid reading beyond school requirements and behavioral responses such as avoidance may become visible in the classroom. Students who struggle to read tend to read less, which leads to reduced reading experiences and can impede vocabulary growth, a dominant predictor of reading comprehension (Ahmed et al. 2016; Cromley and Azevedo 2007). This, in turn, can impact the development of background knowledge and exposure to higher literary elements, resulting in only basic reading awareness and experiences. In addition, for some students, language comprehension can emerge as a secondary consequence of dyslexia (Lyons et al. 2003). When word reading is not automatic, it places significant demands on cognitive resources, as it is challenging to remember what was read when you need to decode all or most of the words on the page. These cascading elements (Figure 3.1) impact one another and can leave a profound and lasting mark on a student's well-being and academic journey.

Understanding the academic impacts is critical, yet many impacts of dyslexia reside below the surface, hidden from view, and their effects can be profound. They hold just as much of a need for our awareness and recognition as the academic pieces. Dr. Samuel Orton, neurologist and founder of the Ortonian Prescription, spoke to the need to address a dyslexic child's well-being and making sure our instruction is emotionally sound. He observed that the emotional aspects of dyslexia began when children entered school and had trouble with letters, sounds, and directions. Over time, the frustration increased and widely impacted the child's social and emotional development. To counter this, Orton's emotionally sound principle fosters emotional growth by emphasizing a safe and supportive environment with highly structured progression with immediate teacher feedback designed to provide high levels of success building confidence and resilience.

Awareness of the social-emotional factors can help the negative and reinforce the positive forces in each learner's life. While these underlying factors may not always be visible to us, students with dyslexia often feel insecure with their reading and writing abilities, leading to other impacts and behaviors.

Some things that lie below the surface of the iceberg may be:

- Feelings of shame or guilt—students often feel insecure in their reading and writing abilities; they may feel shame or guilt that they are having difficulties and may require additional support, taking time and finances away from their family.

- Anxiety—students often feel anxious about being put in a position that highlights their learning challenges, such as reading aloud in front of peers or writing in a public space, such as on the whiteboard or in a group project.

- Exhaustion—many students spend more time completing homework and classwork assignments than their peers (what is considered a thirty-minute assignment may take 1.5 hours to complete).

- Negative self-talk and self-perceived literacy disabilities potentially leading to a higher rate of feelings of anxiety and depression (Maughan & Carroll 2006; Sturm et al. 2021; Bazen et al. 2022; Francis et al. 2019).

- Feelings of isolation.

- Negative impacts on self-esteem.

- Lack of confidence.

- Lack of trust—students may lose faith in themselves and their teachers to know what to do to help and often fall into a fixed mindset that they can't do the work or are "bad" at reading or spelling.

- Difficulty or challenges with social relationships.

- Behaviors/outbursts—students may keep it together during the school day but fall apart at home (after-school restraint collapse) or display behavior issues during the school day, particularly when asked to perform reading or writing tasks.

- School fatigue—students with dyslexia spend more time completing homework assignments and academic tasks, which can lead to fatigue or frustration when their hard work is not recognized or result in higher performance outcomes.

- Frustration.

- Refusal of accommodations or help—often due to feelings of embarrassment or feeling singled out.

- High levels of stress—asking students to read in front of peers is usually a significant stressor, leading to anxiety, as are feelings of perfectionism.

- Fixed mindset.

- Difficulty in expressing oneself.

- Unwillingness to go to school, anxiety, hard time sleeping or eating.

Through my conversations with parents and teachers, it is more common than not that a child begins school happy and excited about learning. As the struggles with reading and writing become more apparent, the impact on the child's emotions may come to the surface. They may withdraw, act out, or struggle in silence—but the effect on their self-esteem and confidence was apparent, leaving parents wondering what to do. When speaking with educators, there is often a thread of concern when we look at comments in the student file or on universal screeners and classroom observations.

For this reason, understanding the cascading or secondary consequences of dyslexia and what we can do to counter this is at the core of the integrated framework approach. The real fear I have for our students with dyslexia is that they will quit on themselves. That without the proper support and instruction the long-lasting impact of repeated failure will forever taint their self-esteem both within and beyond the role of academics, setting them on a path that doesn't serve them.

What are some behaviors or underlying factors for the student?

Mini-Lesson 1: The Dyslexia Iceberg

Bringing awareness to the dyslexia iceberg can open conversations about what the student, parent, or educator perceives about their journey with dyslexia (see Figure 3.2). I use this with students in grades 3 and up and with parents and educators to highlight the multiple impacts that dyslexia has on our students. I then use this awareness to develop learning goals within the integrated framework.

The lesson PDF and The Dyslexia Iceberg poster can be downloaded at www.thed yslexiaclassroom.com/teachingbeyondthediagnosis

1. Provide each participant with The Dyslexia Iceberg outline (PDF and poster).
2. Discuss with participants that we all have challenges in life; some are more visible to others, some are more visible to us as individuals,

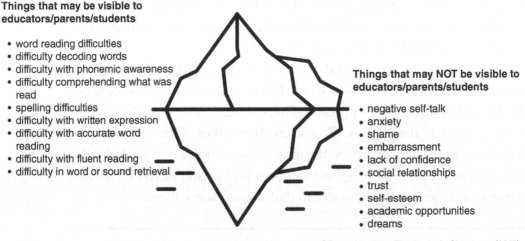

The Dyslexia Iceberg

Things that may be visible to educators/parents/students

- word reading difficulties
- difficulty decoding words
- difficulty with phonemic awareness
- difficulty comprehending what was read
- spelling difficulties
- difficulty with written expression
- difficulty with accurate word reading
- difficulty with fluent reading
- difficulty in word or sound retrieval

Things that may NOT be visible to educators/parents/students

- negative self-talk
- anxiety
- shame
- embarrassment
- lack of confidence
- social relationships
- trust
- self-esteem
- academic opportunities
- dreams

©Casey Harrison, The Dyslexia Classroom (2016)

FIGURE 3.2 The dyslexia iceberg.

and some are not visible but are present. Be sure to discuss how our awareness of these can help us design a path or steps to meet our goals. Provide appropriate examples as needed.

3. Discuss what they see as challenges with dyslexia—what are those things they feel are visible within the school day? Place them in the appropriate place on the iceberg (above, below, or the iceberg itself).

4. Discuss other areas that they feel can be a challenge within or outside of school, such as difficulty remembering phone numbers, feeling anxious, etc., and place those in the appropriate place.

5. Let students know that our work together will help to address these pieces on the dyslexia iceberg and help us generate goals and strategies to use within our lessons. Provide conversations about what is within our control (attitude, participation, etc.) and what is outside of our control (having dyslexia, etc.) There is a mini-lesson which can be downloaded from the website for use.

6. Use this as a springboard for conversations, goal setting, strategy development and awareness, and shifting the narrative surrounding dyslexia.

Conclusion

These underlying impacts on the student's emotional well-being require understanding and awareness from educators, parents, and the child. Insecurity about the school can start early and become broader and more compounded as the child gets older. For these reasons, we need to have a deeper awareness of dyslexia and how it impacts learning and social-emotional development. With this deeper understanding of dyslexia and its impacts, both academic and social-emotional impacts, we can better help students, shift the narrative, and preserve or repair self-esteem. This is at the heart of the integrated model for teaching and empowering dyslexic students. We want to ensure that the dyslexia iceberg does not rip a hole into our students' reading and academic ship so they can sail to new heights.

Key Takeaways

- Dyslexia is lifelong and can have an impact beyond academics.

- Not all parts of the dyslexia journey are visible to others.

- There can be contradictory aspects of dyslexia, which must be considered to ensure that intervention and testing are not delayed and that appropriate supports are provided.

- A deeper understanding of dyslexia is necessary for all educators.

- Dyslexia instruction should be comprehensive in terms of academics and the student's social and emotional well-being.

> Simplify your path to practice. What did you put in your pocket?
> What stepping stones, or nuggets of knowledge, are you taking from this chapter?

CHAPTER FOUR

Understanding Student Learning Profiles

"Children are apt to live up to what you believe of them."

—Lady Bird Johnson

Integrated Framework Component: Understanding Dyslexia

In this part of the journey, we continue to develop and shift our understanding and the narrative around dyslexia as we look at the learner's profile through a more comprehensive and holistic lens. This knowledge leads us to a better understanding of the learner, which results in better instructional decisions regarding academic success and the student's well-being.

With a greater understanding of dyslexia, we can shift the focus to addressing instructional needs while amplifying areas of strength and digging deeper into a student's learning profile. This knowledge is crucial as it helps us to comprehend what each student requires and how to address it best. It also underscores the importance of differentiating learning in meaningful ways, a strategy that can result in a better outcome for those with dyslexia. This approach honors their academic needs and empowers them to know themselves as learners, how to use and advocate for accommodations and tools, and see dyslexia as a part of their journey and not their sole identity. As educators and parents, defining dyslexia solely on areas of weakness is narrow in understanding and limits the possibility of identifying and fostering personal strengths, which each person possesses.

Often, in the area of dyslexia education, conflicting messages surround the impacts of dyslexia. Is dyslexia a different set of strengths in which the world is perceived differently? Or is dyslexia a disability in which the enormity of struggles weighs down the individual? Or is there a space for addressing both the need to remediate the areas of weakness due to dyslexia while amplifying the areas of strength we possess as human beings? I believe the latter to be true, and that the combination of the two is essential: designing schools and lessons that remediate the areas of need and amplify each student's areas of strength. This individualized approach is what our students deserve, and it empowers us, as educators, to help students meet their potential, while also reiterating that dyslexia is not the sole defining factor of who they are.

A Deeper Look at the Student Learning Profile

When asked questions about a student with dyslexia and how to best help them, while there are the guiding principles of the structured literacy components that should be addressed, I often find my response is "It depends," and that idea of "depends" rests on a deeper understanding of the student's learning profile. This is because while the characteristics of dyslexia remain consistent, the impact varies from person to person. A student with a large gap or need in phonological processing tasks and rapid automatic naming, or the inability to retrieve verbal-visual connections, may require more intensity and scaffolded support to address the phonological processing needs linked to reading and spelling. Perhaps a student has adequate phonemic awareness in these elements but shows gaps in Rapid Automatic Naming, under phonological processing, requiring intentional retrieval practices embedded within and between lessons. If a student shows a need for Oral Reading Fluency, have we looked at the level at which the breakdown occurs: Is it at the letter, word, phrase, or sentence level? Is the need in the area of reading the words correctly and accuracy, or with the fluency or phrasing? Is vocabulary and language playing a role? There are many questions we can pose, and the instructional implications reside in assessments and observations, and review of both of these is critical for those who teach students with dyslexia. We must learn to pull data from our resources, determine instructional implications, and put those into appropriate practice. This comes with knowledge of how to read data, keenly observe students, and align these to instruction and lessons within our structured literacy approach. In addition, we must understand the intensity with which to address gaps, the duration of time, and the knowledge of how to scaffold up or down based on the student. This deeper understanding of the student's learning profile allows us to connect with our students on a more empathetic level, tailoring our teaching to their unique needs.

Through a deeper look at the student learning profile, we may utilize formal and informal data as well as observations to identify those critical areas of need, determine areas of strength, and personalize instruction to provide appropriate intervention that remediates needs and amplifies strengths. Typically, a dyslexia assessment would include tests on phonological processing, letter knowledge, word level decoding or word recognition, fluency, rapid automatic naming, and perhaps spelling, vocabulary, comprehension, and oral and written expression. Some may even include some cognitive components to aid in understanding how working memory may impact learning. All data and observations can be used to gather a more holistic or comprehensive understanding of the student's learning profile.

When working with students, I look at the dyslexia report and my own diagnostic assessments and observations to gather as much of a whole picture of the learner as possible. This allows me to have a clear visual of each area of instruction, and determine those components that require intense need, moderate need, or regular instruction or intervention, as well as areas of strength. A report will only be as good as the information that can be extracted and put into instruction. Every student has a unique learning profile, meaning that strengths and areas of need may vary in what we determine as the instructional focus, the level of intensity, and need.

Shifting the focus to remediate areas of need and recognizing and amplifying areas of strength is what our students deserve.

A Sea of Strengths

Dyslexia highlights the struggles in reading, writing, and spelling; yet, when we look more holistically at the student, we see so much more. Dr. Sally Shaywitz famously said, "Dyslexia is an island of weakness in a sea of strengths." This encompasses what we, as educators and parents, see in our children. We see the impact of the daily struggle with dyslexia, and we also see the brilliance that our children hold. We can't ignore or diminish the challenges that learning to read and write imposes on a daily basis, nor the immense pressures to meet up with the expectations of school, work, and life that require fluent reading and writing skills in every aspect of our society. However, suppose we are ensuring that appropriate academic needs are being addressed. In that case, we don't want to let deficiencies dominate the conversation either for fear of individuals being unable to see beyond the struggles of their diagnosis of dyslexia. The big question is, how do we weave these seemingly contradictory pieces into our work to empower students?

Years ago, I worked with a young girl, a third grader, whose intelligence and curiosity were clear when speaking with her, and yet in her classroom, when asked to read or write, I observed a shy and reserved student full of fear and insecurity. When placed in group settings for projects, she rarely spoke, was deeply impacted by other students' comments about her spelling, and was overshadowed by others' quick responses to the task. She was a child experiencing repeated failure in the classroom, and even though she was clearly bright, she couldn't showcase this within the general education classroom as it was being done at that time. When looking at her learning profile, if given additional thinking time and the ability to gather her thoughts, her output was often superior to that of her quick-responding peers. She was also a very curious child who wanted to understand the concepts and had in-depth questions that showed deeper thinking—all wonderful strengths that she was unaware of, nor was the classroom culture making space for this need in her learning.

In our dyslexia therapy sessions outside of the classroom, I purposefully wove into the lessons conversations about these things that I witnessed in her. When she asked questions, I would note aloud how curious she was and that it was wonderful that she was thinking so deeply about things and wondering about what we were learning, to which her response was, "Really? I didn't know that I asked questions like that." This small but thoughtful and authentic comment to the child highlighting an area of strength for her was then made conscious of and, in return, increased her response and engagement within the lessons. She became more aware of her thinking and her curiosity, and we used that strength to dig into deeper learning, increase her confidence, and connect to the skills she was working on. We used that strength to improve deficits.

Dyslexia	
Areas of need	**Areas of strength**
Identify and *target* through explicit systematic instruction in a structured literacy approach.	*Identify* and *amplify* areas of strength within the academic setting and beyond.
Data-driven instruction (quantitative and qualitative)	Build on these strengths.
Dyslexia is unique to the individual, and therefore understanding the learner profile is critical in establishing the needs and strengths and how to address needs and amplify strengths.	

One of the biggest things that we can do for students with dyslexia, or those struggling to learn to read, is to separate these challenges from the person's identity as a whole. We must see the student first before we see their dyslexia. Dyslexia is a lifelong learning difference and, therefore, a part of the person; however, in life, we all experience different struggles and areas in which we shine. While the current definition of dyslexia notes the areas of weakness, we must consider possible assets associated with dyslexia and the individual strengths held by each person, and how these impact the learner's profile of dyslexia. When working with students, we can intentionally integrate this awareness that we are all unique and bring different things into the world. As the educator or parent, keen observation and using small moments to authentically identify areas of strength while noting areas of challenge is important. It can't be a focus on one or the other—we need to combine the two.

Our role is to show students how we can use our strengths, such as curiosity, to build those areas of need. This curious student began to use her curiosity to look at the meaning of words and why words were spelled a certain way—all of which led to increasing her knowledge of spelling, reading, and vocabulary. Sometimes, students who have experienced repeated failures struggle to recognize the areas in which they shine. Perhaps it is due to a lack of opportunities to showcase their unique strengths in the traditional school setting, or perhaps their strengths lie in those small interpersonal skills (Palser et al. 2021; Strum et al. 2021) that may be overlooked. Regardless, as we work with students in this setting, we can make note of these strengths and authentically bring them to light with the students. This self-awareness or metacognitive practice of noting for the student is powerful.

Possible areas of strength (Note: everyone is unique!)	How can we use this to build areas of need?
Creative thinking—often, we refer to this as "thinking outside the box" and coming up with innovative solutions due to their unique thought processes.	We can provide opportunities for students to think about strategies used, how they solved a problem (this may include some unique workarounds, and we need to teach students strategies for solving problems so noting what they are thinking and adjusting from there can be a powerful tool), and share how they are linking knowledge.
Big-Picture thinking—students with dyslexia may often see the larger picture or be able to "see" the big picture. Those with dyslexia may be able to see the big picture but get stuck in the details or the steps. Students benefit from understanding the larger picture as this can give an understanding of how things work and how different components work toward the larger goal or task.	Starting with the goal or big picture in mind can set the stage for learning and help learners understand the purpose that the components serve in achieving the goal of the lesson. Without understanding the bigger picture and how this connects to the smaller components, learning can feel isolated or disconnected.
3-Dimensional and Visual thinking—students with dyslexia may excel at visual thinking, or the ability to quickly engage and perform in non-language visuospatial domains (art, architecture, etc.) (Schneps et al. 2012; Von Karolyi et al. 2003; Wolff & Lundberg 2002)	The use of mind maps, outlines, concept maps, and graphic organizers can help to organize thoughts in a visual representation.

(Continued)

(*Continued*)

Possible areas of strength (Note: everyone is unique!)	How can we use this to build areas of need?
Critical thinking—students may possess a strong ability to use logical reasoning and critical thinking to solve a problem.	Explicit strategies in reading and writing instruction to logically solve problems and then reflect on the use of those strategies.
Other traits or strengths we may see can include: abstract thinking, imaginative, empathy, conversation, leadership skills, puzzle-solving skills, strong memory for stories, reasoning skills, interpersonal skills, storytelling, interconnected reasoning, goal-directed, and many more. Each learner is unique.	

Part of understanding dyslexia is to look at each child's unique learning profile through the lens of identifying strengths and areas of need. We are all good at different things, and no one thing defines us. While we hear about the deficits of dyslexia, it's essential to understand and highlight areas of strength. A teacher who understands the bigger picture of dyslexia can impact our dyslexic learners—academically and emotionally. Many people don't realize the social-emotional impact that dyslexia has on students throughout the day. Our systems rely heavily on the ability to read and write well, highlighting our student's areas of need in every class and every encounter. Every day, our struggling students are surrounded by experiences in school that remind them of their challenges and often overlook their strengths. Expanding our understanding of how dyslexia is impacting a student and using a student's strengths to help with new learning can have a fantastic impact. When we help our students see themselves in this light, everything changes.

Tips for Discussing and Identifying Strengths

Authentically Recognize a Student's Strengths

Children are keen to realize when someone is inauthentic. Speak the truth and identify, highlight, and state the strengths you see in each student. Our children are incredibly smart; one of their strengths is often their interpersonal skills and intuition. Kids know when you aren't being honest. Connect with compassionate empathy (see Chapter 10) and show them through consistent actions that you believe in them and will support them and hold them to put forth their best effort.

Praise Privately and Openly

Building connections and trust with students is important, especially for students who have disengaged or experienced a great deal of failure. They may not yet recognize their talents or skills, and as educators and parents, we can honor the differences each child brings and highlight these talents. This recognition helps students understand there is value in what they bring to the world. Dyslexia doesn't define them, there is no ceiling, and they too can achieve their dreams.

Provide Opportunities for Those Strengths to Shine

Some of the strengths of many dyslexic thinkers are visual-spatial skills (Schneps et al. 2012; Con Karolyi et al. 2003; Wolff & Lundberg 2002), reasoning skills, out-of-the-box problem-solving (Logan 2009), interpersonal skills (Palser et al. 2021; Sturm et al. 2021), declarative memory (Hedenius et al. 2013), and big-picture thinking. Traditional school assignments may not provide students with opportunities to showcase these strengths. We can provide different ways for students to show what they have learned. This may take some reflection and revamping on our part, but the outcome for our students is that it strengthens their self-esteem, reinforces their talents, and promotes a positive learning cycle.

Weave in Discussions About How We All Have Areas of Strength and Need

This helps students understand that all humans, whether dyslexic or not, will face their future with a range of strengths and weaknesses.

Share Your Struggles and Discuss Challenges

Share what struggles you have with something as well as areas in which you feel confident or strong. My students love to hear how many attempts were made in the creation of the lightbulb—learning from each mistake or error is what creates improvement. Some of my older students have struggled or had a hard time accessing the curriculum, but the teachers were telling them how smart they were and that they would get there yet they weren't able to do it with just this well-intended encouragement alone, and this created a sense of self-doubt, but when they understood why they were having the challenges they were able to shift their perspective a bit to learn from the challenges and have it not be their whole identify. Identifying challenging areas provides us with awareness and sets us up to create a plan to address these roadblocks in the path of our learning—an essential part of work in metacognitive processes, which we will address in later chapters.

Acknowledge Efforts and Small Wins

Keeping the focus on the effort being made instead of keeping the sole focus on the outcome will help students recognize the small wins. As humans we can easily become focused on what we can't do or what we are not yet doing—instead keep the focus on recognizing those small improvements, whether it is a gain in reading fluency, application of a decoding or reading strategy, or rereading—anything that is moving learning forward.

Things to Be Mindful of

Currently, there are differing conversations surrounding the word "gift" and dyslexia. Some feel that it creates a Pollyanna effect or minimizes the challenges, while others claim that dyslexic thinking offers benefits and different aspects of thinking. There is a growing body of research that is looking at multifactorial models and the complex interactions as well as the benefits of high-quality mentoring (Haft et al. 2019), growth mindset (Anderson & Neilsen 2016), and emotional resilience (Goldberg et al. 2002; Haft et al. 2016; Zheng et al. 2014) as well as interventions that foster motivation (Lovett et al. 2021; Duke & Cartright 2021) which warrant a consideration of the possible assets or strengths surrounding dyslexia and deserve future exploration (Orkin et al. 2022). I believe we need to be very mindful and understanding when making statements about what is or isn't a gift. When working with students in a therapeutic setting for dyslexia, I see my students' remarkable talents and "out-of-the-box" thinking that are overlooked in a deficit-only mindset or traditional school design.

While I don't use the specific phrasing that "dyslexia is a gift" because dyslexia is challenging, I think we should help students see themselves as more than their dyslexia. We must guide our students in identifying their talents (we all have them!) to preserve self-esteem and realize that every one of us brings something beautiful to this world. So often, our students are surrounded by a sense of failure and can't see their strengths. We can help them see their uniqueness. Also, suppose we understand that dyslexia is under the neurodivergent umbrella. In that case, it is part of who they are and isn't separate—it isn't something that goes away, so a mindset about embracing challenges and strengths can empower students. While I appreciate people's perspectives on using or not using the statements about dyslexia and gifts, I feel that it is not my place to say it is or isn't—that is for the person walking this journey. With that in mind, the following mini-lessons focus on individual strengths which we all hold.

Two Mini-Lessons to Shift the Narrative

Mini-Lesson: Sea of Strengths

Returning to Shaywitz's quote about dyslexia being an island in a sea of strengths and the contradictory signs discussed in previous chapters, as well as the "unexpected" part of the IDA dyslexia definition, we can see how this seemingly paradoxical explanation of dyslexia comes together and why we must address this within our lessons (see Figure 4.1). I speak to my students about this often and weave this notion that we have areas that pose challenges and areas of strength into our lessons.

My Sea of Strengths

Believe in yourself and all that you are. Know that there is something inside of you that is greater than any obstacle. - Christian D. Larson

My dyslexia

©2022, Casey Harrison, The Dyslexia Classroom

FIGURE 4.1 Sea of strengths.

One of my students, when introduced to the lesson on the island of dyslexia and the sea of strengths, started to draw a ship heading toward the island and a dock extending from the island. We discussed the purpose of these two items, and the student shared how the ship, which contained drawings of the two of us, was docking at the island, and together, we would work on the items we listed on the island as we sailed along the waves that contained the student's strengths. This really stuck with me. This student showed just what people mean when they say that dyslexics are "out-of-the-box" thinkers. We then used the ship to illustrate the structured literacy lessons we were conducting and how those would let us sail off the island of what we perceived as our struggles and into our strengths. What a beautiful way to illustrate hope, determination, and strategy as we worked together to break the reading code and better understand what dyslexia means to that child and their journey.

Materials: Student copy of A Sea of Strength and My Dyslexia Island

---

Download the PDF and mini-lesson at www.thedyslexiaclassroom.com/teaching beyondthediagnosis

---

Teacher: We all have areas of strength, or things that we feel we do well, and areas that we may find challenging. For some, dyslexia or learning to read can be a challenge. We are going to put dyslexia (or reading difficulties) on this island. What are some challenges in the area of reading or writing that we are working on or notice? *(Students can write or teacher writes these challenges, for example: spelling, reading aloud, reading, etc.)*

Teacher: Do you see how this island is surrounded by water? This is where all of our strengths are. The challenges are one part of our lives, but we all bring so many wonderful strengths into the world as well. All unique and all needed. Let's think of some things that we notice about ourselves that we can add to our sea of strengths and note these on our charts. *Authentically discuss or bring to light those strengths that you have observed in your students. These can be academic or not—there are many interpersonal skills that students possess and may not be aware of that you can bring to light. For example, ____ is a great listener. This is such an important skill to have in the world—the ability to listen well to others and connect with them is what counselors, therapists, and good friends do.; I have seen ____ play football—wow! You are good!, etc.; I love the way you ask questions, you are always thinking and wondering—which is such a fantastic skill and shows you are curious about the world around you and how things work, etc.*

Tip: Students may not yet be able to identify those things that they feel confident or recognize as strengths. Before this lesson, jot down a few authentic observations about each student that you can highlight as a strength. Students can write down or even sketch their strengths in the sea. This is an ongoing conversation, and I have my students place their charts in the front of their folders, and we revisit this and add to the sea of strength throughout our sessions.

Extension: Our structured Literacy or science of reading ship—Here is where we add what we are doing to help us reach the island— what skills are we working on in class that will get us to our island of dyslexia or reading difficulties? I like to use this connection for my students to see why we are focusing on different skills and practice within our lessons. It keeps them engaged in understanding why we are doing this hard work and how it will get them where we want to go—these skills we are bringing to the island will make our reading challenges less—it will empower us with the skills needed to address or lay claim to the island. Students can draw a ship heading to the island, or you can have a ship for the class in which you note the things the class is working on just as my student who drew a dock on her island with us, waiting for the ship to reach us did. It was such a fantastic image and one we returned to as we did our work to "move the ship" toward the island.

Mini-Lesson: Only One You

> "Believe in yourself and all that you are. Know that there is something inside of you that is greater than any obstacle."
>
> —Christian D. Larson

The book *Only One You*, by Linka Kranz, is a wonderful read-aloud for students as it highlights that we are all unique and wonderful in our own way. Upon reading the book aloud, have discussions surrounding the theme that we are all beautifully unique. As an extension, you can have students generate adjectives to describe themselves and write them on the fish worksheet or complete an acrostic poem with their name or the word dyslexia (see Figure 4.2). Another possible extension is to have students paint a rock as a fish to represent themselves, team up with the art teacher to create a fish as a cross-curricular activity, or even ask parents to send in adjectives describing their child. This is another way to bring awareness that we are all unique and bring different strengths to the world.

The PDFs for these lessons can be downloaded at www.thedyslexiaclassroom.com/teachingbeyondthediagnosis

---

Extension/Connecting to Text: Provide opportunities for questions surrounding dyslexia. Children are inquisitive beings and love knowing more about things impacting their lives. When we talk to children about dyslexia, they often have questions. Weaving conversations about dyslexia into your structured literacy lessons is powerful. It keeps the topic and

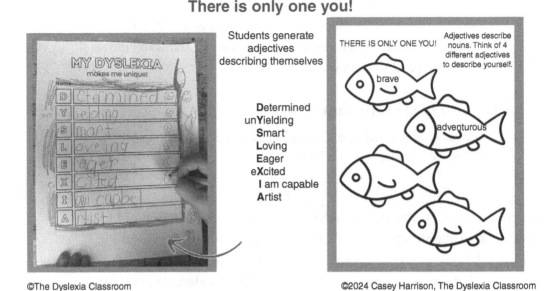

FIGURE 4.2 There is only one you.

word at the center of your lessons, focusing on understanding and not shame. I like to share stories and insights from other dyslexic learners and am grateful for the increase in people sharing their journey.

Books provide opportunities for students to connect to themselves in a safe way and can springboard conversations. Download a comprehensive read aloud book list at www.thedyslexiaclassroom. com/teachingbeyondthediagnosis. Some of my favorite books to read with students that connect to identifying our strengths are:

Maxwell's Mountain—Shari Becker and Nicole Wong

Only One You—Linda Kranz

Beautiful Oops!—Barney Saltzberg

I Am Enough—Grace Byers and Keturah A. Bobo

We're All Wonders—R.J. Palacio

Jabari Jumps—Gaia Cornwall

The Most Magnificent Maker's A to Z—Ashley Spires

Smart Cookie—Jory John and Pete Oswald

Conclusion

When feeling supported, students with dyslexia will know what value they bring to their world. This helps them understand that dyslexia does not define them and that there's no ceiling to what dreams they can achieve.

This deeper understanding of each student and their unique learning profile which focuses on addressing areas of deficit while in tandem promoting and amplifying areas of strength is key for remediation of dyslexia.

By having a deeper knowledge of dyslexia, both academically and emotionally, we can guide students to understand their unique and amazing brains better.

Key Takeaways

- Student learning profiles should include insights into strengths and needs.

- Use understanding of student learning profile to guide instruction.

- Guide students in understanding dyslexia and self-reflection on areas to "grow" and areas of strength.

> Simplify your path to practice. What did you put in your pocket?
> What stepping stones, or nuggets of knowledge, are you taking from this chapter?

The Reading Brain

"Each new reader comes to reading with a 'fresh' brain—one that is programmed to speak, see, and think, but not read. Reading requires the brain to rearrange its original parts to learn something new."

—Maryanne Wolf

Integrated Framework Component: Academics and Support

In this part of the journey, we look at how reading comes to be, what this means for building neural pathways in the brain, and how this acts as a bridge to link our understanding of dyslexia to our academic journey (see Figure 5.1).

Reading well is something that many of us may take for granted. The ability to automatically see letters and, within milliseconds, have that transfer to a word connected to meaning. And yet, 43 million adults in the US (US Department of Education 2019), or 1 in 5, possess low literacy skills. We see a similar trend in our children, with the United States National Assessment of Educational Progress showing that only 33% of fourth graders and 31% of eighth graders across the country performed at or above the basic proficiency level (US Department of Education 2022). This raises many questions about reading acquisition, reading

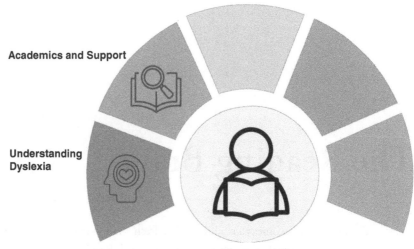

THE INTEGRATED FRAMEWORK
©2019 - The Dyslexia Classroom, Casey Harrison

FIGURE 5.1 The integrated framework—academics and support.

instruction, and reading disabilities. Indeed, not all 67% of students struggling with reading proficiency on the national exam have dyslexia, even with dyslexia being the most common of the learning differences, which has led to more research about how we learn to read, especially in the area of neuroscience.

When I first went to school to become a teacher, little conversation or research was shared about what occurs in the brain as we learn to read and write. Instead, much of our studies focused on reading comprehension, with little on how we learn to break the reading code and the alphabetic principle or what occurs in the brain to make reading possible. Before the National Reading Panel Report (2000), conversations in education continued to support the idea that reading was a natural thing (it's not) and that struggling students will pick it up when they are ready (they won't). Even after the report came out showing educators the research behind what was needed within instruction, and legislative funding was put into place, the professional development and curriculums used within schools were not always aligned with best evidence-based practices. The findings from the NRP supported what was being done in dyslexia interventions grounded in the Orton-Gillingham approach, but these were overwhelmingly left out of classroom instructional practices and schools, contributing to the trend in our reading scores. We are seeing shifts, but I know that I am not unique in this story of frustration within our field. We don't need to be researchers or neuroscientists to impact change for our children. Educators and parents, when we have more knowledge about how we learn, are the bridge between research and practice, and we can better advocate for effective change within our schools and classrooms.

What Do We Know About How We Learn to Read?

The Simple View of Reading (SVR) Model and Beyond

The ultimate goal of reading is for our children to achieve high levels of comprehension. To have reading be a path to opportunity. We want this for ALL children, regardless of the ease with which they acquire reading and writing, yet we are leaving many students behind in our current state of reading instruction. One of the theoretical models that has brought awareness to the necessary components of reading is the Simple View of Reading. Researchers Gough and Tunmer's Simple View of Reading provides a useful reference for conveying the importance of both word recognition and linguistic comprehension.

Word Recognition (WR) × Language Comprehension (LC)
= Reading Comprehension (RC)

While first created 35 years ago, the Simple View of Reading by Gough and Tunmer (1986) breaks apart the complex reading elements into two broad categories: word recognition and linguistic comprehension, posing the concept that reading comprehension is a product of printed word recognition and linguistic comprehension (Gough & Tunmer 1986). This theory proposed that weakness in either (or both) domains leads to weak reading comprehension and showed this through the equation of $D \times C = R$, where D = decoding and C = comprehension, specifically linguistic comprehension, and R = reading. The R in this equation was in reference to comprehension of written text (Gough & Tunmer 1986; Hoover & Gough 1990). Since this time the model has been revisited by Hoover and Tunmer (2020) with a shift in the terms used for Word Recognition (formerly Decoding) × Language Comprehension (formerly Linguistic Comprehension) = Reading Comprehension to provide a broader view of the constructs represented in reading acquisition. This framework connects to the domains of language and reinforces the idea that an individual's knowledge of both phonological awareness (an aspect of spoken language) and semantics in language supports reading and writing skills.

Word recognition, or the accurate and fast retrieval of decoded word forms, is essential for developing reading comprehension, and is the primary area of need for students with dyslexia. Students who cannot accurately read the words on the page will not fully comprehend what is being read. Proficient readers must be able to access the written word accurately and automatically. This automated word reading frees up mental resources and allows for close attention to the meaning of the text. The skills acquired under word recognition (decoding, word-level reading, and phonological awareness) are paramount for beginning and novice readers, and typically, this is the core area of instructional need for those with dyslexia. Students with dyslexia need additional support and instruction focusing on the word recognition domain. While ALL students benefit from an explicit and systematic approach to connecting speech to print, it is essential for dyslexic and struggling readers.

Additionally, Gough and Tunmer state through this equation that if a student lacks proficiency in understanding language, then reading comprehension is impacted. As educators, we need to understand that these two components are interdependent in some sense, and we should be mindful of how our understanding of the SVR translates to reading instruction.

As we disseminate the findings from multiple researchers and disciplines, we see the complexity within reading instruction and the need to continue to dig deeper into the components of word recognition, language comprehension, reading comprehension, and other factors such as metacognitive processes.

A Look at Scarborough's Reading Rope and the Active View of Reading

Scarborough's Reading Rope is a visual metaphor for reading development created by Dr. Hollis Scarborough that is often used when discussing reading both within schools and with parents (see Figure 5.2). I find this visual representation of what the research highlights in reading instruction and the development over time in the core areas to be a useful tool when speaking with parents about their child's journey in reading acquisition. This image clearly breaks down reading into two bundles, which allows the viewer to organize the complexities into manageable components and understand that every strand on the rope plays some role in becoming a proficient reader. Scarborough's two bundles are broken into word recognition and language comprehension, and although they are the same categories as the SVR, Dr. Scarborough says the creation of the rope was made without any connection to the SVR, which highlights the importance of these two broad categories in reading instruction. While the SVR proposed that the WR and LC remained and developed separately, Scarborough highlights that the two strands reinforce one another and weave together to produce a skilled reader,

THE MANY STRANDS THAT ARE WOVEN INTO SKILLED READING

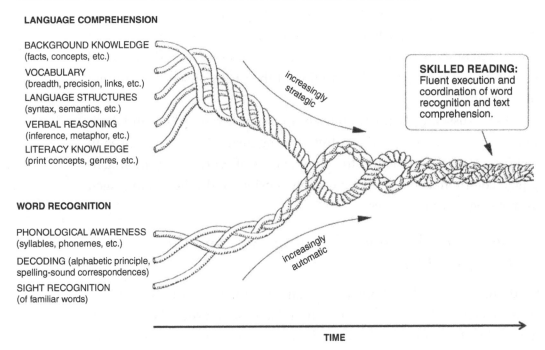

LANGUAGE COMPREHENSION

BACKGROUND KNOWLEDGE
(facts, concepts, etc.)

VOCABULARY
(breadth, precision, links, etc.)

LANGUAGE STRUCTURES
(syntax, semantics, etc.)

VERBAL REASONING
(inference, metaphor, etc.)

LITERACY KNOWLEDGE
(print concepts, genres, etc.)

increasingly strategic

SKILLED READING:
Fluent execution and coordination of word recognition and text comprehension.

WORD RECOGNITION

PHONOLOGICAL AWARENESS
(syllables, phonemes, etc.)

DECODING (alphabetic principle, spelling-sound correspondences)

SIGHT RECOGNITION
(of familiar words)

increasingly automatic

TIME

FIGURE 5.2 The reading rope.
Source: Scarborough, H.S. (2001). Connecting early language and literacy to later reading (dis)abilities: Evidence, theory, and practice. In S. Neuman & D. Dickinson (Eds.), *Handbook for Research in Early Literacy* (pp. 97–110). New York: Guilford Press.

noting that this doesn't happen quickly nor in isolation of one another, but rather over time with practice.

When providing instruction for struggling readers or those with dyslexia, understanding each child's learning profile determines where the focus of intervention needs to occur. Students with dyslexia will need additional instruction in the word recognition strands. However, this doesn't mean that we ignore the language comprehension strands, as both must be addressed within lessons, providing a comprehensive scope and framework in its approach to literacy instruction. When the foundational reading skills, those under the word recognition band, are strong, it affords more opportunities to acquire more knowledge and engagement with the upper strands, and when language skills are strong, it allows for faster and more accurate decoding of unfamiliar words as students connect the pronunciation, orthographic representation (spelling) and meaning together through the orthographic mapping process. As the strands develop, they interact with one another, reinforcing the need to teach both strands for skilled reading comprehension to occur. If strands are frayed, then the development of these reading skills can be negatively impacted and cause the widening between the two bands instead of coming together to create proficient reading.

As we continue to gain knowledge and research in reading and learning, new theoretical models have emerged. Researchers Duke and Cartwright offer the Active View of Reading (AVR) model (2021) to reflect advances in research to include additional disciplines and factors that determine children's success in reading (see Figure 5.3). Their work expands on elements of the Reading Rope to include components within active self-regulation, executive function skills, the importance of bridging processes between word recognition and language comprehension, cultural and content knowledge, and theory of mind or social reasoning. These bridging processes reflect an overlap found in many studies regarding reading comprehension and intentionally note that "each construct named in the model is instructionally malleable; that is practitioners can affect it" (Duke & Cartwright 2021), highlighting the need for educators to understand the instructional implications within each component and how that impacts the delivery of lessons to aid students.

The Active View of Reading expands upon the broad isolated bands of WR and LC found in the SVR and the interwoven strands within the Reading Rope to include the constructs of active self-regulation, including motivation and engagement, as well as executive function skills and strategy use. In addition, the AVR model notes that difficulties in reading acquisition may exist beyond isolated categories of WR and LC. For those working with dyslexia, where we understand the complexity of

ACTIVE VIEW OF READING

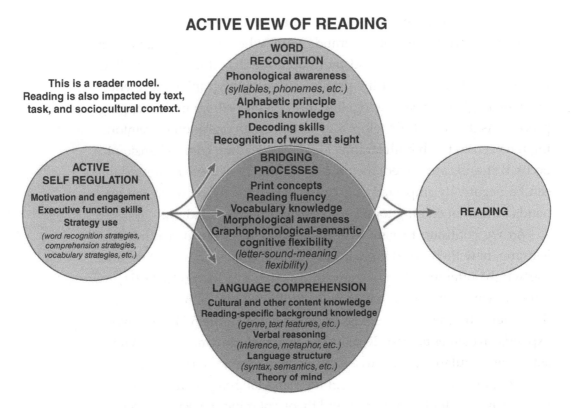

This is a reader model. Reading is also impacted by text, task, and sociocultural context.

WORD RECOGNITION
Phonological awareness
(syllables, phonemes, etc.)
Alphabetic principle
Phonics knowledge
Decoding skills
Recognition of words at sight

ACTIVE SELF REGULATION
Motivation and engagement
Executive function skills
Strategy use
(word recognition strategies, comprehension strategies, vocabulary strategies, etc.)

BRIDGING PROCESSES
Print concepts
Reading fluency
Vocabulary knowledge
Morphological awareness
Graphophonological-semantic cognitive flexibility
(letter-sound-meaning flexibility)

READING

LANGUAGE COMPREHENSION
Cultural and other content knowledge
Reading-specific background knowledge
(genre, text features, etc.)
Verbal reasoning
(inference, metaphor, etc.)
Language structure
(syntax, semantics, etc.)
Theory of mind

FIGURE 5.3 The active view of reading.
Source: Reprinted from "The science of reading progresses: Communicating advances beyond the Simple View of Reading," by N.K. Duke and K.B. Cartwright, 2021, *Reading Research Quarterly* 56(S1), S25–S44. Copyright 2021 Authors. Reprinted with permission. Note: Several workings in this model are adapted from Scarborough (2001).

learning profiles, this makes sense. Some students with dyslexia will have a primary need in the area of WR, while others may have additional needs in LC and/or EF skills. Remember that while characteristics of dyslexia remain consistent, the range in which dyslexia impacts the individual may vary, and coexisting areas of need may also exist. For this reason, I like the Active View of Reading as another theoretical model that looks beyond simple categories and honors the students' journey. Another aspect of the AVR is the goal of guiding practitioners in their work with students. In addition, you will see the constructs found within the AVR, such as executive function skills, metacognitive processes, and bridging processes in connection to word recognition and language comprehension, align with those found in the integrated framework within this book and will be addressed throughout the chapters.

The Reading Brain and Dyslexia

I have been fascinated with the information coming out of cognitive neuroscience regarding dyslexia and reading. The use of fMRI to analyze the ongoings in the typical reading brain and the dyslexic brain and then to see the changes that occur from appropriate reading remediation is mind-blowing. The areas responsible for phonological and language processing (Broca's and Wernicke's language areas, and word analysis area) show a difference in the dyslexic brain both before and after interventions. While I am not a researcher or neuroscientist, the impact of understanding the ongoings in the brain has enhanced how I teach students in connection to academics and emotional regulation. I also use this information in a mini-lesson with students, included in this chapter, to deepen their own understanding of why we complete certain tasks within our dyslexia intervention and as an anchor for the expectation of taking an active role in their own learning.

Why do we need to look at the brain through the lens of learning and reading? Reading is a complex process that requires different regions of the brain to perform specific jobs in concert with one another. Our brains were designed for language, vision, and cognition, not for reading. Reading is a man-made construct and, therefore, does not have a designated area of the brain designed as the reading center. Instead, the brain relies on a network of systems, each designed for different things (language, vision, cognition), but together create a whole new circuitry so that we may read. We rely on these networks to convert language into printed form for reading and writing. Student success in reading relies on establishing this new circuit system and continuing to add more sophisticated linguistic, cognitive, and affective processes over time as we create complex circuits. The critical thing to note here is that ALL readers must build a new reading circuitry. We all need to create a reading circuitry that connects the regions of the brain to make reading accessible. This means that every single student learns to read the same way; however, we may need to teach reading with different strategies, scaffolds, intensity, and repetition. Those students with dyslexia will require an intensive approach to create this circuitry system. This basic understanding of the brain and its workings is key for educators so that we can match our instructional practices to what we know about how the brain learns—for all students—and especially for those with learning differences.

While we want our work to be research-driven and evidence-based, it needs to make sense to teachers, parents, and most importantly, the students! The reality is that the right kind of instruction and intervention changes the brain to become more efficient in connecting oral language to written code. Explicit instruction in linking speech to print is necessary because our brains are not programmed to read. The brain can create neural pathways, or a series of connections that send signals from one part of the brain to another, to unlock the written code and connect reading to the words written on a page. These neural pathways are built over time with the practice of specific skills so that we create, in essence, a superhighway in which information is transferred at incredibly fast speeds, less than a quarter of a second, so that reading can appear to be natural for some, and arduous for others, when in reality it is the efficiency of the connection of these neural networks that determines the ease with which reading occurs. Most of what is being learned about in the field of reading and the brain is acquired through neuroimaging, but for educators, it is the connection to classroom application that is essential to understand and bring into instruction.

Researchers are conducting studies about the brain and impacts from related reading methods to help determine instructional impacts, and while this is ongoing, and science is dynamic, understanding a simplified view of the reading brain can assist our instructional decisions and lessons. This information can also be shared with students to engage them in the process of learning and actively bring them into the work.

Our purposeful, explicit, and systematic approach to teaching reading addresses the complex process that requires different regions of the brain to perform specific jobs in connection with one another (see Figure 5.4). The right-and-left hemispheres of the brain are connected with a band of cell fibers called the *corpus callosum,* and while we used to think that information remained within each hemisphere, the newest research shows that our brains connect across the hemispheres when reading, although the left hemisphere is the most involved in reading and where we will focus our attention.

Major Regions Underlying Processes in the Reading Brain Circuit

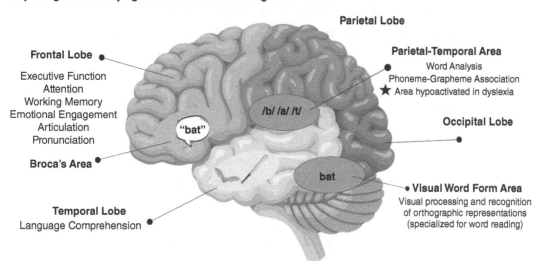

The brain creates neural circuitry for reading

FIGURE 5.4 Major regions underlying processes in the reading brain circuit.
Source: Adapted from Stanislas Dehaene (2009).

The Frontal Lobe

The frontal lobe is responsible for decision-making, planning, and focus shifting. These Executive Function (EF) skills develop over time, as does the demand for them. It is the last area of our brain to fully develop. The executive function's role may be the greatest detriment to success (Harris & Graham 1996) and warrants educators addressing the executive function skills within literacy instruction, and the Active View of Reading is a model that addresses these executive function skills. In addition to EF skills, the frontal lobe addresses language. Language provides the foundation for reading, and when we look at the left hemisphere, the primary side for language and reading, within the frontal lobe, there is a portion referred to as Broca's area. It is responsible for pronunciation, articulation, and word analysis. We can think of this as language in/language out. This is in part where the (approximate) 44 speech sounds of the English language are processed. As students gain knowledge and skills in the alphabetic principle, how we link letters and sounds, they are connecting or creating a highway between the different areas of the brain to connect the speech sounds to the written words and the meaning of those words—a lot is happening as we build the neural pathways in the brain!

The Parietal-Temporal Lobe

The parietal lobe helps us process sensory information. What we see, taste, and touch is processed in this area. When we think of reading, the overlap of the parietal lobe and the temporal lobe, the parietal-temporal lobe is responsible for the phoneme–grapheme association—the connection of the sounds to the letters. This is also where phoneme analysis occurs—all part of the phonological processing system. For those with dyslexia, underlying difficulties in the area of phonological and phonemic awareness are housed here. On fMRI scans, we can see the difference in engagement within this brain region between typical readers and those with dyslexia, where those with dyslexia have hypoactivation.

Students who have received appropriate remediation or instruction will later show a new engagement in this area of the brain during the fMRI scan. Researchers have used this information to determine areas of instructional implications and focus to address student needs.

The Occipital-Temporal Lobe

Have you heard the expression "you have eyes in the back of your head"? Well, the area of the brain responsible for vision is located in the occipital lobe, at the back of your head. When reading, there is a specific area of the brain, the visual word form area within the occipital-temporal junction, which holds a critical role in our ability to store and retrieve letters and words. This is a specific area of visual processing accountable for the orthographic representations (spelling), the recognition of letters, letter patterns, and written words; it is stored in a special area of the brain here, different from vision. The word form area, or what Dr. Stanislas Dehaene refers to as the "letterbox" allows for automatic retrieval of words when reading so that it appears as if we read by sight. Through imaging studies, the occipital-temporal lobe, our visual-word form area, has shown that the brain region is also implicated in dyslexia in multiple languages (Wolf et al. 2024).

The Temporal Lobe

Language comprehension helps us store and retrieve meaning, which is stored within the temporal lobe. This works as our mental dictionary. Once readers are proficient and automatic, all of this information transfers along the brain's superhighway at such high speeds that it seems effortless. For those with dyslexia, this creation of the brain's superhighway may take longer to create, and therefore, we need to understand what is happening in the brain and why and address this through appropriate instruction that targets the specific needs of those with dyslexia. This understanding is critical for educators so that we can match our instructional practices to what we know about how the brain learns, and it is important for those with dyslexia to understand better how their brain organizes and processes information. Those with dyslexia need explicit and systematic instruction in all components of linguistic knowledge and a heightened focus on deficit areas to help link the different circuits to access the reading code. When we understand dyslexia and all of the pieces come together, our children can take flight both academically and emotionally.

Understanding the Dyslexic Brain

One of the biggest concerns for parents and dyslexia educators is the statement that a student just needs more time, that they will eventually get it, or they need to try harder. Dyslexia is not due to a developmental reading lag. It is a specific learning disability that is neurobiological in origin. Neuroimaging studies have shown a difference in the processing systems in people with and without dyslexia and the changes in the neuropathways once appropriate instruction and intervention are provided. We are literally rewiring brains!

This information about the brain processing systems and the need to create new circuits, as well as the identification of those areas typically less engaged for those with dyslexia, deepens our understanding of dyslexia and should directly impact our instructional practices. In addition, applying this understanding to the review of educational reports and looking at the student's learning profile allows educators to pinpoint areas of focus and better understand how the reading processes come together. After looking at the reading brain, we understand that reading is a man-made construct, and no one area of the brain is responsible for reading. The task of reading involves multiple cognitive processes within our brain organization systems. People with dyslexia have difficulty making quick connections between the critical areas of the brain when reading, but appropriate instruction creates neural pathways for this information to transfer quickly. Therefore, intentional instruction that encompasses teaching is needed to foster neural pathways in the brain and provide enough practice to bridge knowledge to application. For students with dyslexia, the amount of practice may vary from student to student, often requiring numerous repetitions within lessons and spaced practice, highlighting that it is imperative that we provide enough practice or application to create the necessary neural pathways. This is something that I come back to often when I reflect on my lessons. Am I providing enough practice for my students to solidify their learning and gain automaticity?

What Do Students Need to Understand About the Brain?

Whew! The brain is a lot to understand—and really, we need to understand it not from a scientist's point of view but from what this means for our work with students and how to bring students into conversations about the brain. Engaging students in conversations about their brains is beneficial for many reasons. Why? Students with dyslexia often want to understand why certain aspects of reading and writing are so difficult for them. Shedding light on the ongoings in their brain helps them in several ways.

First, it provides an opportunity for students to understand themselves. We all have a unique brain signature—there is some variance in each of us—but we know the areas we need to grow, or connect through explicit instruction and multisensory (multimodal) experiences, to make reading and writing easier. Bringing students into conversations about the reading brain can explain why the task of learning to read and write may be challenging. When we can separate the challenges or needs from our whole self, we can begin to look objectively at what we can do and what we need to work on to create these connections in our brains.

Talking with students about the reading brain connects to the metacognitive processes in the integrated framework.

Another benefit of discussions about the reading brain is that it provides opportunities to connect to our instruction. My students, especially my older inquisitive students, want to understand why we do certain tasks in our structured literacy sessions. Connecting components of the lesson to the areas and connections in the brain involves the student in the learning process and metacognitive processes, and supports the importance of engagement. When building automaticity in letter knowledge, we strengthen our orthographic processor to retrieve and recognize written letters stored in the visual word form area. When we work on phonemic awareness tasks, such as segmenting and blending phonemes, we strengthen our parietal-temporal lobe, which is often needed for those with dyslexia! I don't need to use the brain terminology with students, but I have them participate in coloring their brain poster as we learn why we do certain tasks and reference the brain poster when needed (see Figures 5.5 and 5.6 and the mini-lesson in the next section).

Understanding how our brain works and connects to the tasks in the lessons aids in student buy-in and engagement.

Some students may not see the value in the tasks or activities we do within our structured literacy lesson, and need to develop habits of attention to establish student behaviors and high expectations for learning. Discussing the brain processing systems can get buy-in for the hard work. The Reading Brain picture/worksheet can be used as a task management and behavior awareness tool within lessons to remind students of their role in active participation. Creating and managing clear expectations with students through the brain highlights their role in the work. Aligning with the AVR and best practices, in lessons, students are expected to actively engage by looking, listening, verbalizing, and thinking. We can't do the work for them—we can walk alongside them and provide guidance—but they do the work that needs to happen in their brain through the activities in our lessons. Using the brain to aid in engagement or buy-in helps to anchor participation expectations in lessons.

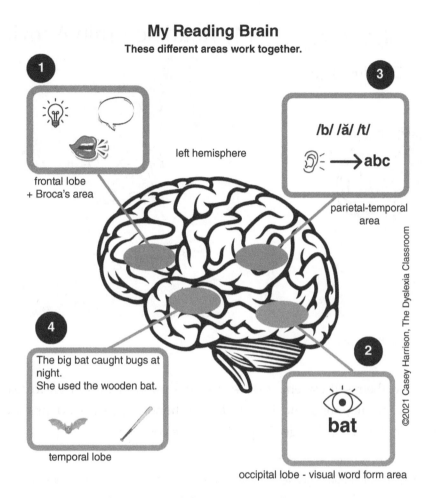

FIGURE 5.5 My Reading Brain worksheet.

Developing awareness of how active engagement aids in personal development and leads to self-awareness and advocacy skills is important for students. The more students understand the unique workings of their brain, the more they can begin to identify those tasks that are challenging, easier for them, and those that they are growing. We want students to recognize that the unique workings of their brain system also provide them with strengths that can be nurtured as we build the areas of need. In addition, working on areas of need leads to student success, which gives students confidence, helping students achieve their full potential and

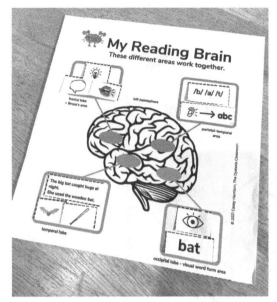

My Reading Brain Activity

FIGURE 5.6 My Reading Brain activity.

preserve their self-esteem. Addressing the mindset moves us to teach beyond the diagnosis and into a place of honoring each student's journey. Chapters 11 and 12 go deeper into these concepts.

Having metacognitive awareness and understanding oneself as a learner leads to agency and self-advocacy skills.

Mini-Lesson: My Reading Brain

Goal: For students to understand the connections that need to be made in the brain when learning to read as well as their role in making this happen.

Materials: student My Reading Brain worksheet, scissors, glue

Download the lesson plan and PDF at www.thedyslexiaclassroom. com/teachingbeyondthediagnosis.

Discussions and quick activities that build awareness of the brain workings for reading can be used to engage students in participation of all the pieces within a structured literacy lesson as they build the connections in their brains.

Mini-Lesson Teacher Script:

Teacher: *Today we are going to talk about our reading brain! There is a lot that happens when we learn to read. Did you know that there is no one spot in our brain made for learning to read? It's true! We need to create a new road to connect these areas of our brain (point to the four areas on the brain sheet).*

(point to the turquoise area/#1) This is the frontal area of our brain. It is dedicated to thinking, problem-solving, and our sentence production and speech. This lets us produce the 44 speech sounds in our language. Let's put the speech bubble, mouth, and thinking lightbulb in this area.

(point to the green area/#2) Did you know that when you see something like a letter or a tree, the information is sent to the back part of your brain? It's true! This area of our brain takes in what we see and lets us understand it. When we see a letter or word, it takes that information in and makes sense of what we see, and stores it in a special area of the brain called the word form area or letter box. Let's put the eye picture and the word "bat" in this area.

(point to the pink area/#3) Now, we said we need to make connections from one area to the next—so we need to pass through the pink area to connect our sounds to the letters (name what is appropriate for students, for example: parietal-temporal area, sound to letter area, etc.). When we do this, we are connecting what we are hearing to the sounds and letters in our language and playing with those sounds. This is an area that for many with dyslexia is one that we need to build up—so we will do a lot of activities to strengthen this area of our brains and make strong

connections. Let's put the ear with the arrow to letters and the sounds /b/ /ă/ /t/ in this section.

(point to the yellow area/#4) The reason that we want to learn to read and write is to understand what is written down. Our brain wants to make sense of what we hear and read, so we have this area that helps us connect meaning. If I say the word "bat," what comes to your mind? (students respond) When we hear the word "bat" right away we may have an image pop into our brain connected with that word. You may even have more than one! We use the language of our sentences to help us determine which meaning is intended (read the sentences on the small cut out piece and discuss the meaning of bat in each). Let's put the two pictures of the bats and the sentences in this section.

Wow! There is a lot going on in our brains when we learn to read! The more we build connections between these areas, the better readers we become. Our goal is to have our brain connect all of these areas *snap* just like that! It takes practice to forge these new paths in our brains, and that is what we will be doing in our lessons—building our reading brains! (Have students draw a line connecting all of the colored ovals.)

Every day, when we look, listen, speak, and think, we are growing our brains and creating connections between these areas needed for reading! In our lessons, I will refer to the brain picture and this is the expectation for our lessons—that we look, listen, speak, and think.

*You can also have students act out the neurons of the brain sending information to one another by holding their hands facing one another and wiggling their fingers.

You can change the analogy to meet the interest of the students. Some of my students like to build things like robots, so we discuss what is needed when we create a circuitry system. What happens if one of the circuits misfires? The circuit doesn't work and needs to be reconnected. This is the same thing that occurs in our brain when we are learning to read. For dyslexia, often there is a need to focus on the parietal-temporal area of the brain worksheet (pink/#3) to create strong connections between sounds and letters and manipulate those sounds within words. Another analogy that I use with my students is that we are driving a car. Often our dyslexic brain is like taking the country or scenic route. It may be slower, or leisurely, and while lovely at times, we need to create a super highway when reading and writing. If we take too long to get to where we are wanting to go, we are not creating the necessary path or route in our brain to make reading easily accessible. You can connect to music, art, or anything of interest to the student that requires a connection to achieve a goal. Once this lesson is covered, I then use it to generate student buy-in, self-awareness, and responsibility within the tasks of our lessons.

---

*Teacher Tip: You can use the brain activity to set the stage for lesson expectations. For example, when students are in their dyslexia intervention lesson, the expectation is that they actively build neural networks/their reading road throughout the lesson by looking, listening, speaking, and thinking. This provides a visual cue to support high student engagement and expectations within the lesson—and this supports the metacognitive processes and brings awareness to our own learning, a large part of the integrated framework.

Learning about the brain can be something you continue to embed in your lessons. Below are some of my favorite extension books and materials to use when taking about the brain with students.

Extensions:

- *The Brian Hemisphere Hat* by Ellen McHenry—https://ellenjmchenry. com/brain-hemisphere-hat/

- *Your Fantastic Elastic Brain* by JoAnn Deak, PhD

- *The Brain: All About Our Nervous System and More!* by Seymour Simon

- *Dyslexia Explained* by Mike Jones

- *Wonderfully Wired Brains: An Introduction to the World of Neurodiversity* by Louise Gooding

Conclusion

Speaking about the brain with students doesn't need to be in-depth. However, there is power in helping dyslexic learners unlock the workings of their brain so they can begin to shift their own narrative and gain an understanding of how their brain works, what instruction, accommodations, and strategies are most beneficial, and ultimately, their self-advocacy skills and knowledge. Knowing that the brain can change and knowing about how the instruction being provided by the teacher helps to change the brain—to make those necessary connections for reading to occur—actually encourages students to engage and be successful. Anchoring our learning in this knowledge provides students with enough information for empowerment.

Key Takeaways

- All students need to create a new circuitry system in the brain to read.
- We all learn to read the same way but with varying degrees of ease.
- Students with dyslexia require explicit, systematic, intensive, and multimodal instruction in delivery.
- Talking to students about the reading brain increases engagement.

Simplify your path to practice. What did you put in your pocket?
What stepping stones, or nuggets of knowledge, are you taking from this chapter?

CHAPTER SIX

Structured Literacy in Dyslexia Education

"The remedial teacher works in an area of specialty. It requires specific training, a willingness to acknowledge and accept children's strengths and weaknesses, and the ability to be an encouraging, supportive advocate at all times."

—Anna Gillingham and Bessie W. Stillman, *The Gillingham Manual*

Integrated Framework Component: Academics and Support

In this part of the journey, we deepen our understanding of the tenets of literacy instruction, which encompasses a Structured Literacy approach and evidence-based practices that explicitly and systematically teach all components of literacy development to set students up for success. Proper instruction, scaffolds, and support must be grounded in a deep understanding of research and evidence-based instructional practices encompassing multisensory, explicit instruction in all components of literacy development.

Engaging with and understanding the scientific knowledge surrounding reading instruction is one thing. It is another to put it into practice. How do we translate the findings to help students with dyslexia become proficient readers and writers? Strong evidence shows that the majority of students learn to read better with explicit and structured teaching of foundational language skills, which address all aspects of literacy and are critical for students with reading disabilities, including dyslexia. This structured approach to literacy instruction is not "phonics-only" but comprehensive and includes reading and writing acquisition, focusing on the teacher responding through diagnostic and prescriptive measures. When teaching with a structured approach to literacy, the lesson encompasses critical areas of language and literacy, including an integrated approach to instruction in phonology, phonics, orthography, morphology, vocabulary, syntax, discourse comprehension, and written compositions, all connected to the student's learning profile. While new research is dynamic, this effective instruction for students with dyslexia has been in place for some time, grounded in the work of Dr. Orton and Anna Gillingham and decades of work from other researchers to become what we now call a Structured Literacy approach.

Structured literacy is not just a reading approach; it's a comprehensive strategy that can benefit a wide range of students. Coined by the International Dyslexia Association, it's designed to be effective for all students, including those with reading disabilities, English learners, and struggling adolescents. Structured literacy provides a systematic and explicit approach to language learning for English learners, helping them develop strong literacy skills. Similarly, for struggling adolescents, structured literacy can offer a clear and structured framework for literacy instruction, potentially improving their reading and writing abilities. This comprehensive nature of structured literacy should reassure educators that it is a powerful tool in their teaching arsenal, especially when working with dyslexic learners.

A critical understanding is that structured literacy does not equate to a program, and "structured literacy" is not designed to replace Orton-Gillingham, multisensory or other terms in common use (Cowen 2016; Moats 2020), which all share an emphasis on the instructional content and essential features, but rather to unify our terminology in hopes of generating a better understanding of instructional practices.

A Structured Literacy approach provides educators with an avenue grounded in the science of reading research that emphasizes the core instructional features and elements along with the guiding principles that play a key role in literacy development. The most effective programs will include all of the components of structured literacy, with comprehensive training and ongoing support for those teaching it. We cannot expect educators to be handed a program sans training or with limited training and expect high-yield outcomes for students. There is also an art to teaching; what the teacher understands is the key! Regardless of which evidence-based program is in use, it is vital for educators to deeply understand and, therefore, implement these elements and principles with students effectively. Knowledge is key. Implementation is the path. And educators are the life force behind bringing instruction to students.

The integrated framework helps bring to light the fact that dyslexia is not something to address in isolation; instead, it should focus on addressing all components of the framework.

Knowledge is not just power, it's the key to effective teaching. But knowledge alone is not enough. Implementation is the path to success. By understanding and implementing the principles of structured literacy, educators can empower themselves and their students.

There is so much research available to educators that if we are not mindful, we can drown in the vast amount of information, theory, and advice, which can sometimes feel contradictory. While theoretical models provide the necessary insights into the research of what does and doesn't work for instructing students in reading, writing, and learning, without the knowledge of how to translate research findings to instructional practices, there remains a wide gap, and children are the unfortunate ones who fall into the chasm. Instead, as those working directly with children, I want us to focus on how we best support the implementation of these established best practices of a Structured Literacy approach that are grounded in the research and act as translators to bring the research to life. A solid understanding of a reading lesson's instructional content and essential principles can lead us in the right direction. This chapter builds this foundational understanding of the instructional content and guiding principles. Then, in the following chapters, we aim to support implementation with scaffolds and support in a clear and concise manner so that teachers can take this knowledge and bring it right into their instruction.

Instructional Content of Structured Literacy

All students with dyslexia must receive explicit and systematic instruction that is cumulative and data-driven. This approach, which addresses all layers of reading acquisition, requires a deep understanding that the dosage and intensity of instruction may vary from student to student, and that more targeted systematic approaches may be needed even if students receive intervention in an evidence-based program. The instructional content and essential principles of a Structured Literacy approach necessitate teachers to be diligent in individualizing instruction (even within groups) based on careful and continuous informal and formal assessment and observations. Students must master the content to the degree of automaticity needed to free attention and cognitive resources for comprehension and oral and written language.

The International Dyslexia Association has created a new infographic grounding structured literacy in the science of reading research in connection to the instructional foundations and practices which we implement within our reading instruction (see Figures 6.1 and 6.2) (IDA 2024). The *What* and *How* are where the research comes into practice and are vital for educators to understand deeply. The teacher's knowledge of dyslexia and structured literacy must anchor the work and remain at the

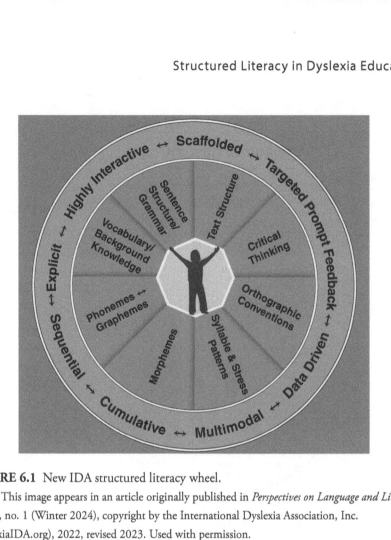

FIGURE 6.1 New IDA structured literacy wheel.
Source: This image appears in an article originally published in *Perspectives on Language and Literacy*, vol. 50, no. 1 (Winter 2024), copyright by the International Dyslexia Association, Inc. (DyslexiaIDA.org), 2022, revised 2023. Used with permission.

forefront when choosing curricula, delivering instruction, monitoring student progress, and understanding how dyslexia may impact learning across content areas. The teaching elements of a structured literacy lesson purposefully focus on integrating language with reading, written expression, handwriting, composition, and comprehension to support automaticity, fluency, and reading proficiency (IDA), noting that oral language occurs from the very start.

The inside of the wheel addresses the instructional components for establishing solid foundational reading skills, and a quick breakdown of these elements follows.

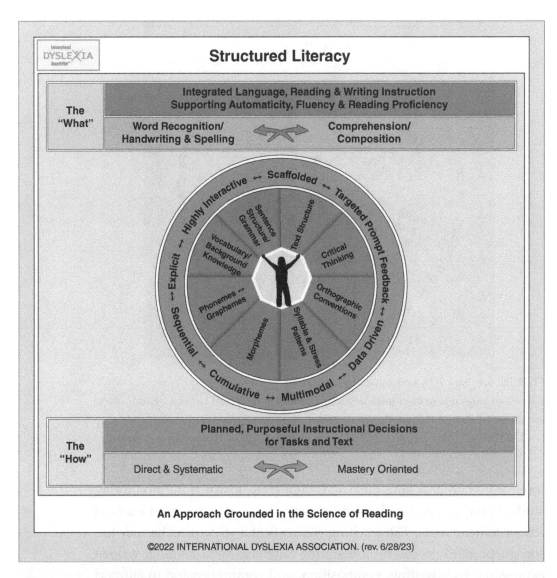

FIGURE 6.2 Structured literacy—an approach grounded in the science of reading.
Source: This image appears in an article originally published in *Perspectives on Language and Literacy*, vol. 50, no. 1 (Winter 2024), copyright by the International Dyslexia Association, Inc. (DyslexiaIDA.org), 2022, revised 2023. Used with permission.

Alphabet knowledge is a cornerstone of literacy development, and knowing letter names provides a springboard for learning and remembering sound-letter relationships (Ehri 2005; Foulin 2005; National Reading Panel 2000). While the mastery of letter knowledge and the ability to identify, name, and eventually write all of the alphabet letters are often mastered in mid-kindergarten or before, students with dyslexia commonly struggle to recall the alphabet sequence and letter names. Research indicates that students who struggle with acquiring alphabet knowledge tend to later be diagnosed with learning disabilities (Gallagher, Frith, & Snowling 2000; O'Malley, et al. 2012). The knowledge of letter names and the fluency in recalling and identifying them are among the best predictors of learning to read and later reading success (Caravolas, Hulme, & Snowling 2001; Leppanen et al. 2008; Schatschneider et al. 2004; Catts et al. 2015) indicating the importance of including alphabet knowledge in lessons until mastered by the student. For students who are not yet automatic in alphabet naming, this should be a part of the dyslexia intervention lesson, and teachers should analyze where students are having difficulty mastering this foundational skill (naming, retrieving the sequence, automaticity, letter confusion, etc.) and provide effective support to students as they gain automaticity of letter knowledge.

Phoneme-grapheme correspondences (phonology, phonics, alphabetic principle) addresses the connection between the smallest unit of sound (phoneme) linked to the grapheme (letter or letters), which represents the spoken sound in written form (e.g., the sound /k/ can be represented with <k> as in *kite*, <c> as in *cat*, <ck> as in *duck*, <ch> as in *echo*, <que> as in *boutique*). Students learn these sound-letter linkages and knowledge that letters and letter patterns represent the sounds of the spoken language (called the alphabetic principle) through explicit phonics instruction in a sequential scope and sequence that builds from easier concepts to more challenging ones. It should be noted that there is not a set scope and sequence for phonics instruction. However, programs should move from earlier sound-symbol correspondences to more challenging ones, including spelling and morphology. Teachers and interventions should follow a scope and sequence that is explicit, systematic, and progresses in a logical sequence. You can download a suggested scope and sequence at www.thedyslexiaclassroom.com/teachingbeyon dthediagnosis.

English is a morphophonemic language, meaning that we have elements of phonemes (sounds) and meaning (morphemes) that impact our spelling system. **Morphemes** refer to the smallest unit of meaning that exists in our language such as suffix -s as a plural in *cats*, -ia noting noun usage *dyslexia*, or pre- indicating "before" in *preschool*, as well as Latin roots like "rupt" meaning to break as in *erupt, interrupt, disrupt*, and Greek combining forms like "therm, bio, and geo." Some morphemes may stand alone as a word (free morpheme), also called base words. These base words can be content words (jump, run, daylight) or grammatical words (the, of). Some morphemes are combined with other morphemes to make words. These can be categorized as prefixes, suffixes, roots, and combining forms. Student knowledge of morphemes enhances their reading, vocabulary, and spelling (Moats 2020), and building students' morphological awareness should occur early on within oral language and in reading and writing instruction.

In addition to phonemes and morphemes, **syllables** and the **stress patterns** in our language impact our writing system. A syllable refers to a unit of spoken language that includes one vowel sound, such as *nap-kin*, or even unwritten vowel sounds, like in *rhy-thm* in which the *thm* represents a syllabic consonant. The vowel sounds are the most resonant or sonorous sounds in a syllable. Knowledge of syllables and syllable types aids in word reading and spelling. As students gain awareness of the syllables and syllable patterns and stress patterns, also referred to as accent, students acquire reading and writing skills surrounding how stress or emphasis on a syllable within a word can impact spelling, pronunciation, syntax, and meaning.

English orthography (spelling) includes the rules governing written language (spelling, spelling generalizations, high-frequency and irregularly spelled words) and the reason behind spelling generalizations and variations. These **orthographic conventions** include guiding principles with phoneme-grapheme correspondences as well as how the position of a phoneme or grapheme may impact spelling (final /ch/ can be spelled <tch> in a one-syllable base word after a short vowel sound as in *match*, or <ch> after a consonant letter or long vowel sound as in *lunch*, and *screech*); the impact of the language of origin such as /sh/ spelled as <sh> in *shell* from Old and Middle English versus /sh/ spelled as <ch> in *chef* from French origin influence; spelling pattern impacts linked with morphology (such as doubling the <p> in *mopping*, dropping the <e> in *sliding*, and just adding suffix -s in *cats*), and more arbitrary spellings such as *have, love,* and *give*, where the <e> is written because English words don't end in the letter <v>.

A Structured Literacy approach encompasses all strands of Scarborough's Reading Rope, and therefore, language comprehension is addressed throughout lessons from the beginning. These include direct and systematic instruction that addresses multiple components, including vocabulary and background knowledge. **Vocabulary** refers to the knowledge of word meanings, ranging from partial to deep understanding of the word in oral and written application, and plays a key role in reading comprehension. Educators who understand how vocabulary develops and how to teach through direct and indirect methods can best support learners in vocabulary development. The development of word consciousness is an integrated part of structured literacy lessons.

Background knowledge refers to the knowledge the students hold and what they bring to reading tasks. Students will have varying background knowledge of topics, including possible misunderstandings, which purposeful instruction should address at the oral and written levels.

Sentence structure, or how the structure of language occurs at the word, phrase, sentence, and text level, is taught through direct instruction. Students learn about meaningful phrases, prosody, fluency in reading, and composing and decomposing sentences. In addition, students analyze sentence construction and written conventions.

Text structure, or how an author organizes text (narrative, informational, etc.), is also addressed through explicit instruction and aids student reading comprehension.

In addition, explicit instruction in **critical thinking**, including executive function skills, metacognitive awareness, and strategies that encourage students to think deeply about what they are reading and apply it, is included in lessons. Written responses and compositions are also a part of this approach. This encourages students to engage in deeper thinking about their learning. This critical thinking is a vital component of the integrated framework.

Essential Principles of Structured Literacy

The teaching principle of a structured literacy lesson focuses on intentional and purposeful instructional decisions to create planned lessons, including tasks and text used. These guiding principles are core tenets of dyslexia instruction and highlight how we teach the content and bring structured literacy to life. It requires deep knowledge on the part of the teacher and is grounded in the need for explicit, systematic, and cumulative instruction that addresses the following. Each of these principles is woven into the work we do—they provide the foundation for how we teach students and are essential for student success.

Explicit instruction is foundational to multisensory language skills and structured literacy. It is purposefully designed to provide clear instruction and delivery to maximize learning. Explicit instruction aims to secure student attention, focus on active participation, and foster independence and mastery through regular checking for understanding and promoting high levels of success. A cornerstone of dyslexia interventions is explicit and systematic instruction that is carefully **sequenced** and designed to ensure that students are provided with the necessary skills to build learning—it leaves nothing to chance. In addition, the implementation of explicit instruction is designed for high levels of application and practice, with at least 80% accuracy, and requires frequent responses from everyone. This is key in delivering the lesson—the students need to be actively engaging in the lesson. Think back to the Reading Brain activity, which encourages high levels of student engagement. When implementing the lesson, a general framework for responses should focus on a careful design of the flow between teacher presentation and student responses where the teacher delivers the information in small parts, students are actively engaged in group and individual responses while the teacher monitors responses and provides immediate feedback so that the interaction works as a back-and-forth between teacher and student. The teacher then scaffolds as needed, with the goal of students moving to independent application. The lessons are quick-paced but carefully monitored for high levels of success leading to student engagement, motivation, and a continued desire to learn (see Figure 6.3).

The **cumulative** instruction is purposefully designed and presented in a sequence where skills and concepts build on one another through a progression that systematically moves from easier concepts and skills to more challenging ones. Educators ensure that prerequisite skills are attained and then clearly create connections from previous knowledge and learning to new learning, always building on what students have learned.

Key elements include engaging and **highly interactive** teaching, where the students actively participate in meaningful **multimodal** (multisensory) experiences. They are held accountable for their learning through this engagement of responding orally, in written form, or participating in a specific task. Research supports reading intervention

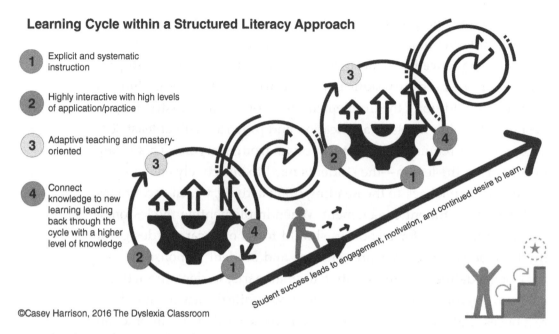

Learning Cycle within a Structured Literacy Approach

1. Explicit and systematic instruction
2. Highly interactive with high levels of application/practice
3. Adaptive teaching and mastery-oriented
4. Connect knowledge to new learning leading back through the cycle with a higher level of knowledge

Student success leads to engagement, motivation, and continued desire to learn.

©Casey Harrison, 2016 The Dyslexia Classroom

FIGURE 6.3 Explicit instruction learning cycle.

that uses explicit instruction as effective for improving student reading skills in both younger and older students (Flynn et al. 2012; Gersten et al. 2020; Herrera et al. 2016). **Precise language** and thoughtful planning with built-in **reflection** and thinking aloud to reveal a thought process modeled by the teacher and providing **targeted prompt feedback** are all elements of explicit and direct instruction. This feedback is both affirmative ("I see that you boxed the prefixes and suffixes to figure out that word") and corrective. ("Let's look at this word *ship*. The letters sh make one sound /sh/. What sound? Yes, /sh/. Let's sound out this word and read again.") In addition, the teacher can ask specific questions linked to the feedback to elicit reflection ("I love how you figured out that word. What did you do to help you?") or model thinking aloud in connection to a strategy used which both set the stage for metacognitive processes.

Dyslexia instruction encompasses **multimodal** experiences. This refers to intentional multisensory instruction in which students simultaneously engage in two or more sensory modalities to take in and express information. These modalities are visual, auditory, kinesthetic/motor, and tactile. Multisensory teaching is often emphasized by those who work with dyslexic learners. These instructional practices embed multisensory strategies into lessons to engage the learner in techniques that connect visual, auditory, kinesthetic/motor, and tactile (VAKT) connections and will be addressed more in chapter 7 and 8.

One of the goals of explicit, direct instruction is for students to gain automaticity and fluency or mastery of the skills taught. This **mastery-oriented** focus ensures that the pace of the lessons matches what the student needs—not too fast or too slow, but set at a pace in which learners will gain mastery of the skills and concepts taught. Due to the dyslexia continuum, some students will need a higher dose of application of practice or repetition in specific areas of reading and writing acquisition often with scaffolding. **Scaffolding** provides purposeful instruction that leads to new learning and is a big part of adapting instruction and moving students who are struggling to apply the tasks and concepts independently forward which we will address in detail in chapter 8.

In dyslexia instruction, **data-driven** instruction is at the heart of our work. It should be the springboard for instructional decisions and incorporate formal and informal assessments and observations. We can generate better instructional decisions by utilizing data from multiple areas. Again, knowledge of the learner and keen observation of student behavior, learning, and response to instruction in tandem with data collection are dominant in determining the next steps for instruction. While summative assessments provide teachers, students, and parents with general information, formative assessments give educators the information at the moment and allow them to utilize this to be diagnostic and prescriptive in real-time. You may find that most of your students with dyslexia who require intervention will be flagged on reading screeners, as these are given to help determine a student's performance trajectory on benchmark expectations and if a student requires reading interventions. Therefore, within our interventions, using diagnostic screeners that pinpoint the specific skills to address and then planning and monitoring student learning will provide the teacher with the necessary information to differentiate instruction to meet the needs of their students. This focus on mastery-oriented work within structured literacy is an essential component. It includes **data-driven** instruction, targeted prompt feedback, is highly interactive and engaging with the student, and the teacher utilizes meaningful scaffolds and supports to differentiate instruction.

When fully implemented, the Structured Literacy approach provides students with a comprehensive reading and writing foundation and enhances student self-esteem as it is emotionally sound instruction. These tenets have been around for decades and have been at the heart of the work of those in the field of dyslexia. "To ensure that all children have access to effective reading instruction, we must ensure that their teachers have BOTH the deep content knowledge and specific experiences to teach these elements according to these principles" (International Dyslexia Association). All of these elements work together, and it is clear that a Structured Literacy approach comprehensively addresses not only phonics but all of the layers of reading.

Creating a Path for Learning

The ease with which students respond to intervention may vary, and teachers must be equipped with the knowledge to address student needs within their programs based on diagnostic and prescriptive measures. Students with dyslexia who are not meeting expected learning outcomes should receive intervention at the most intensive level to support literacy outcomes. This includes integrated instruction in phonemic awareness, letter and word recognition, spelling, text comprehension, writing composition strategies, and metacognitive processes such as self-regulation and self-monitoring of learning. As stated by Dr. Louisa Moats, "We should abandon the expectations that serious reading disabilities can be fixed or remediated in a few short lessons per week or over a year or so. If evidence is going to drive our thinking, then all indicators point to teach all students who are at risk, skillfully and intensively; and maintain the effect for as long as it takes" (Moats 2016).

As educators serving those with dyslexia, we must deeply embrace at the core that this approach is not a quick fix or a simple task. The deep work that we do through this approach may be slow to build, but it is critical that our students have the skills, strategies, and routines to use independently. We are building learners—students who are empowered with self-awareness and skills to drive their own learning and advocacy. This is our goal, but our path must be intentional and meaningful for students and include all of these components, plus self-advocacy and metacognitive processes.

The research grounds us and informs our practice, but what we do with that knowledge allows students to soar. As educators we must hold knowledge beyond the programs we teach so that we can address student need and make informed decisions to enhance student outcomes. This includes:

1. Know the learner profile
2. Establish goals based on data (observational, diagnostic, and formal)
3. Determine areas of strength and need
4. Follow a clear scope and sequence (systematic, sequential, and cumulative)
5. Determine additional elements and scaffolds needed to build knowledge and understanding

6. Lesson plan—visual schedule, consistent growth, daily observation, clear language and anchor charts, high expectations, practice to automaticity, intentional retrieval practices, morphology, spelling, and writing (explicit instruction)

7. Daily ongoing observation and evaluation are needed to determine the next steps

Conclusion

Every program following the elements of structured literacy should include the components of structured literacy and deliver instruction through evidence-based practices. Regardless of the program we teach, as educators, therapists, or specialists, we must be empowered with the knowledge of the key delivery skills of explicit instruction and how to differentiate and scaffold within the reading program to address the individual needs of our students. This is of critical importance and cannot be overlooked. In the following chapters, we look at the elements of structured literacy and the effective ways to scaffold based on student needs and offer some strategies within each of the components of structured literacy.

Key Takeaways

- Structured literacy is more than phonics.
- A comprehensive approach is necessary.
- Instruction for dyslexia intervention must be comprehensive, intensive, explicit, and systematic.
- Knowledge is key. Implementation is the path.

Simplify your path to practice. What did you put in your pocket?
What stepping stones, or nuggets of knowledge, are you taking from this chapter?

CHAPTER SEVEN

Meaningful Multimodal Experiences to Support Learning

"Simultaneous multisensory instruction purposefully integrates visual, auditory, and kinesthetic-motor (for speech and writing) pathways to support memory and learning of both oral and written language skills."

—Mary L. Farrell and Nancy Cushen White,
Multisensory Teaching of Basic Language Skills, p. 48.

Integrated Framework Component: Academics and Support

In this part of the journey, we look at the impact that intentional and purposefully planned multimodal experiences within our instruction create meaningful learning opportunities, and how this approach is a core component of dyslexia instruction.

The world is a place where we engage the senses to enhance our understanding. Learning has never been a unisensory process. From the time of our birth, our brain learns and operates in our natural environments, often guided by information integrated across multiple sensory modalities. This multisensory learning is a natural occurrence, as seen when we watch a baby or toddler explore their world. We see the integration of senses as they take in all around them. Looking, listening, touching, and tasting occur as children interact with their world.

As caregivers, we naturally point or show children new objects, name them, and have our children touch or taste and manipulate to build connections and understanding. In addition, children are exposed to repeated practice as they learn new things. Think of how many times a child falls down when learning to walk, only to go through those steps again, increasing awareness each time and learning from the experience as they move toward independence. The same concept of integrated or multisensory inputs occurs within instruction but with the purposeful intention of engaging specific modalities to create the necessary neural pathways for reading and writing to occur. As you read through this chapter, think back to the mini-lesson about the reading brain and the expectations for students to actively engage in learning by looking, listening, speaking, and thinking—in other words, engaging different modalities simultaneously.

Multimodal instruction is one of the essential principles of instruction within the structured literacy approach (IDA 2024), commonly referred to as multisensory instruction. Currently, there is a shift in language to use the term **multimodal** to focus on instructional experiences that simultaneously target the use of two or more modalities (senses). Effective programs for dyslexic learners are rooted in the Orton-Gillingham and structured literacy principles and include the direct, structured, systematic, and explicit teaching of the organization of language, also referred to as Multisensory Structured Language Education (MSLE). Dr. Samuel Orton wrote about the use of multisensory strategies in connection to teaching reading to students with dyslexia in the 1900s. His work, which advocated the use of all sensory pathways to reinforce weak memory patterns and called for education methods based on the simultaneous association of visual, auditory, and kinesthetic fields, remains highly relevant today. Through the work of Anna Gillingham, Dr. Orton, and Bessie Stillman, specific multimodal experiences were applied to reading instruction in the 1930s and continued throughout their work. As research evolves, we sharpen our instructional practices to incorporate specific and targeted multi-sensory strategies as part of structured literacy lessons. These instructional practices embed multisensory strategies into lessons to engage the learner in techniques that connect visual, auditory, kinesthetic/motor, and tactile (VAKT) connections.

A Link Between Multimodal Experiences and Cognitive Engagement

Our capacity to remember does not exist in a discrete niche of the brain but involves several areas working together to make sense of our experiences. Current research on working memory and cognition demonstrates the benefits of multimodal experiences with literacy elements. Incorporating multisensory strategies within a structured literacy approach benefits students by providing opportunities for cognitive engagement, for example, through active participation (strategies that encourage physical, written, and oral interaction), habits of attention with the reading brain lesson (focusing on routines and attentional expectations), worked examples (step-by-step demonstrations with visual aids, think-aloud, smaller steps, etc.), scaffolding, and the intentional connection of visual and verbal stimuli to activate learning. Many students with learning differences, such as dyslexia, have coexisting deficits in working memory, and multimodal strategies may aid in meeting their cognitive demands. One specific deficit for many of those with dyslexia is difficulties in phonological skills, and many students also struggle with rapid retrieval and short-term memory recall of verbal information. Using multisensory strategies supports connecting the oral language with visual language structures due to the activation of circuitry systems during language learning using a multimodal approach. When teaching reading and spelling, these multisensory experiences with linguistic units can activate more circuitry during language learning than if we only use one singular sensory experience. This multimodal teaching integrates information across sensory modalities, which provides multiple opportunities to create new neural pathways.

In reading, we engage our **visual memory** to retain the visual image of a two-dimensional symbol (letter/word), especially the sequence of symbols in words. The orthographic patterns, the spellings, and the sequence of words in phrases and sentences are gathered through the visual sensory input system. The occipital lobe is engaged in the visual cortex; therefore, we must look at the letters, words, and text as we read, engaging our sense of sight.

At the root of the **auditory modality** in reading is the ability to listen and remember phonemes, words, sentences, and stories or information in a specific sequence. For example, the auditory sensory input system engages listening and the ability to discriminate between similar-sounding phonemes, identify the position of a sound within a word, or recall the number of words in a sentence. For many students, this auditory memory, specifically the phonological memory, is impacted by dyslexia, one of the root characteristics of dyslexia. Planning for meaningful multimodal experiences, such as targeting listening for specific phonemes (sounds) within the phonemic awareness component of the lesson while connecting to graphemes (letter representation), engages two sensory input systems (auditory listening and visual reading). This activation of the visual channel and the auditory/verbal channel to create a connection helps establish a memory trace that is both word-based and image-based, which is then dual-coded in our long-term memory (Lovell 2021). Teachers can intentionally engage the verbal and auditory channels by presenting information through both words and images, such as the keyword linked to the sound production or the use of mnemonic devices or a rhyme/chant to recall facts or concepts such as "/ĭ/ makes you grin and /ĕ/ drops the chin" (see Figure 7.1). Carefully chosen representations should be made to help elicit recall, as memories are often inaccessible due to missing or ambiguous cues (Willingham 2010), highlighting the importance of meaningful representations and modalities.

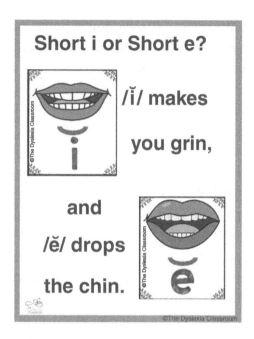

FIGURE 7.1 Short i or short e.
Source: Retrieved with permission from The Dyslexia Classroom.

To understand the K in VAKT, the root of kinesthetic, "keie," means set in motion. **Kinesthetic/motor memory** in reading instruction refers to the sense of body and muscle movements focused on the ability to produce and retain the sound and shape of a letter/ grapheme. Effective instruction engaging this modality focuses on the muscle movements of the formation of the sound as well as the letter formation to automaticity. Introducing students to phonemes (sounds) by using a mirror to identify the place of articulation, where the sound comes from within our mouth (front, middle, or back of the mouth), the manner of articulation (what the teeth, lips, and tongue do), and awareness voiced or unvoiced sound production strengthens phonological awareness through multiple modalities (look, listen, feel) facilitates what Castiglioni-Spalten and Ehri called "graphophonemic connections" to help students secure letter-sound connections in their memory (Castiglioni-Spalten and Ehri 2003). An articulation chart can be downloaded at www.thedyslexiaclassroom. com/teachingbeyondthediagnosis.

Tip: Videos of articulatory features and sound production can be found at https:// www.thedyslexiaclassroom.com/sound-production-support.

At the root of Tactile, *tag* refers to touch. Using meaningful hands-on materials and instruction aids in learning about the world around us, including language and reading tasks, is crucial in the structured approach to literacy. Meaningful activities should increase student engagement, opportunities for application and learning and planned with intention with a focus on building to automaticity and mastery. For example, as students learn to identify, name, and write the letters of the alphabet, the shape and feel of a letter in 3-D form or written form connects to the **tactile modality**. Writing requires the skill of manually forming the letters that represent our written language. This act of manually writing letters engages the graphomotor system, which is linked to the same language centers in the brain that support reading. As we gain automaticity in letter formation, the application becomes automatic, allowing us to complete this learned task without trying much. We see this skill in other areas of our lives, like walking, riding a bike, or even typing. Once this has been learned to automaticity, it alleviates the cognitive load for letter formation and frees up the mental desk space to focus on other areas of instruction and learning. In literacy instruction, letter formation automaticity in written form or typing is essential to free up our working desk space, allowing thinking to occur.

Purposeful integration of multimodal experiences is key! (See Figure 7.2.) For example, when students first begin to develop their sound-symbol correspondences and are linking the sound production to the letter, we use a mirror to look at what the mouth, tongue, teeth, and lips are doing as we produce the sound in isolation. In doing so, the

Integrating multimodal experiences in lessons should be intentional, meaningful, and carefully designed.

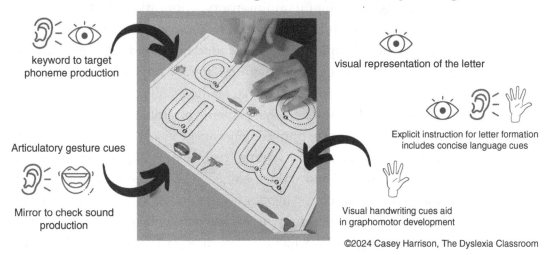

keyword to target phoneme production

visual representation of the letter

Articulatory gesture cues

Explicit instruction for letter formation includes concise language cues

Mirror to check sound production

Visual handwriting cues aid in graphomotor development

©2024 Casey Harrison, The Dyslexia Classroom

FIGURE 7.2 Integrating multimodal experiences.

auditory, kinesthetic/motor modalities are engaged when students look in the mirror to identify their mouth position, tongue movement, and breath when a sound is produced. The student is provided with a keyword to connect with the letter and sound (the letter a, keyword apple, sound /ă/). Students look at the letter, name it, and connect the sound to the letter. They write the letter in isolation as we focus on the proper letter formation and ask that students say the sound and letter name as they write the letter on a chalk board or white board, on a tactile surface such as sandpaper, or lined paper through the use of explicit and concise verbal and visual cues. This integrated approach to linking sound to letter names and letter formation creates a connection, or linkage, for students through two motor output systems (oral motor productions through the mouth and graphomotor productions through the hand). The visible letters that they assemble or write help to retain the memory of pronouncing the letter or word. In addition, handwriting is then linked to the retrieval of the phoneme and grapheme. This physical act of writing the letter adds to learning through a multimodal approach, incorporating meaningful multisensory application, and targets the integration of speech to print, which helps students gain awareness of the alphabetic principle and lays the foundation for decoding, word recognition, and spelling. The structured literacy approach focuses on an integrated approach to foundational reading skills.

The key here is the intentional planning of simultaneous VAKT strategies within our lessons to purposefully engage visual, auditory, and kinesthetic-motor (or speech and writing) pathways to support memory and learning of both oral and written language skills (see Figure 7.3). When planning for our structured literacy lessons and embedding multisensory strategies, we must consider why we use different components and how they aid learning and teaching. Within these tasks are layers of support

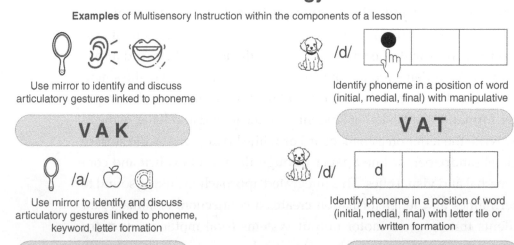

FIGURE 7.3 Phonology.

that should be used based on the student's needs and the lesson's targeted skill. For example, when introducing a phoneme, students can use a mirror to identify and discuss the articulatory gestures and manner of movement in the mouth, activating the V-A-K connections. Then, linking the grapheme to the phoneme with a keyword as a visual memory aid in connection to explicit instruction in letter formation activated the V-A-K-T connection. In segmenting tasks, using manipulatives or letters with Elkonin boxes (sound boxes) to identify the position of the sound within a word can utilize meaningful multimodal connections within the lesson to enhance phonemic awareness. Multisensory strategies planned beforehand can ensure that the chosen strategy supports students, their age and development, and moves learning forward towards independent application.

Many of these multimodal experiences can provide a scaffold or support within the lesson, such as a tool for reteaching, provide additional application of a skill or concept, or even as a support for error correction. For example, as students gain automaticity in phoneme-grapheme correspondences, the use of articulatory gestures can be faded and used as a cue if an error in reading or spelling occurs. If a student is saying or writing "chop" for shop, or "cach" for cash (see Figure 7.4), a

A student is writing <u>ch</u>op for <u>sh</u>op, and ca<u>ch</u> for ca<u>sh</u>.
Use explicit instruction with mouth cards as an aid in sound production and confusions.

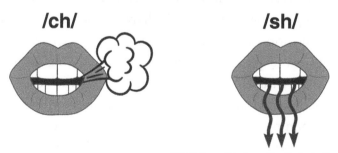

©2024 Casey Harrison, The Dyslexia Classroom

FIGURE 7.4 Articulatory knowledge aiding phoneme-grapheme correspondences.

multimodal lesson focusing on articulatory features can aid in correcting phoneme confusion by bringing awareness to the differences in articulatory gestures, including airflow. The "ch" and "sh" sounds are commonly confused; both are unvoiced and are made with the same mouth formation, like a pucker of the lips. However, they differ in how the air leaves the mouth. Students can place their hand in front of their mouths and feel the quick puff of air as they make the "ch" sound and compare that to the soft flow of air when making the "sh" sound. Teachers can use this explicit instruction to teach students the features of individual phonemes, which supports reading and spelling. Teachers will also want to determine if the student can produce the sounds in isolation, within a word, or in a sentence, and provide appropriate practice to aid in sound differentiation, allowing students to analyze target words through pictures or word sorts. Multimodal tasks focusing on segmenting and blending target words with ch/sh and reading and spelling words comparing ch/sh would be appropriate to address the confusion in a meaningful and multisensory way.

The goal of multimodal instruction is to integrate two or more modalities that highlight the necessity of providing active participation that engages learning pathways in the brain during language tasks. Special consideration should be taken when planning meaningful multimodal experiences. It is not connected to learning styles, a debunked idea where a perceived preferred learning avenue is the focus, nor does multisensory simply mean putting kids' hands in sand or other manipulatives. As educators and schools embrace the science of reading research and put into practice instruction and activities grounded in research, we must be mindful of the multimodal experiences used to aid students in creating neural linkages in reading and writing to ensure instructional planning of meaningful multisensory or **multimodal experiences** is implemented with intention, as multimodal experiences encompass good, effective teaching and should be used across all ages. Meaningful multisensory experiences don't stop in early elementary school. Our older students look at a passage, listen to the language of lectures, take notes, and actively interact with the text. The multimodal approach will still be engaged, but the tools and strategies will vary. As proficient readers and writers, you may highlight, annotate, or take notes as you read this book. These are multisensory strategies that engage multiple modalities. We use notes and graphic organizers to help us make sense of things we read. When asked to write, we may use an outline to organize our thoughts—all of these are multisensory strategies that help us, yet we may not realize we are engaging the senses to aid learning. So, while multisensory strategies may look different at different stages of reading development, at the root, multisensory means engaging two or more senses simultaneously to engage and learn information.

Things to think about:

What impact does multisensory instruction, specifically multimodal instruction, have in structured literacy lessons?

Does this chosen multimodal task provide appropriate practice for the application of the target concept/skill?

Is this multimodal strategy increasing learning? Distracting? Needed?

When should I integrate multimodal strategies into my lessons?

How can I scaffold multimodal strategies?

Purposeful integration is key.

As we saw in the previous chapter, the components of structured literacy include an integrated and comprehensive approach to instruction in phonology, phoneme-grapheme correspondences, syllable and stress patterns, spelling, morphemes, syntax, and semantics. Because the structured literacy approach focuses on simultaneously teaching written language skills with reading comprehension, the importance of language, reading, writing, and comprehension are all integrated from the start. The how of our practice is the application of these concepts and skills through meaningful multimodal experiences. As we break down the common components of a structured lesson, we see how intertwined multimodal strategies are with learning to read and write. These strategies connect and activate the regions of the brain and aid in creating a new neural circuitry system for reading to occur. By carefully choosing and integrating these targeted multimodal strategies within the lesson, we can actively engage the senses to create new neural pathways. It is crucial to be mindful of which strategies and supports we use with students in our structured literacy lessons. This will vary based on your student needs, the concept or skill of focus, and the learner profile. Not all multimodal activities are created equal, and they should evolve to meet the needs of the lesson and student. In addition, we must reflect on when, how, and if we gradually release those supports, as well as how do we continue to integrate the multimodal activation in meaningful ways? In the following chapters, you will find information and examples highlighting the implementation of multimodal experiences within the components of structured literacy lessons and ideas for scaffolding.

Conclusion

When using an intentional multimodal approach, we engage multiple areas of the brain, forming complex connections among the areas engaged, which are highly activated and widely distributed across the brain. It is essential for teachers to explicitly teach the structure of our language to engage in multiple senses and promote reading success by integrating both explicit instruction and multimodal experiences to enhance instruction.

While more research needs to be conducted on the benefits of specific multimodal experiences on reading outputs, multimodal instruction encompasses good teaching strategies. It is difficult for researchers to tease out multisensory strategies from structured literacy instruction. Within the cognitive and neurological sciences, research about the impact of multisensory/multimodal experiences, and theoretical support for the positive impacts of specific multimodal methods has been conducted, though more research is needed. Through clinical and practical application of structured literacy lessons, encompassing multimodal strategies, teachers can capitalize on how the brain activates and responds when students integrate multiple engagement modalities during active learning.

Key Takeaways

- Multimodal experiences engage two or more senses simultaneously.
- Integrating multimodal experiences in lessons should be intentional, meaningful, and carefully designed.

> Simplify your path to practice. What did you put in your pocket?
> What stepping stones, or nuggets of knowledge, are you taking from this chapter?

...

Key Takeaways

Scaffolds in Structured Literacy

"Effective teachers constantly monitor student understanding and adjust their instruction."

—Anita Archer

Integrated Framework Component: Academics and Support

In this part of the journey, we dive into the heart of intervention work—the ability to provide scaffolds, adaptive teaching, and support for students as part of explicit instruction, which sets students up for success.

Scaffolds

If you have ever had work done on your house, such as building an addition, or walked the city streets as a new building is being erected, you have seen the scaffolding set up to aid those constructing the building. These usually consist of basic metal frameworks and boards that have been used many times as they are often not pristine and may even be considered an eyesore. They are not permanent. They are not fancy or pretty. Yet they have an important role in ensuring that the completion of the task occurs and that the support is quickly removed. Their purpose is simple—to provide the support to complete the task at hand.

Due to student learning needs, the wide range of severity of dyslexia, varying working memory capacities, etc., there is no "one-size-fits-all" program, highlighting the need for intentional scaffolding. While every evidence-based program designed as a dyslexia intervention should contain explicit, systematic instruction grounded in the components and elements of structured literacy to support learners in a clear and concise progression, we will find that sometimes students need additional support to move along the scope and sequence of skills. For these students, the additional step or layer of support, including breaking information into smaller chunks and providing a tool, structure, or strategy to help them grasp new materials or concepts so they can tackle increasingly more complex skills or materials, is necessary.

Scaffolding is one of the principles of effective instruction that enables teachers to accommodate individual students' needs (Larkin 2002) and add support for students to enhance learning and aid in the mastery of tasks (see Figure 8.1). These scaffolds should be customized based on the specific needs of the individual learner and highlight the need for a deeper understanding of the learner's profile and observations by those educators who serve them with a focus on student understanding and learning. In the scaffolding process, the teacher helps the student master a task or concept that the student is initially unable to grasp independently, or that may seem insurmountable, giving support until they can apply new skills and strategies independently (Rosenshine & Meister 1992) effectively fostering the emotional safety needed to learn (Tajeddin & Kamali 2020). Types of scaffolding can include reteaching a concept or skill, allowing more time to apply a concept of skill, breaking the concept down into smaller discrete parts, and providing guided practice with each component. Teacher knowledge of the what, why, and how is critical for student success.

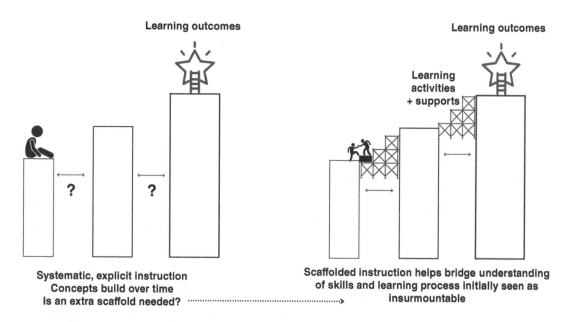

FIGURE 8.1 Scaffold learning outcomes.

What learning outcome goal will be achieved through this lesson within the systematic and sequential focus?

Why may a student struggle to make the necessary connections to learning within the lesson?

How can the teacher, then, at that moment provide the required steps or scaffolds to bridge student learning?

The art of teaching lies in experiential knowledge in tandem with evidence-informed practices to determine what, when, and how to deliver these meaningful scaffolds and when to fade them. This responsive or adaptive teaching requires us to pay keen attention to students and provide *just* the right amount of support to help them learn the concept or skill. Instructional scaffolding, much like scaffolding on a building, applies a specific tool, strategy, or technique within the lesson to support students. When students reach the intended level of understanding or mastery, the teacher can step back and gradually fade their support.

"Scaffolding is actually a bridge used to build upon what students already know to arrive at something they do not know. If scaffolding is properly administered, it will act as an enabler, not as a disabler"

(Benson 1997).

The Keys to Scaffolding Success

Many modern-day cars have an adaptive cruise control setting that takes in information and predicts when the car may need to slow down based on the environment around us and make adjustments that keep us on the right path or road, ensuring we reach our final destination. Adaptive teaching, or in-the-moment scaffolds and supports, acts in much of the same way, and the ability of teachers to adapt their teaching at the moment is crucial to making learning accessible. Scaffolding in dyslexia intervention links together planned, purposeful instructional decisions systematically building on students' experiences and knowledge as they learn new skills, within an explicit-guided-independent mode, also referred to as the Gradual Release of Responsibility model (Pearson & Gallagher 1983; Frey & Fisher 2013) or the "I-do, We-do, You-do" model. The teacher demonstrates and explicitly shows the learner how the skill is done, and then they repeat the skill together. At the same time, the teacher monitors, offers immediate corrective and specific feedback, coaches, reteaches, observes, and offers more scaffolds if needed, all the while gradually transferring the skill to the student. Seeing the big picture, we can break each component down to aid in instructional planning.

Start with the learner in mind. Keep the scaffolds based on planned, purposeful instructional decisions. We must keep the student at the forefront of the lesson and ask ourselves, what does *this* student need (see Figure 8.2)? What does their learning profile tell me about

What to keep in mind - a simplified version

Specific goal + explicit instruction

Planned, purposeful instructional decisions

Intentional opportunities for deliberate practice by learner

Scaffolds are temporary - fade out*

Independent application - meets goal

FIGURE 8.2 What to keep in mind.

instruction? What is the ease with which this child is acquiring reading, writing, and language? When planning lessons, I focus on the concept that I want students to understand and how I want them to apply this new knowledge. Within that lesson planning, I think of possible areas where the student may require additional support, reteaching, clarification, and what this requires. For example, would the student benefit from an anchor chart to address the steps of syllable division? Or does the student need the support of handwriting formation cards to help recall the motor planning steps when forming letters?

In addition, I want to determine if my scaffolds need to occur within a specific task, content, or materials or perhaps across these elements. Materials should be carefully chosen to address the components of literacy instruction and align with the expectations. Material scaffolding focuses on using materials to help with strategies and steps necessary to perform the learning task. It can include writing or visual prompts, anchor charts, steps, and strategies, such as word attack strategies, use of decodable text, etc.; these should all be considered when planning in addition to how this material provides opportunities for practice and application. In our planning, carefully chosen content that strategically builds on previous learning that is not too difficult for students to connect to a new skill should be strategically determined. In addition, carefully choosing tasks that align with the goal should be considered as scaffolds are planned. Planning surrounding how instruction will be explicitly taught and modeled, the language used to break down the steps, how to verify and clarify understanding, and what fading instruction will look like should all be considered.

There are many ways in which we provide support and scaffolds for students throughout the lessons, and therefore, the question becomes, does the student require this support, or can it be released? What do my observations and assessments tell me? It is important to note that not all areas of a structured literacy lesson will require additional scaffolds or support. We need to base these on what our students need. The intentional planning and placement of scaffolds keep the focus on learning and close the gap between what the student cannot yet do and what they need to do independently and relies on teachers to be empowered with knowledge beyond their resources and curriculum.

Specific goal + Explicit instruction. Explicit instruction makes lessons clearer to students by teaching skills sequentially and modeling what is needed. In the "I-do" phase of this model, the teacher plays a prominent role in delivering the lesson information and providing the necessary knowledge. Learning is not left to chance. The teacher acts as the expert and provides the necessary information about what is being learned, why it is being learned (tapping into the metacognitive processes), and when and how to use it, all while modeling the steps or strategy. Determining what type of modeling your students need should be part of the planning process. Modeling may include a think-aloud, where the teacher verbalizes their thought process and gives students a window to their thinking, allowing novice students to observe how an expert thinks. Another beneficial type of modeling is talking through the process while demonstrating the correct way to solve the task. In addition, we may find modeling without verbal instruction to be the best approach or a combination of these types. Explicit instruction with modeling is essential for struggling readers. It sequentially provides students with the skills to build a solid foundation for reading and writing through explicit instruction that clearly breaks down learning into smaller chunks of information as it builds to a larger task.

Intentional opportunities for deliberate practice by the learner. Practice, number of repetitions, and application of skills and concepts in reading and writing instruction for those with dyslexia matter. Structured literacy is designed to weave in multiple practices within a lesson and review previously learned skills. The opportunity to intentionally practice a skill or task with meaningful experiences while being provided with coaching or feedback from the teacher makes the new learning stick. We need opportunities to bridge knowledge to practice. Without monitored practice, there is no improvement. Repetition and practice create change at the synaptic level where the neurons meet. Remember the chapters about the reading brain and meaningful multimodal experiences? Our brain needs to make new neural pathways when learning to read and write, which takes practice. In the "We-do" phase, the teacher guides the student through the application or practice of the skill or concept that was demonstrated in the "I-do" portion of the lesson. The teacher provides layers of support as needed and immediate feedback during this guided practice. It is important to note that for students with dyslexia, high levels of application are required to solidify reading and writing skills, especially in deficit areas.

Scaffolds require careful monitoring and adaptive teaching. Within the guided practice ("We-do") portion of the lesson, the focus is on the application or practice of the target concept. It is here that intentional scaffolding is provided, which can include: intentional multimodal experiences, different levels of support (cues, anchor charts, etc.), intensity of practice, teacher monitoring and clarifying as well as reteaching and consolidating learning, immediate corrective feedback, and critical thinking and metacognitive processes. There may be fluidity between the direct instruction and the guided practice and scaffolds throughout the lesson. Scaffolding is a critical element in the teaching of instructional strategies and is essential for dyslexic learners. As a reminder, it is important that scaffolds are customized (Frey, Fisher, and Almarode 2023), based on student needs, are data-driven (formal, informal, and observational), and remain fluid.

Scaffolding as Response

Teachers must carefully monitor student application of the strategy/ concept/task and, in response to student performance, adapt the teaching in the moment. Even within our response to students, we can think of ways to scaffold our prompts or cues (see Figure 8.3). Prompts and cues are strategies that educators use to provide cues (hints) or more

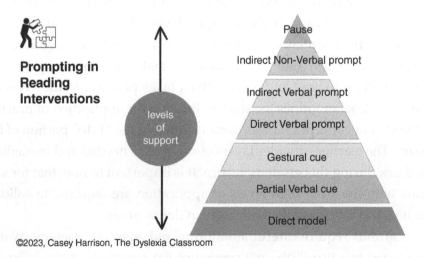

©2023, Casey Harrison, The Dyslexia Classroom

FIGURE 8.3 Prompting in reading interventions.

direct prompts to help students get to the correct answer or learning objective. While educators tend to use these within their lessons, reflecting on these purposeful interactions can ensure we are not overly cueing or prompting, as over-scaffolding can negatively impact student learning. However, knowing when and how to provide just the right amount of support to students through cues or prompts helps students recall or retrieve and apply knowledge. If the student needs more time to formulate their response or think time, then perhaps a pause is the appropriate level of support. Or does the student need a reteach or direct model? Is there a gesture cue that would benefit the student? How do these cues align with the multimodal experiences of visual-auditory-kinesthetic-tactile to elicit retrieval practices, aid working memory, and support feedback? We may move from least-to-most support when reviewing concepts previously learned or from most-to-least when explicitly teaching new concepts. Below, we look more explicitly at the combination of cues and prompts within a general hierarchy as a broader view of assisting students with pause being the least amount of support (see Fig. 8.3).

Pause—This can be providing appropriate think time (three to five seconds), or extended think time for a student. Often, students with dyslexia will have the answer on the tip of their tongue and need time to retrieve the information.

Example: Student is trying to recall the keyword for a sound (coin, /oi/). Give student think time before additional prompting cue.

Indirect Non-Verbal prompt—This can be visual prompts such as images, visual schedules, picture, etc., as well as body and facial expressions to support the student in the expectations of a response. Cues like a smile, thumbs-up, facial expressions, an auditory cue like a clap or snap to note a response is expected, such as reading the word aloud, nodding, etc., are examples of an indirect non-verbal support.

Indirect Verbal prompt—An indirect verbal support will hint at the answer but not give all of the answer to the student. It is designed to prompt the student to recall the information. For example, "What's next?" or another verbal prompt to lead the student to the correct response.

> Example: In spelling-sound dictation, if the teacher provides the sound /oi/ and the student says <oi> but doesn't give the other spelling, the teacher can prompt with, "And?" to remind the student that there is also the <oy> spelling.

Direct Verbal prompt—A direct verbal prompt helps the student get to the answer with direct questions or prompts.

> Example: A student made an error in the unvoiced sound of /th/ and said /f/ instead. A direct prompt when working with a student on /th/ could be to show the student the thumb key-word card and tell the student, "Put your tongue between your teeth. Blow out air /th/."

Gestural cue—A gestural cue is a non-verbal cue given by the teacher to the student, such as pointing, using physical cues or gestures, etc., that provides more direct support.

> Example: A student working on identifying digraph ck eliminated one of the letters; a gestural cue could be the teacher using their arm to draw a line in the air noting the digraph. This would align with the student then underlining the digraph ck in the word. The gestural cues can be as simple as the teacher pointing to the word misread by the student.

Partial Verbal cue—A partial verbal cue can include a sentence starter, a cloze sentence or reading, etc., to remind the student or aid them in the correct response.

> Example: A student is stuck in recalling the letter formation of the cursive a. The partial verbal cue could be "Curve under,

over, stop ..." as the start of the verbal directions for the approach stroke to make the cursive a. This could also be combined with a gestural cue in which the teacher in the air gestures the approach stroke as they verbally say the partial cue. If student was still stuck, then continue with the full verbal cue, and if still needed, move to the direct model.

Direct model—A direct model is modeling explicitly for the student. Direct models can include verbal, visual, and gestural cues to provide multiple pathways to learning.

Observing the student's application of the target skill or concept should determine the cueing or prompt used. This in-the-moment adaptive teaching provides students with immediate corrective feedback, cues, and prompts to then practice the concept correctly. The ebb and flow of this within the lesson requires active learning and engagement from the student and keen observation from the teacher.

Scaffolding with Gradual Release

Gradual release within guided practice. The scaffolds used in the lesson can move fluidly from the most support to the least support based on student need. As the student acquires new skills and knowledge at the mastery level, the teacher fades away. In addition, the level of scaffold or support may fade away, or some scaffolds or supports may become accommodations for students and will continue to be available as students move to the independent application. In the following chapters, I share possible scaffolds within the elements of a structured literacy lesson.

Meeting the goal with a mastery-oriented application. As students rely less on the teacher, they begin to apply new skills to their learning. The teacher monitors learning constantly and moves fluidly back and forth through the model as needed. Within the "You-do" or independent application portion of the lesson, students are meeting the goal or the steps needed to attain the larger task. For example, a student working on increasing accuracy in word reading whose lesson included the use of diacritical marking (coding words with a breve, macron, etc.) to aid in word reading, will use this skill independently at this stage with the larger goal being to release this scaffold as the student becomes more automatic in word reading. This gradual release of responsibility sets students up for success, explicitly models and teaches the necessary skills and concepts needed to move to independent practice, and provides ongoing monitoring and teaching. This form of teaching is essential for struggling students and provides them with a solid foundation upon which to build their reading and writing knowledge and reinforces the importance of fluidity within the model.

To aid teachers, additional items to consider in planning instruction and reflecting on the GRR model include:

Items to consider	Phase of instruction (I-do, we-do, you-do)	What is the intentional practice used?
What is being modeled? What is the core focus or expected outcome?		
How much time is dedicated to the explicit instruction or modeling part/s of the lesson?		
What follows the modeling ("I-do") portion of the lesson?		
What is the concise language used within my explicit and direct instruction?		
What is my plan and language for immediate corrective feedback within each component of lesson?		
What are some possible supports needed based on the student profile?		

Items to consider	Phase of instruction (I-do, we-do, you-do)	What is the intentional practice used?
What are meaningful multimodal experiences used within this lesson? How many opportunities for application are the students given?		
How will students show mastery oriented? How and when will scaffolds or supports be removed?		

Areas of Caution

In education, especially within interventions, we must be cautious and mindful of using scaffolds for students to ensure that:

1. The support is needed
2. We release the support as soon as possible

Often, I see the implementation of scaffolds within reading interventions far past the point at which they support students. For example, if a student can segment phonemes within words proficiently and apply this knowledge in reading and spelling, then having them use Elkonin boxes or tapping it out is no longer serving them—it is not a scaffold that is needed anymore for the child. The same could be said for identifying the syllable types—if students can decode the word automatically, then there is no need for having the student label these—we must be aware of our instructional practices and where our students are on their path or journey to the independent application of reading and writing skills.

The purpose of implementing scaffolds is to support students in the moment. Determine if there is a need, how to customize it to the goal, and how to release the support. This requires educators to plan for support that may be needed within a lesson, but with intention and caution so as not to over-scaffold. In addition, we must be mindful of the intensity of the support that we are providing, the frequency of the support, and the duration of its use. Planning ahead with these three things in mind keeps the learning at the forefront and can mitigate the pitfalls of over-scaffolding.

Scaffolds are designed to support students within the moment of frustration or struggle. Only use a scaffold or support when the task at hand is not possible without it. When determining if a scaffold or support is needed, we must ask ourselves:

- Can the student complete the task without that support?
- Is the support customized based on the student's needs?
- What will be the determination for the release of this temporary support?

Students with dyslexia or other learning differences may require intentional instructional scaffolds and support to break the reading code, to aid in fluency development, spelling, etc. By understanding the role of appropriate scaffolds within the GRR model and the structured literacy framework in connection to prescriptive and diagnostic measures, educators can feel empowered to individualize instruction to support.

We must keep the student at the forefront of the conversation. What does this child need? What does their learning profile tell us about instruction? What is the ease with which this child is acquiring reading, writing, or language? Children learn to read the same way, but the path will look different for different students.

Conclusion

The use of scaffolds and supports, including the Gradual Release of Responsibility model, is at the heart of reading and writing instruction for students with dyslexia. These are built into the framework of structured literacy, and it is critical for educators to understand and hone it as their craft while grounding their work in the research.

Key Takeaways

- Scaffolds are temporary supports that will vary based on the student profile, intensity, frequency, and duration.
- Scaffolds require the learner to actively engage in deliberate practice.
- Educators should plan for meaningful supports within their structured literacy lessons through the lens of diagnostic and prescriptive measures while also being adaptive in their teaching in the moment.
- The role of the educator is to move students to independent application of skills and knowledge through the Gradual Release of Responsibility model.

> Simplify your path to practice. What did you put in your pocket?
> What stepping stones, or nuggets of knowledge, are you taking from this chapter?

A Snapshot of Support in Action

"Our basic task in education is to find strategies which will take individual differences into consideration but which will do so in such a way as to promote the fullest development of the individual."

—(Bloom 1968)

Integrated Framework Component: Academics and Support

In this part of the journey, we continue our dive into the heart of academic intervention work—the ability to provide scaffolds, adaptive teaching, and support for students as part of explicit instruction based on student needs concerning assessments and observations.

Dyslexia intervention requires all elements of structured literacy, with intentional application and design taught by a highly knowledgeable and skilled teacher trained in dyslexia, to make meaningful decisions regarding instruction based on diagnostic and prescriptive measures. This means looking to assessments and observations to pinpoint specific areas of need (diagnostic) and using this information to guide instruction (prescriptive).

The large lesson components typically included in dyslexia interventions are alphabet sequence and knowledge, phonemic awareness, handwriting, phonics, history of the language, spelling, fluency, comprehension, and written expression. This is a lot to include in lessons, and the foundational skills are built systematically, increasing in difficulty and concepts over time. There is a reciprocal nature to reading development in that foundational skills support higher skills, and higher skills support lower ones. Think of this as a spiral in which when we come back, we pick up higher-level skills and continue on in this cumulative manner (see Figure 6.3 in Chapter 6).

This chapter examines examples of evidence-based practices, scaffolds, and supports within a structured literacy lesson plan with the student at the forefront. What does this student need? What is the ease with which this child is acquiring reading, writing, or language? What does their learning profile (assessments and observations) tell me about instruction?

As we move through this chapter, you will see examples of student data and how this relates to instruction as well as scaffolds and supports that would be appropriate for that student. Because this book focuses on the integrated framework, I share *some* scaffolds and supports. This is a partial list or set of examples, as the book would far exceed the allotted pages. However, it is my goal that the reader feels empowered to reflect on best practices for addressing areas of need within the lesson, raise awareness of the power of instruction and prescriptive and adaptive teaching through meaningful scaffolds and supports, and begin to grow their teaching toolkit for supporting students. The best thing we can do for our students is to have the knowledge and know-how to understand what is needed—to teach beyond programs—and to understand the student in front of us to ensure we provide the best services possible.

Keep in mind the following questions when planning connected to the Scaffolding in Dyslexia Intervention image in Figure 9.1 as we move

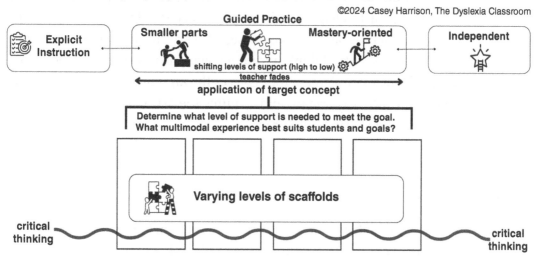

FIGURE 9.1 Scaffolding in dyslexia intervention.

through these examples and components commonly found within dyslexia intervention instruction. Making planned and purposeful instructional decisions for reading and writing tasks encompasses explicit instruction and guided practice where the level of support moves from higher to lower levels as the teacher support fades, leading to mastery-oriented and independent application. In planning, there are some questions to consider.

Explicit instruction questions to consider: What target concept am I teaching? How will I explicitly teach this concept? How will I collect data throughout the lesson to monitor student understanding and application? What scaffolds and supports does this student need or likely need to complete the task?

Guided practice questions to consider: How will I move students from the smaller parts to the application? How will I determine when to fade support? What multimodal experience best suits students and their goals?

These levels of scaffolding adjust with practice and includes: intentional multimodal experiences, hierarchy of prompts and cues, materials supports (charts, etc.), intensity of practice, consistent monitoring, clarifying, reteaching and consolidating of learning, immediate corrective feedback, and critical thinking and metacognitive processes. The knowledge of how to implement these pieces through purposeful instructional decisions takes experience and requires the art of teaching—the ability to bridge the research into practice.

Student 1

Letter knowledge is an important building block of literacy, and knowing letter names provides a springboard for learning and remembering letter-sound relationships—the alphabetic principle—a foundational skill for learning to read (Ehri 2005; Foulin 2005; National Reading Panel 2000) and the ability to hold a sequence of letters in memory anchors our orthography or spelling system.

Let's look at this foundational skill through data, both diagnostic and observational, of a student with dyslexia.

Student #1 Data—In the fall of first grade, student letter naming indicates that the child can automatically identify and name 36/52 letters (upper-lower case), unable to recall the alphabet outside of singing the song; unable to write the sequence of the alphabet or place letters in order. Observations show common confusion of j for g, s for c (the letter name when said produces the less common phoneme, the letter g begins with the sound of /j/), b/d/p/q (confusion in letters with similar visual markers); inconsistent recalling letters, even those in name indicating additional retrieval practices are needed.

Instructional goals: Student will identify and recall upper-and-lowercase letter names in less than two minutes. Student will independently sequence the letters of the alphabet with automaticity with letter tiles and in written form.

Instructional Scaffolds and Supports for Student #1: Daily explicit instruction and practice with alphabet knowledge and sequence (2–5 min.) at the start of the lesson with constant observation, modeling, and corrective feedback. Because the student is not yet able to work with the entire alphabet sequence, appropriate scaffolds could include:

- Work with a smaller sequence of letters (ABCDE, etc.)
- Provide a paper outline of the sequence and moveable letters for the student to engage with the letter sequence in a multimodal way (see the letter—name the letter—feel the letter shape)
- Write the smaller sequence of letters (say the letter as it is written)
- Teacher calls out letter names and student identifies and points to the letter and says the name (Find the letter ___)

note the high level of retrieval practices within this small portion of the lesson

---

As the student increases automaticity, alphabet knowledge tasks increase in stages of gradual release of supports to include: alphabet arc with letters outlined, alphabet arc with only A-MN-Z visible, alphabet strip as reference only, placing plastic letters in sequence and writing the alphabet from memory, and on to more advanced work with the alphabet such as missing letters (moving within a sequence of easier to more challenging such as ab_, a_c, _bc, _b_) or alphabetizing skills (see Figure 9.2).

Phonemic Awareness, Handwriting, Letter Knowledge, and Early Phonics

We want our instruction targeted toward learning strategies and activities with the highest learning outcomes for the student. Our students with dyslexia don't have time for anything else. To make the most of our work with students utilizing purposeful integration of speech to print through a multimodal approach that connects the phoneme (sound) to the grapheme (letter representation) in connection to explicit letter formation and application within reading and writing solidifies the

Scaffolding In Dyslexia Intervention in Practice
Goal - Identify and sequence the alphabet (upper-case).
What multimodal experience best suits students and goals?

small sequence of letters (matching)	arc with letters (matching)	letter strip	anchor letters	independent sequencing of alphabet

most support   **less support**

©Casey Harrison, 2024

FIGURE 9.2 Scaffolding in dyslexia intervention in practice.

foundational skill of phoneme-grapheme connections. Each piece links or connects, as shown in Figure 9.3. When we explicitly teach these linkages, we help students gain awareness of the alphabetic principle, the knowledge that letters and letter patterns represent spoken language and lays the foundation for reading and spelling.

> When taught explicit letter formation linked to the concept that letters represent speech sounds, syllables, and words, these images are stored in the brain's language center (Berninger & Wolf 2015).

Once students are engaged in formal reading instruction, the instructional focus for developing reading and writing of words should be done through an integrated approach of foundational reading skills. Research indicates that targeting an integrated approach to explicitly and systematically teaching phoneme awareness linked to articulatory

**Purposefully integrating Phonemic Awareness,
Letter Knowledge, and Handwriting through multimodal instruction
(in connection to word reading and spelling)**

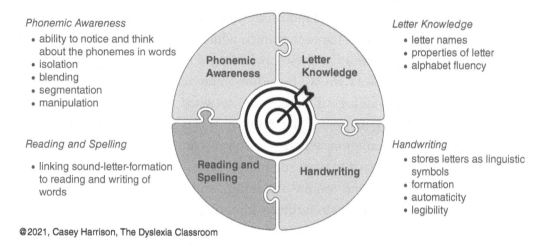

Phonemic Awareness
- ability to notice and think about the phonemes in words
- isolation
- blending
- segmentation
- manipulation

Letter Knowledge
- letter names
- properties of letter
- alphabet fluency

Reading and Spelling
- linking sound-letter-formation to reading and writing of words

Handwriting
- stores letters as linguistic symbols
- formation
- automaticity
- legibility

@2021, Casey Harrison, The Dyslexia Classroom

FIGURE 9.3 Purposeful integration.

features (Castiglioni-Spalten & Ehri 2003), with systematic synthetic phonics (NRP 2000), explicit instruction in letter formation (Berninger & Wolf 2015), and deliberate practice and application of the sound-symbol correspondences in decoding and encoding (reading and spelling), we establish this bond between speech and print.

Intentional instruction in this part of the lesson should focus on:

- Phonemic awareness that links the phoneme to the articulatory features and focuses on isolation, segmentation, and blending (phonemic awareness)

- Direct teaching of letter representation or representations (letter knowledge + phonics)

- Explicit instruction in letter formation (letter knowledge + handwriting)

- Deliberate practice and application of sound-symbol knowledge within intentional decoding and encoding practice (reading and spelling)

Articulatory features refers to use of voice, placement, and manner of our tongue, lips, and mouth as we make individual speech sounds. In English there are 44 speech sounds which are linked to letter representations (graphemes) and these can be sorted into categories based on these characteristics. When we introduce students to phonemes, we can activate the phonological processing network by explicitly teaching the articulatory gestures of the phoneme. Using a mirror to identify the place of articulation, where the sound comes from within our mouth (front, middle, or back of the mouth), the manner of articulation (what the teeth, lips, and tongue are doing), and the use of voice or unvoiced sound production strengthens phonological awareness. These mouth cues are important for anchoring sounds to letter representations, especially for struggling readers, and can act as a cue for recall and error correction within the lesson.

Note that videos describing these articulatory cues can be found at www.thedys lexiaclassroom.com/teachingbeyondthediagnosis

---

As you explicitly teach the articulation feature for the sound, link this understanding to the grapheme. This includes explicit instruction and practice in letter naming, and isolated phoneme production in connection to letter formation, focusing on the grapheme, as handwriting helps students store letters as linguistic symbols. For example, if learning the digraph sh, students would look in a mirror and say "sh," noting the puckering of the lips and the long stream of air that is felt when saying the sound. This knowledge is connected to the grapheme <sh> while learning and practicing the letter formations of <s> and <h>. An effective process for a multimodal interconnected approach to introducing phoneme-grapheme correspondences gets students thinking critically about the sound-letter relationships in language as they participate in uncovering the concept and connecting the new learning with previously learned concepts (Cox 1992; Gillingham & Stillman 1997) through explicit instruction.

Multimodal Mini-Lesson

Sample of a multimodal interconnected instructional routine of phoneme-grapheme introduction (5–8 min. instructional time in the lesson).
*Note the high level of back-and-forth engagement between teacher and student.

Materials: student mirror, keyword card with written grapheme, letter card, handwriting paper or board.

Auditory and Visual Modalities (students listening and looking at the teacher)

1. Teacher says three to five target words. Example: *fish, fan, fox, fat*

   *scaffold—say one word at a time and have students echo.
   Note if student has difficulty in pronunciation; correct and repeat word as needed.

2. Teacher asks what sound was alike in all the words. (yes, /f/)

   *scaffolds—repeat the words emphasizing the sound /f/; elongate the word to highlight the sound ffffffffffffffiiiiiiiiiiish.

Auditory, Visual, Kinesthetic (articulatory cue) Modalities

3. Direct students to look in mirror and produce the sound. *(students look in mirror at mouth and say /f/)*

4. Teacher asks students to note the position and movement in the mouth. *Example: Are your teeth close to your bottom lip? (student responds) Yes, this sound is partially blocked by our lips. (show students the mouth card for /f/)*

5. Teacher asks students to place hand in front of mouth and say sound. *(What do you notice? /f/. Yes, air is coming out.)*
6. Teacher asks more detailed questions about the feel of the sound, such as the flow of air. *(What does the air feel like? A puff? A flow of air? Yes, a flow of air)*
7. Students are asked to place three fingers lightly on their voice box/ throat and say the sound, noting if the voice is engaged. *(Say /f/. Do you feel vibrations? No. Is your voice on or off? off.)*
8. Teacher notes for students if the sound is a consonant or vowel sound and the articulatory features. *(This is a consonant sound. The sound is partially blocked by our teeth and lips.)*

Auditory, Visual, Kinesthetic (articulatory cue) Modalities

9. Teacher writes the three to five target words on the board and asks students to identify the letter that is alike. Example: *fish, fan, fox, fat.*

    *scaffolds—use teacher "think aloud" to model this metacognitive process. *"Hmmm. I see the letter a in two of the words, but not all of them. I see the letter f in this word at the beginning. Oh, I see the letter f in all these words!"* Note: if students don't know the letter, explicitly tell them: This is the letter *f*—and point to the letter *f* in each word.
10. Teacher shows the letter *f* card.

Auditory, Visual, Kinesthetic, Keyword Assimilation Cue, Handwriting Cue

11. Teacher highlights the keyword and links it to the sound by giving clues to the keyword, or directly telling the students the keyword. The keyword should include the target sound. (fish, /f/)
12. Teacher explicitly models how to write the letter (print or cursive) using consistent and explicit verbal instructions as they write the letter (f, /f/, *"curve way up, loop left, pull straight down, curve up to the*

right and release" to make a cursive f). Students practice writing the letter and saying the letter name and sound. Teacher provides corrective feedback on letter formation and gives verbal cue as they write.

*scaffolds—teacher determines the best path for writing materials for students; skywriting, tactile surface, paper, etc. with the focus on letter formation and linking sound to grapheme.

Student 2

Student #2 Data—Second grade student with consistent errors in reading and writing, including omission of sounds, adding sounds, and distorting sounds in words. On phonological processing assessments, the student was unable to consistently segment phonemes and showed a normative weakness in phonological awareness and phonological memory (the ability to hold sounds, words, sentences in the working memory). In class, spelling provides a window into many of these errors with vowel sound substitutions (*help* written as *halp, thing* written as *fing*). It should be noted that there can be a dialectal impact on some of these sound productions, however this is not the case for this student. Student was screened for speech and did not qualify as errors are not within spoken language.

Instructional Scaffolds and Supports for Student #2: Daily explicit instruction and practice with segmenting and blending words in reading and spelling with mouth cards to aid in phoneme confusion. Explicit instruction using the integrated multimodal approach to link phonemes to graphemes with articulatory features, keyword, grapheme, letter formation, and application to reading and spelling.

Things to consider and observe in the lesson (see Figure 9.4):

- Can the student pronounce the sound in isolation? Within a word where the sound is in the initial/medial/final position?
- Practice targeted speech sound identification with picture or word sorts comparing target sounds.
- Provide ample opportunities to practice reading and spelling.

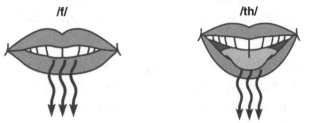

A student is saying "fin" for thin, and "baf" for bath.

Use mouth cards as an error correction in phoneme confusion.

©2024 Casey Harrison, The Dyslexia Classroom

FIGURE 9.4 Phoneme confusion.

- Provide practice with segmenting, or breaking apart, each phoneme in the word. Elkonin (sound) boxes act as parking spots for the sounds to support phonological working memory (see Figure 9.5a and 9.5b).

- Scaffolding with the use of sound boxes may include using chips and objects to represent each phoneme. If students are not yet able to segment consistently, providing sound boxes with the correct number of boxes is a higher level of support (eg. if segmenting cat, provide a sound box with 3 boxes for /k/ /ă/ /t/). This level of support fades as students gain automaticity in segmenting phonemes. The support can be pulled back in stages—providing preset sound boxes, choice of preset sound boxes (up: 2 boxes, bat: 3 boxes), a row of boxes, moving to lines, and then no boxes needed.

- Use pictures to build vocabulary and linguistic knowledge. This can include words, sentences, and also highlight multiple meanings (see bat in Figure 9.5a).

- Move to letter connections as they are taught and have students use letter tiles or handwrite the phonemes in the sound boxes (see chat in Figure 9.5b).

- Students with dyslexia also benefit from using the articulatory feature mouth cards during these segmentation tasks to analyze sounds in connection to these features (see Figure 9.6). This strategy is beneficial for students with dyslexia as they gain sound-symbol knowledge.

---

*scaffolds noted in images, and downloadable student worksheets can be found at www.thedyslexiaclassroom.com/teaching-beyond-the-diagnosis

---

- Student focuses on segmenting sounds, using scaffolds noted above, and writing the word to solidify phoneme-grapheme correspondences.

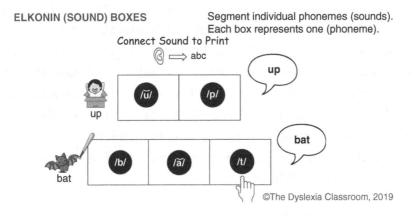

FIGURE 9.5a Early sound boxes phonemic awareness.

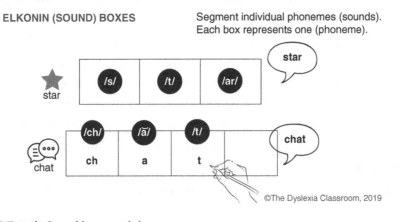

FIGURE 9.5b Sound boxes with letters.

PHONEMIC AWARENESS WITH MOUTH CARDS

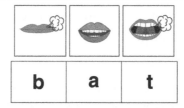

©The Dyslexia Classroom, 2019

FIGURE 9.6 Segmenting with mouth cards.

Using mouth cards for phonemic awareness segmenting tasks is a scaffold that supports phonemic awareness with students by bringing awareness to the articulatory features of individual phonemes as we link sounds to print. According to Ehri and Castiglioni-Spalten (2003), establishing an "awareness of articulatory gestures facilitates the activation of graphophonemic connections that helps children identify written words and secure them in memory." The procedures are the same as above with sound boxes, but now students match mouth cards to the sounds as they segment each phoneme, then link those mouth cards to letter representations (Figure 9.6).

Reading and Spelling

Reading, or decoding, is applying the sound-symbol relationships and successfully blending them to read a word. Spelling, or encoding, is the ability to segment words by individual sounds and use the correct sound-symbol correspondences in written form. Teaching reading and spelling together strengthens the phoneme-grapheme correspondence and spelling instruction. Spelling should include dictation at the sound level (repeat the sound, and write the letter representation), word level, and sentence level. Spelling should increase in difficulty as students gain mastery, and include spelling generalizations (such as when to use k, c, ck), spelling multisyllabic words, and application of morphemes.

Decoding Strategies

Students with dyslexia often have difficulty with word reading, decoding at the word level, and fluent and accurate reading of words, sentences, and text. Students learning to read need to spend time decoding—the practice of linking speech sounds to print. This decoding is the heavy lifting required during reading instruction to allow for the orthographic mapping process, a cognitive process that bonds sound to print, and students should have ample opportunities for this practice. Dyslexic students learning to read require more instructional time and practice, often hundreds of applications, addressing decoding and spelling applications, and may require scaffolds to aid in decoding skills.

Student 3

Student #3 Data—Third grade student presenting at the early stages of reading application of single syllable words with consonant clusters (st, str, dr, etc.) on a diagnostic assessment. Observations show that the student correctly segments the sounds in the word, but when blending sounds to read, will omit sounds and substitute sounds, causing much frustration for the student.

Instructional Scaffolds and Supports for Student #3: Daily explicit instruction and practice in strategies to move the student to blending the sounds fluently when reading. Student should have practice applying the strategy at the word, phrase, sentence, and text level. The use of decodable text that focuses on the phoneme-grapheme correspondences taught provides students with opportunities to apply strategies and build fluency.

Decoding Scaffolds to Use with Student #3

- Successive blending is an early scaffold for students who tend to drop the initial phoneme. This strategy is best for students to work with short vowel sounds where you do not have a vowel situation like silent e or vowel team since you are uncovering one grapheme at a time. Students identify the initial phoneme, then add the second phoneme, and read from the beginning to

(Continued)

(Continued)

the second phoneme. Then, students add the next phoneme and so on until they have read the word. This strategy is beneficial for students who struggle with phonological working memory or who need additional help with blending. Example: /l/, /la/, /las/, /last/, last.

- Continuous blending or connected phonation is a great strategy to help students connect sounds with decoding. Students that struggle with holding individual speech sounds with their phonological memory benefit from this instruction. Within this scaffold, it is recommended that you start with continuous sounds (those sounds that are able to be stretched out until you run out of breath–/m/, /s/, /f/. mmmmmmmmmmmmaaaaaaaat
- Backward blending is the strategy to use when a student struggles with vowel sound production or sound omission. Cover the beginning portion of the word up to the vowel and have the student begin with the vowel sound and read to the end. Uncover each grapheme, one at a time, that comes before the vowel, blending the word as we go. Student reads word as a whole. (word to read is: crab. students will begin by reading: -ab, -rab, crab)

*PDF of decoding strategies can be downloaded at www.thedyslexiaclassroom.com/teachingbeyondthediagnosis

---

Morphology and Multisyllabic Word Reading

Morphology work connects to spelling conventions, meaning, and pronunciation, so we can't wait to introduce this concept, and we need to provide students with reliable decoding strategies that include morphology (see Figure 9.7). Research shows that students who received morphological awareness instruction "significantly increased comprehension and spelling of morphologically complex words in fourth-and-fifth grade children with dyslexia" (Arnbak & Elbro 1996/2000). Early instruction with morphology can begin in the younger grades with inflectional suffixes. These suffixes, such as *-ed, -s, -ing, -es, -er*, and *-est* do not change the part of speech of the word when added. Morphology work connects to spelling conventions, meaning, and pronunciation and should be a part

Start morphology work
early in your instruction.

Using real word parts
(morphemes) to sort, read,
and build real words.

FIGURE 9.7 Morphology.

Source: Retrieved with permission from The Dyslexia Classroom.

of structured literacy lessons across the grades, moving from early Anglo-Saxon affixes to Latin roots and Greek combining forms.

Student 4

Student #4 Data—Seventh grade student presenting with reading fluency of 104 words correct per minute, comprehension is adequate and student gets the gist of what is read; multisyllabic words pose a challenge and student will guess at unknown words showing limited word attack strategies. Student has knowledge of sound-symbol correspondences and has some syllable knowledge.

Instructional Scaffolds and Supports for Student #4: Explicit instruction in morphemes and word attack strategies at the word level. Application of strategies to move student to automatic and accurate word reading in words, sentences, and text. Student should have practice to apply the strategy at the word, phrase, sentence, and text level. Use of decodable and connected text that focuses on the phoneme-grapheme correspondences taught provide student with opportunities to apply strategies and build fluency.

- Use a scaffold of coding words. Coding is a strategy that empowers students to connect their learning of syllable types, phoneme-grapheme knowledge, and morphological awareness by underlining, circling, or noting parts of words using diacritical markings, like those found in the

(Continued)

(Continued)

dictionary (see Figure 9.8a). I have my students box the suffix and prefix for morphology work and then move to the base word. This strategy can be carried throughout all multisyllabic word reading and work with Latin roots and Greek combining forms.

- Explicit instruction in the steps for decoding multisyllabic words. Providing students with a reliable word attack strategy to read new unknown words includes the following steps (see Figure 9.8b):
  1. Box prefixes and suffixes.
  2. Look for consonant digraphs, vowel teams, syllable patterns (vowel-r, vowel-consonant-e, silent e, etc.).
  3. Underline or mark the vowels to be sounded.
  4. Identify and label the syllable pattern (VC/CV, VCV, etc.) *Note: this labeling is a scaffold to be removed as students gain proficiency, moving to scooping of syllables and then fade out all scaffolds.

- Divide between the syllables and read the word.

Basic Diacritical Marks - How to Code

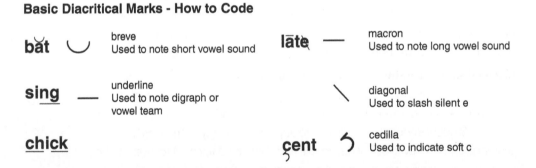

bǎt ∪   breve
Used to note short vowel sound

lāte —   macron
Used to note long vowel sound

sing —   underline
Used to note digraph or vowel team

╲   diagonal
Used to slash silent e

chick   (underlined)

çent ↄ   cedilla
Used to indicate soft c

NOTE: This is not all of the diacritical marks used in dyslexia intervention programs

FIGURE 9.8a Basic diacritical marks.

Steps for decoding multisyllabic words

1. Box prefixes and suffixes
2. Look for syllable patterns (VCe, Vr, Cle), consonant digraphs, vowel teams, silent e
3. Underline the vowels to be sounded
4. Identify and label the syllable pattern (VC/CV, VCV, etc.)

*note - this labeling is a scaffold - remove as students gain proficiency

5. Divide between syllables and read the word

FIGURE 9.8b Steps for decoding multisyllabic words.

Fluency

Many students think that fluency is the act of reading fast. However, researchers Hasbrouck and Glaser (2012) refer to fluency as "reasonably accurate reading at an appropriate rate with suitable prosody that leads to accurate and deep comprehension and motivation to read." This deep comprehension should be our ultimate goal in teaching fluency.

Accuracy means reading words correctly, and the goal for student reading should be 98% accuracy. An appropriate rate is a pace that allows the student to understand the content with proper prosody. Prosody is a linguistic term for the sounds of speech that convey meaning across multiple words, such as the tone at the end of a question or how tone can indicate sarcasm. As students increase fluency, they demonstrate substantial prosodic variability and can make distinctions to match meaning to text from these. Since fluency levels may vary based on text, background knowledge, vocabulary, motivation, and purpose working with a fluency range is beneficial. For this reason, I teach my students about what I call the Goldilocks Fluency Zone.

Student 5

Student #5 Data—Middle school student is racing through text, not heeding punctuation or phrases for meaning; views reading fast as good reading; some errors in word accuracy.

Instructional Scaffolds and Supports for Student #5: Explicit instruction in what fluency includes (accuracy, automaticity, and prosody); set goals for prosody, the intonation, rhythm and emphasis; practice with text (phrases, sentences, and paragraphs/text); progress monitor with attention on the components of fluency.

- Fluency levels may vary based on text, background knowledge, vocabulary, motivation, and purpose so that we read within a range of rate while maintaining high accuracy and prosody. For this reason, I teach my students about what I call the Goldilocks Fluency Zone. They can connect to either the Goldilocks Zone as noted in their science classes—they understand this concept that life exists only in this zone—or in the traditional fairy tale in which the desired bowl of porridge is just right. This concept can be used to teach students that this is the zone where we can easily read the text (addressing accuracy, automaticity, phrasing, and prosody) and comprehend—it's our goal for bringing life into our reading (see Figure 9.9a and 9.9b).

Download these posters at www.thedyslexiaclassroom.com/teaching beyondthediagnosis

- Model appropriate prosody and have students practice with phrases, sentences, and text (see Figure 9.10). Scaffolds could include scooping phrases and phrase-cued marking (O'Shea & Sindelar 1983) in which slashes indicate the amount of pause to use when reading to aid in meaning and prosody.
- Monitor student fluency, noting rate, accuracy, and prosody. Student progress monitoring using a grade-level passage, such as those found from Acadience® provides valuable information and should be used for goal setting and instructional planning. When monitoring student oral reading fluency, take note of the accuracy in reading and mark errors to aid in instructional decisions, determine the words correct per minute and provide a prosody score. A simple prosody rubric can be used to determine student application of phrasing, stress, intonation, expression and pauses when reading. A progress monitoring form can be downloaded at www.thedyslexiaclassroom.com/teachingbeyond thediagnosis

(a)

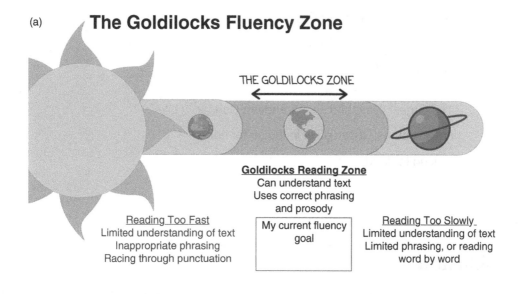

(b)

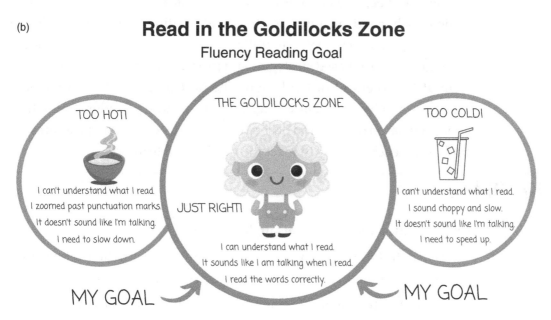

FIGURE 9.9 The Goldilocks zone of reading fluency.

Source: Retrieved with permission from The Dyslexia Classroom.

Instructional Scaffoldings for Prosody in Reading

Phrase-cued text markings
O'Shea & Sindelar (1983)

The largest flying bird /is the Andean Condor. // Like

most vultures,/ it can glide in the air for hours /

looking for food.

/ = short pause
// = longer pause

FIGURE 9.10 Prosody.

Conclusion

We need to keep the child at the center of our teaching. The ease with which each child acquires reading and writing can vary. Dyslexia instruction requires that we utilize a structured literacy approach through evidence-based strategies and programs while keeping the student at the forefront of the lesson. The best thing we can do for our students is to have the knowledge and know-how to understand what is needed based on data and observations—to teach beyond programs—and honor each journey to meet the needs of all learners.

Key Takeaways

- Scaffolds support students in the lesson.
- Use data (all types) to make adjustments to instruction within the structured literacy lesson to meet the needs of students.
- Keep the student at the center of the work—what does this student need to move learning forward?

Simplify your path to practice. What did you put in your pocket?
What stepping stones, or nuggets of knowledge, are you taking from this chapter?

CHAPTER TEN

Call for a Champion

"What makes something better is connection."

—Brene Brown

Integrated Framework Component: Metacognitive Processes

In this part of the journey, we look at how educators can foster metacognitive processes to support student learning and performance (see Figure 10.1). This begins with the call for reflection and focus on our part as a sort of dyslexia coach and how we thoughtfully bring high expectations and support to students. Fostering metacognition and critical thinking skills for both teachers and students is a key part of the integrated framework that supports student learning performance.

Many years ago, I had a student who was diagnosed with dyslexia in elementary school. He spent his fourth and fifth grade in reading interventions with me during the school day in a dyslexia therapy model program. During this time, he completed the program. He left fifth grade, having closed most of the academic gaps, passed all the state standardized tests and reading grade-level material with accommodations and a continued plan of what to access as accommodations in middle school. In our work together, we constantly wove into our conversations and

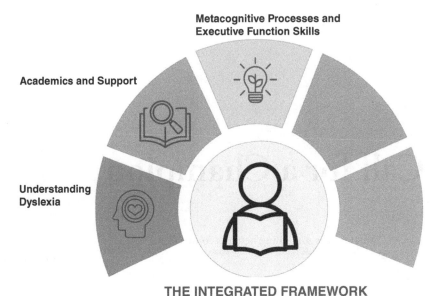

FIGURE 10.1 The integrated framework—metacognitive processes and executive function skills.

lessons knowledge about dyslexia, what that means for each learner, what accommodations are available, which ones work well to address specific barriers due to dyslexia, and when and how to ask for access to these—all the things to set this child up for success in his academic journey. Due to misunderstandings about dyslexia, it took some time and years of struggle on the child's part for the parents and system to reach an agreement for an educational evaluation, which determined a qualification of dyslexia and dysgraphia. I spent countless hours working with the family and child to shift the narrative around dyslexia and what that means for the child. The family's role in this journey was not just crucial, it was pivotal. Their support was instrumental in the child's success, and their involvement underscored the importance of a united front in supporting a child with dyslexia. This child left elementary school as a happy and confident student ready to step into their academic path with an understanding of the role dyslexia may play.

In the fall, after some time in middle school, he returned to tell me that his middle school teacher told him that he was not dyslexic and probably had been misdiagnosed and didn't need any accommodations in her classroom. He was upset because he struggled with accessing some of the curriculum due to his learning disability and felt certain accommodations would be helpful. As I sat there listening to the student, I could see the impact that those words had on his confidence and how they planted a seed of doubt in what he thought he knew about himself. Mind you, the teacher was not a diagnostician nor a neuropsychologist, and the statement made, while perhaps not meant to cause harm, did, in fact, do that. It highlighted the teacher's misunderstanding of the impacts of dyslexia and took away from the students their identity of how they understood their learning path. This same sentiment was shared with the family, who had just embraced the diagnosis of dyslexia and were shifting their narrative around the word, setting us back to a level of uncertainty and thinking the child was lazy or unintelligent.

Statements like this made to students highlight much about what occurs in classrooms, the accessibility of legally required accommodations, and overall misunderstanding and long-held stigma surrounding dyslexia. While this is one of many similar stories from children and families I work with, I don't think ill intentions were behind the teacher's words, but as Charles M. Blow says, "One doesn't have to operate with great malice to do great harm. The absence of empathy and understanding are sufficient." There is power in the words we use. What we say to students and families matters. They look to educators for guidance and expect that we know best for their child. Often, we do, but sometimes we do not, and we must be willing to step into our journey as lifelong learners to figure out what we still need to learn, what dyslexia is, its impacts on the whole child, and what it means for our classrooms and instruction. Before my dyslexia therapy training, I had little knowledge of dyslexia despite being a reading intervention teacher and facilitator, and I know this is true for many in the education field. With dyslexia being the most common learning disability, it is absolutely necessary that we deepen our understanding of dyslexia—both academically and the emotional impacts—within our communities and classrooms to build bridges of knowledge and support. A teacher that understands dyslexia can make all the difference.

The Role of Empathy in Education

Empathy encompasses a broad concept of cognitive and emotional reactions to us and our world. It is a crucial component in connections with others and the ability to take the perspective of another without judgment, to recognize emotions in others, and to communicate your understanding of those emotions. It is a skill that grows and strengthens with practice, a building block of morality and successful relationships. Researcher Brene Brown, speaking from a human and vulnerability perspective, says that empathy is communicating that incredible healing message of "you're not alone," which is why it is powerful for students to understand the prevalence of dyslexia—they are not alone. When working with dyslexic learners, along with academic knowledge of reading and dyslexia, empathy needs to be held to help guide students on their learning journey toward high educational outcomes. This requires us as educators and parents to reflect on our role in understanding and connecting with students, ensuring we hold high expectations, and always keeping the student at the forefront. In addition, we as adults need to have the emotional maturity to guide our children, but what does this mean?

While the study of empathy is ongoing, researchers often differentiate between types of empathy: cognitive, emotional, and compassionate.

Cognitive empathy, or logical empathy, is the ability to know how the other person feels and what they may be thinking. It is often referred to as "perspective talking"—when we are using our cognitive empathy, we are able to see another person's perspective (Ratka 2018). It's the idea of "putting yourself in another person's shoes" and understanding on an intellectual level how someone is feeling. Children begin to develop this empathy around three to four years of age, roughly when they start to develop an elementary "theory of mind" (Wellman et al. 2001). This "theory of mind" allows us to understand that, as people, we all hold different experiences in the world. In the Active View of Reading model (Figure 5.3 in Chapter 5), "theory of mind" is noted in the Language Comprehension bubble. We continue to develop more complex forms of the theory of mind, often through literature and the building of content and background knowledge of different cultures and the world we live in. Engaging in student discussions when we ask our students to be aware of this when discussing literature and character perspective-taking is another way in which we develop this cognitive empathy. Through reflective practices, we can bring this awareness into our work with students as they learn to empathize, understand different perspectives, and accept differences in others and themselves.

Emotional empathy is when we are well attuned to another person's inner emotions. It allows us to readily understand how that person feels and move into a shared emotional experience. You can relate to the other person—it's a natural response to feeling the pull of emotion in certain situations—this kind of connection forms a strong bond. It is often the first response with our loved ones and children. Sometimes, this type of empathy can become overwhelming and lead to personal distress and burnout because you are actually feeling along with the person, matching their emotional state. This is sometimes not a helpful response, especially if a student is overcome with big emotions, and you find yourself in the emotional trenches with them unable to step back from that state. Emotional empathy can also lead to burnout or the inability to respond. As educators, we often take on the worries of our students and may experience this kind of emotional response. I can't count the number of days in which I had sleepless nights as I lay worrying about a student or constantly felt the pull into a state of extreme emotion due to a situation at school. Educators have the biggest hearts and give so much to their students and classrooms, but finding the right balance, or compassionate empathy, is healthy for all parties and what we seek.

Compassionate empathy leads us to connect logic and the heart and is the type of compassion usually sought after. With compassionate empathy, we can understand a person's predicament and feel with them, but we are also moved to help take action or help solve a problem. Compassionate empathy generates an outward-focused empathy and desire to care for and help others in our society. This is what most people seek when looking for an empathetic response: someone who can understand what they are going through and sympathize with them while still maintaining their own emotional response so that they can provide appropriate support and action to move towards action or resolution. Compassionate empathy is what our children need from us—the ability to balance understanding and emotion so that we can guide and support their academic struggles and emotional responses that tend to arise when having dyslexia.

Understanding where we are in our own awareness of responses and guidance with students is key to compassionate empathy. Having the ability to be reflective, or a metacognitive awareness of our thought processes, can help us shift our responses and continue to use those strategies that are serving us and our students well. I have experienced all of these types of empathy in my education career. I often reflect on how I feel in response to a given situation and check in with myself about my empathy response. Take a moment to reflect on your empathy type when working with students. This is an exercise in awareness.

> **Reflection:**
>
> What type of empathy am I currently bringing to my lessons? What characteristics do I see in myself? Are there places where I can move to compassionate empathy?

Meeting the Needs of Students

"Shame dies when stories are told in safe places."

—Ann Voskamp

Including empathy-building strategies within our lessons, especially through text, discussions, and "theory of mind," deepens comprehension and provides opportunities to model compassionate empathy and cultivate an environment of trust, respect, and equity. Creating a bridge of connection and trust with students to forge meaningful relationships can address many of the underlying impacts of dyslexia, which are rooted in shame, disconnect, and fear, which we saw in the Dyslexia Iceberg.

Within our classrooms, we address many student needs. Students who feel safe in a classroom are more willing to take academic risks and push themselves in their learning, and all students want to feel connected and accepted in their classrooms. For educators, meeting the needs of belonging within the intervention lessons focuses on connecting, developing social relationships and interpersonal skills, and feelings of belonging and understanding embedded within the structured literacy/OG lesson. We address these by fostering relationships and building a community where emotions, achievement, respect, and confidence are fostered through authentic connections and knowledge of dyslexia and its impacts on academics and emotions. This encompasses all aspects of the lesson—from holding high expectations and setting the stage for success to explicitly teaching and providing practice with appropriate support to inviting the student into the awareness of what worked to achieve the skill or task. Each of these pieces leads to success, and success leads to higher engagement and motivation. While peak experiences, such as doing well on an exam, getting into a selected college, landing a key job, or sporting achievement, are examples of self-fulfillment needs and address longer-term goals, students with dyslexia should be made aware of the smaller daily successes they make—those moments of success in a lesson no matter how small that are moving students toward a larger goal. Modeling and leading students to reflect on these small moments of success in the lesson fosters the development of self-actualization, awareness, and acceptance of where the student is academically and where they want to be without holding onto feelings of guilt or shame for being a human with areas of strength and challenges. This self-actualization is a large part of the work we want to embed into our lessons—we do this through the metacognitive processes integrated throughout the framework as we become the champion in the classroom.

Warm Demanders—Champions in the Classroom

> "Warm demanders expect a great deal of their students, convince them of their own brilliance, and help them to reach their potential in a disciplined and structured environment."
>
> —Lisa Delpit

As we connect our understanding of compassionate empathy with meeting students' needs, we also want to ensure that we have high expectations for students and are culturally responsive. We have all been in those classrooms, coaching, or mentoring sessions where the students are highly engaged, willing to take chances, and believe that the teacher believes in them and will continue to increase the expected outcomes for the student to reach their highest potential. These are the places that feel magical—the connection between the students and teacher is authentic, with clear and high levels of expectations, and learning is occurring.

I can think of many mentors and coaches who created an authentic connection, remained in a compassionate empathy state, and held high expectations for me. At times, this may have looked like them taking me aside and having an honest conversation about the work I was doing, asking where I may need help, or seeing an area of need and providing support, encouraging and offering specific praise so that I continued with that strategy or skill, ensuring the foundational pieces were in place to build upon, etc. These people encompassed all the things we want to bring into the classroom. They are all warm demanders.

> Take a moment to think about a teacher, coach, or mentor who impacted your life. What were some of their characteristics? What was it about that teacher that made an impact on you? On your work? On your self-esteem?

Over the years, I have consistently conducted informal surveys, exit tickets, and mini-interviews with students surrounding some of the characteristics of their favorite teachers or those whom they felt impacted their learning. I purposefully weave conversations that cultivate the reflective process and get students thinking about their learning, what role teachers/students play, and how together we each play a pivotal part in the learning process. While the bullet list that follows is but a sampling of student responses, you can see that much of what the students shared was along the lines of a warm demander or a champion in the classroom. A teacher who clearly held high expectations for them while also understanding them as learners and humans. Some of these characteristics include:

- Believed in me
- Pushed me to do my best

- Recognized and developed potential
- Cared about their students
- Scaffolded instruction
- Was hard on me when I needed it
- Created an environment that welcomed taking risks
- Built real connections
- Had clear expectations and boundaries
- Respect was at the center of the classroom environment
- Held high standards
- Found ways to make each student successful

Did you note things like believing in me, holding high expectations, insisting on best effort, having a deep understanding of their skill/craft, offering emotional support, breaking things down into meaningful parts, using appropriate and supportive tones, and helping? There is a term for someone who encompasses the ability to raise the bar for students, meet them where they are, and walk alongside them while holding compassionate empathy. This is a warm demander. Being a warm demander requires both confidence and humility—this connection of compassionate empathy with high expectations is the goal of creating equity-based education (see Figure 10.2). We can think of this as care plus active demandingness or a champion for our children, and is necessary in dyslexia education.

Lisa Delpit, American educationalist, researcher, author, and scholar at the Center for Urban Educational Excellence, describes warm demanders as those who "expect a great deal of their students, convince them of their own brilliance, and help them to reach their potential in a disciplined and structured environment."

Good coaches tend to do this with their players, and so do teachers. Teachers, tutors, specialists, and therapists are all academic coaches in the classroom. We have the goal of helping each student reach their

Warm Demanders in Today's Classrooms

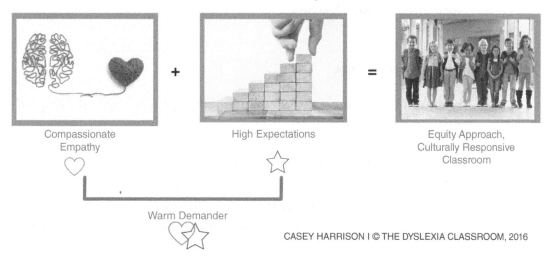

Compassionate
Empathy

High Expectations

Equity Approach,
Culturally Responsive
Classroom

Warm Demander

FIGURE 10.2 Warm demanders.

potential. As academic coaches or champions in the classroom, we know that students need to do the work, take responsibility, and engage, but this also recognizes our critical role in helping them on their path to success is based on connection and expectation.

The idea of warm demanders is not new, but one that is vital for us to conscientiously bring into our work as we support students. Judith Kleinfeld, a professor at the University of Alaska, coined the term "warm demanders" in 1975 when describing teachers who were most effective in student achievement. For some, "demanders" may elicit negative connotations or authoritative design. However, the research behind this is about the insistence on excellence and academic effort while providing the necessary experiences and support for the student to reach success. This aligns with how we teach structured literacy and scaffolds to help bridge the gap between what a student knows and what is not known through the guidance and encouragement of the teacher. This provides students with experiences with appropriate cognitive challenges that stimulate neurons and prevents students from slipping into learned helplessness. It is the heart of our structured literacy lessons.

Kleinfeld's Quadrants

Kleinfeld breaks the warm demander concept down into these quadrants (see Figure 10.3):

Sophisticates are those who hold low expectations and have low relationships/connections with students. They are often considered aloof and undemanding. We can think of the teacher who may say, "I delivered the information; either you get it or you don't."

Traditionalists are those who hold high expectations and have low connections with students. These educators hold high academic expectations but see little value in developing relationships with students or may feel that they are inappropriate or outside of

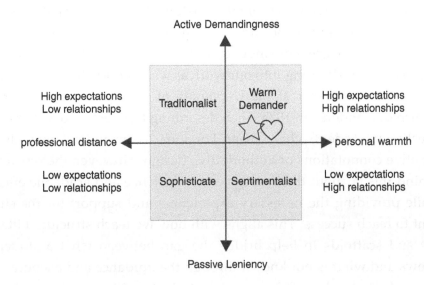

FIGURE 10.3 Kleinfeld's quadrants. Based on the work from Judith Kleinfeld (1975).

their role as teachers. Some refer to this as professional distance. The focus is on academics rather than rapport.

Sentimentalists hold low expectations but focus on high connections/relationships. These educators may lie within the emotional empathy that we discussed earlier in the chapter. They may become overly emotional or sympathetic because they "feel bad" for the students and may find they inadvertently lower the expectations. We may see this in goals set forth on an IEP where the expectation of growth is minimal, or the students, although able, are not required to complete certain tasks within their classroom. The sentimentalist allows for passive leniency. Often, this comes from a belief that they are being kind, but instead, it removes the learning from the child. My students will frequently refer to teachers who fall into this category as "nice, but I don't really learn a lot, or nice, but the class runs over them, they have no control, and really I can just turn in my work whenever; it's not a big deal." As educators, we need to reflect and determine if we may be falling into this quadrant and look at our own biases that may be underlying here—do we really believe that this child can reach high expectations? Do we feel we have an active role in that path to help a child reach their potential? Or are we dumbing it down or feeling sorry for students and lowering expectations? It can be uncomfortable to take a step back and look at our own behaviors and roles in our student's learning—but I believe that even as educators, we can continue to grow, develop, and refine our craft, which means being reflective in our teaching and our own biases.

The sentimentalist quadrant is one that in reflection I unknowingly fell into, especially when I think back to my first year of teaching and an incident that occurred. I had a little girl in my classroom whose background and story were ones that would bring tears to anyone who heard it. My heart broke for this child, and I was definitely emotionally empathetic to her path and story often worrying about her beyond the school day. During class, she would often display avoidance behaviors and because I felt bad for her, I wouldn't push her to complete her work or do her best, and I wasn't yet knowledgeable enough to put into place scaffolds to best help her. In reflection, I actually had low expectations for her; however, at the time, I would have argued that I didn't and was meeting her needs. On some level, yes, I was meeting most of her emotional needs, but definitely not her academic ones. As a first-year teacher, my mentor teacher, a very experienced colleague, saw my regular interaction allowing this student whom she also taught to get a free pass on work, and she pulled me aside and told me, "No. You cannot do that. You need to push her to complete the work and expect that she does it. We can work together to figure out how to get her there, but you cannot keep letting her slide by. You are not doing her any favors. In fact, you are feeding her the idea that she isn't good enough, that she can't do the work, and that you don't believe that she can." Well, I remember being embarrassed about her talking to me, but because I truly believe in growing as a person and her willingness to help me grow, I took that conversation to heart and had a real soul search with myself, my ideas about teaching, and what role I was playing in helping my students meet their potential. I needed to make a shift.

What I needed was to become a warm demander.

The **warm demander** holds high expectations <u>and</u> has strong relationships/connections with students. Kleinfeld calls this a combined "high personal warmth and high active demandingness." These teachers develop mutual respect with their students, along with clear expectations for academics and behaviors. They are very competent in their instructional approaches and scaffold instruction to support and push students to meet the expectations. As educators, we must become experts in the area we teach, and for those teaching students with dyslexia or those needing additional support, the expertise and academic knowledge of the content and how children learn is of high importance.

In addition to the academic knowledge held by the warm demander, the teacher's personal warmth and authentic concern earn her the right to demand engagement and effort through the idea that the teacher is an ally in this journey. This is what Cushman (2005) noted as a sign that the "teacher has your back." This, in fact, was exactly what my colleague was doing with me as a novice teacher. She could have closed her door, rolled her eyes, and had chats about my techniques in the teacher break room, but instead, she stepped into this uncomfortable conversation and, through this, showed me where, in fact, I was holding my students back, but also, she offered that support to mentor me. She basically expressed her high standards for what she expected of her colleagues and the vulnerability to have that conversation in a warm but matter-of-fact way and offered to assist.

In response, I was willing to be coached. To learn and to step into this new role of developing the skills to be a warm demander. I went to her classroom, observed, and saw that this same student in her room did the work and how the teacher engaged with the student, offered support, and held high standards, all while maintaining a strong relationship with the student. This mentor teacher showed me how to be both warm (show empathy) and hold high expectations, and her honesty and willingness to step into that space with me is one that I am truly grateful for as it shifted my teaching forever. She made me a better teacher.

> Think back to a teacher who made an impact on you. Where did they land on this quadrant of expectations and relationships?
> Where do you find yourself in this chart?

We all, as educators and parents, may fluctuate between all of these quadrants, but our goal is to have our primary pedagogy, or beliefs about learning and students, fall within the warm demander quadrant.

We must strive for high connections/relationships while also holding high expectations for all students.

You can download this reflection chart (see Figure 10.4) in the book resources at www.thedyslexiaclassroom.com/teachingbeyondthediagnosis.

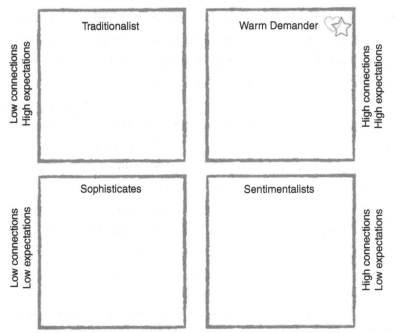

WARM DEMANDERS - CHAMPIONS IN THE CLASSROOM

Warm Demanders, quadrants, Judith Kleinfield (1975)

Reflections:
Where do I see myself on the model? What characteristics do I connect with?
Thinking of mentor teachers, what characteristics do they display? Where do I want to grow as an educator/parent? What do I need to do to achieve this?

FIGURE 10.4 Quadrant reflection.

Characteristics of a Warm Demander in the Classroom

Every teacher can become a warm demander. It may look a little different in each of us because we all have our leniencies, but some common characteristics are held by those who are viewed as warm demanders. Stepping into the role of a warm demander requires us as educators/parents to reflect on what areas we need to cultivate to help our students best and embrace the warm demander role in creating equitable education.

Some key components can be considered when developing our personal warm demander approach (Hammond 2014; Safir 2019) and may include some key characteristics that include:

- Believes that all students can learn.

- The ability to create paths for student success because they are competent with their curriculum and can provide appropriate scaffolding and instructional needs to support students to become their very best.

- Displays compassionate empathy to all students.

- Creates a safe environment for failure and risk-taking.

- Appreciates and understands the uniqueness of each student.

- Uses appropriate and supportive tones which create a community of mutual respect.

- Holds students to high standards for student academics and behavior, explicitly teaches those.

- Looks for areas of improvement, not perfection.

- Has a positive attitude.

Developing a classroom community where students are kept from disengaging and, therefore, setting students up for success by designing systems that hold students accountable for engagement and effort aligns with the high engagement principle of structured literacy. When students find success, that leads to engagement and motivation, which is acquired through a systematic, structured literacy approach (see Figure 6.3 in Chapter 6). I tell my students that I am their learning coach and their biggest cheerleader but also one who will ensure that we are moving towards our goals. It is my job to use explicit instruction to teach in a way that students understand, have the knowledge to provide meaningful scaffolds and supports, differentiate the instruction and ensure all students are learning. However, the heavy lifting of the learning needs to be done by the students. They need to do the work. I tell my students that I will stand with them, help them, guide them, and support them, but I won't do the work for them. We are part of the same team, and we all have a role. This is a great time to refer to the brain lesson in Chapter 5 and bring students into the learning process through this dynamic relationship. Holding the idea of compassionate empathy with the warm demander (or champion) approach leads us as educators to a reflective state in which we can have uncomfortable conversations with ourselves as we reflect on our practices and biases that we may hold (whether academic or rooted in sympathy or anything else) so that we can genuinely provide best practices and implementation to help all students find success. Embracing the role of a warm demander is championing all students.

Some big questions we can reflect on include: What role does being a warm demander have in our classrooms today? Specifically for our children who are struggling with reading or dyslexia.

Take some time to reflect on what you feel displays your warm demander characteristics as a teacher and as a person. You can use the checklist to help in the reflection process (www.thedyslexiaclassroom.com/teachingbeyondthediagnosis). Then, think about what your expectations are for your students. What do those sound like when speaking to students? About students? What do those expectations look Like in your classroom? How are they visible to students?

Creating High Expectations in the Classroom

Empathy and the deep belief that all children can learn—and our role in both of these—is something we weave throughout our inter-actions, instruction, and conversations. Holding ourselves as educa-tors in the role of compassionate empathy and a warm classroom coach/warm demander is woven through the culture we create for our children, whether in the classroom, in intervention sessions, or as administrators.

Our students who are struggling or who have dyslexia often carry a great deal of shame and embarrassment with them. They know they are struggling. They know they are behind, just like that little boy on the beach in Donnelly's artwork (Figure 1 in the Intro-duction). So, our role, especially with these children, is to connect with them on an authentic level through compassionate empathy and create evidence-based systems and approaches to help them find success. There are some strategies and mindsets that we can develop to help with this.

First, we have to believe that all children can succeed and that we have a vital role in this messaging with our students.

In order to help students find their capacity to improve, we need to reflect on our own understanding and any biases we may hold. As edu-cators, it is our job to reflect on how we are able to reach or not reach each student and then adjust our plans to help them find success. This means continuing to be students ourselves, growing, and learning more about the science behind learning to read and the necessary skills we need as teachers.

So, as we deepen our understanding of dyslexia and reading instr-uction, we can better connect and provide effective instruction and scaffolding needed to help each child reach their personal best. When we develop this understanding, we are also developing our cognitive empathy—we have a deeper understanding of our children and their needs because we have logical knowledge of what they are experiencing and what they need, which can lead us to compassionate empathy as we move to action.

Why? Thinking back to that little boy left in the sand, we know we have a vital role in helping him find success and keep his self-esteem intact or build it back up.

Take some time to reflect on these questions. You can use the reflection sheet at www.thedyslexiaclassroom.com/teachingbeyondthediagnosis
or jot down your answers here:

1. Focus on your why. What is at the heart of your goals for your students?
2. What is at the heart of your goals for your classroom?
3. How do you envision reaching this goal with your students?
4. What are your core beliefs about student learning?
5. How does empathy and understanding support success and self-confidence?
6. What expectations do you hold for your students?
7. What expectations do you hold for yourself? What is the role of the educator in this framework?
8. What is your path to reach this goal?
9. What do you need to grow?

A key to being a warm demander is holding compassionate empathy and believing in the success of all children.

Conclusion

Teaching students with dyslexia or those needing extra support to acquire reading and writing requires constant reflection on our role in the work. The ability to be vulnerable with ourselves and reflect on practices and the expectations we hold creates the opportunity for us to step into a deeper understanding and hold compassionate empathy in tandem with high expectations for students. It is necessary that we embrace being a warm demander. Our teaching creates the path to connect these important parts—the knowledge we hold of dyslexia, the expertise that we bring into the lesson about effectively teaching reading and writing, and embracing the role of warm demander set our students up for success. Without these, we risk the inability to connect our knowledge/logic and emotions to create well-rounded plans based on the science of reading to help us ensure that we are setting high standards for our children while providing the necessary instruction to help them succeed. For those teaching students with dyslexia, we must intentionally weave compassionate empathy and high personal warmth with high active demandingness into our culture of learning.

Key Takeaways

- The role of the teacher matters a great deal in the education setting—and must include both compassionate empathy and high active demandingness—or what is called a warm demander.

- Reflection of our teaching practices is an active part of our profession.

- Embracing the role of a warm demander is championing for all students.

> Simplify your path to practice. What did you put in your pocket?
> What stepping stones, or nuggets of knowledge, are you taking from this chapter?

Critical Thinking and Executive Function

"The world as we have created it is a process of our thinking. It cannot be changed without changing our thinking."

—Albert Einstein

Integrated Framework Component: Metacognitive Processes

In this part of the journey, we look at how educators can foster and develop critical thinking, executive function skills, and metacognitive practices before, during, and after the lesson with the goal of fostering self-awareness, reflective practices, deepening comprehension, and lifelong learning.

Each year of teaching, I am reminded of the crucial role we, as educators, play in guiding our students toward independence. Some come to us like baby birds, content or conditioned to sit in the safety of the nest and wait for the adults to provide answers, comfort them, and keep them safe from any risk. As adults, we may cater to this behavior, and doing this for students may come from a place of wanting to prevent the child from having negative feelings or thinking this will boost their self-esteem; however, we must reflect on the more significant outcome and desire we hold for our children and how sheltering them from the work of the learning process or reflection can negatively impact their ability to learn and reach their potential and independence. In education, we want students to self-regulate their thoughts, emotions, and perceptions to be self-directed in the present to achieve academic goals. As professionals and parents, we want to support our children in developing independence and self-direction toward their future goals. Still, we may need to build awareness and strategies to help students leave the safety of the nest as they encounter new learning and beyond.

Why Critical Thinking in Dyslexia Education?

"Learning how to learn cannot be left to students. It must be taught."
—Gall et al. (1990)

The ultimate goal of structured literacy instruction within dyslexia interventions is the development of deep levels of comprehension, the ability to critically think about what is read with focused thought, developing a connection to knowledge with strategies of logical reasoning, and reflection and awareness of self-understanding and metacognitive reasoning. In other words, our primary purpose for teaching reading is to engage students in understanding and thinking to transfer this beyond the intervention classroom and become lifelong learners. It requires students to actively engage with what they read, draw from their background knowledge and schemas, adjust their thinking, and connect new learning to previous knowledge.

Just as we see the many layers of instructional components under the elements and principles of a structured approach to literacy necessary for students to become proficient readers and writers, there are cognitive layers to weave into lessons that set students up for success. These underpinnings of academic reading success are Executive Function (EF) Strategies, Metacognitive Awareness (Self-Understanding), and Effort and Strategy Skills (see Figure 11.1). These processes are the foundation

Critical Thinking in reading instruction includes

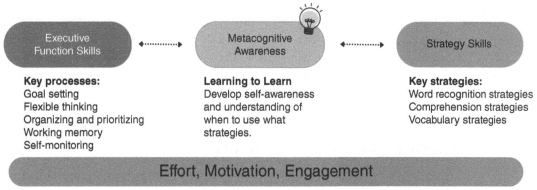

Executive Function Skills	Metacognitive Awareness	Strategy Skills
Key processes: Goal setting Flexible thinking Organizing and prioritizing Working memory Self-monitoring	**Learning to Learn** Develop self-awareness and understanding of when to use what strategies.	**Key strategies:** Word recognition strategies Comprehension strategies Vocabulary strategies

Effort, Motivation, Engagement

©2022, Casey Harrison, The Dyslexia Classroom

FIGURE 11.1 Critical thinking.

for all learning and cannot be separated from our instruction as cognitive processes work together. Think of them as linked gears. When you turn one, the others also move. These processes are interconnected, and teaching one affects the others. For students with dyslexia, addressing and developing EF skills and the awareness of metacognitive strategies is particularly important as they move into self-advocacy.

While this has many components beyond what we can cover in this book, we will focus on key learning pieces and five executive function skills (goal setting, flexible thinking, organization and prioritizing, working memory, and self-monitoring) to support literacy within our lessons. In the chapter, these are broken down with examples of implementation and mini-lessons. It should be noted that it is beyond the scope of this chapter to go into great depth about all-encompassing metacognitive processes and EF skills such as inhibition, selective attention, and activation; however, it does dig into metacognitive and language-based strategies to help students with dyslexia find success in academics and empowerment to take that knowledge beyond the intervention setting. As we move forward, I hope that the interconnectedness of these processes in reading instruction, along with the integrated framework, is evident.

Academic success for all students, particularly those with learning and attention difficulties, is connected with their motivation, academic self-concept, and self-efficacy. (Brunstein, Schultheiss, & Grässmann 1998; Helliwell 2003; Kasser & Ryan 1996; Meltzer et al. 2004; Pajares & Schunk 2001; Sheldon & Elliott 1999).

Executive Function (EF) Skills

Teaching a dyslexia intervention reading lesson requires that the teacher be highly engaged with the lesson and students, explicitly teach the lessons with concise language, monitor student responses, behaviors, and understanding, provide immediate feedback, watch the pacing of the lesson, ensure all components are covered effectively, and meet the learning outcomes. In other words, it's a lot! Teaching and learning require a lot of juggling of cognitive demands, and whether realized or not, it requires constant use of executive function skills on both the part of the teacher and the students.

Executive function skills set the stage for learning. Executive Function (EF) is an umbrella term for the set of brain-based skills, or cognitive processes, that allow individuals to regulate behaviors and thinking. These include cognitive processes such as working memory, cognitive flexibility, and inhibitory control, enabling students to pay attention, plan or organize, strategize, prioritize, reason, self-regulate, and govern their thinking and behaviors. These complex processes take years, often fully developing around age 25, and are connected and work together, often impacting other processing systems, such as speech, literacy, language, emotions, and thoughts. While everyone has strengths and weaknesses in their executive function profile, weaknesses can significantly impact students' ability to accomplish tasks independently. For many students, insufficient development of these skills can, over time, negatively affect their learning outcomes and highlight the need for embedding intentional strategies within literacy instruction (Kapa & Plante 2015).

Reading comprehension, the ultimate goal of our educational efforts, heavily relies on executive function skills. It requires students to actively engage with what they read, draw from their background knowledge, adjust their thinking, and connect new learning to previous knowledge. As educators, we play a crucial and valued role in fostering this engagement and motivation. When students effectively use executive function strategies, they become more efficient learners, boosting their self-esteem and motivation. This cycle of success is particularly evident when learning is explicitly linked to a focus on their efforts and the application and reflection of strategies versus solely a product outcome, such as a written response or essay. In addition, the executive function system develops two key skills for future success: self-determination and resilience (Steinberg 2014). It's important to remember that the executive function system is not fixed. It can be supported and improved with modeling, instruction, and opportunities for practice within lessons. Embedded in this chapter are mini-lessons and ideas for ways to weave the EF skills supporting literacy: goal setting, flexible thinking, organizing and prioritizing, working memory, and self-monitoring. This potential for improvement should empower us as educators, motivating us to actively take responsibility for our instruction and guidance and ensure we have the knowledge to aid students on this journey into critical thinking.

Metacognitive Awareness

Metacognitive awareness links executive function skills and strategies and is related to a better theory of mind (Feurer et al. 2015). It is the ability to monitor and assess one's understanding, determine if it is adequate, take steps and plan to improve understanding, and reflect on growth. It leads the learner to seek knowledge, adapt their thinking, plan, organize, and reassess their understanding and use of strategies. Helping students understand their learning profile, both their strengths and areas of growth, as well as their knowledge of what, when, where, and why strategies are used and analyze how the strategy benefited them are examples of metacognitive practices that build motivation and persistence in learning and support the critical awareness of oneself as a learner. Metacognition, in the simplified definition, is often referenced as "thinking about your thinking" and encompasses critical awareness of thinking about learning and understanding oneself as a thinker and learner.

Student understanding of themselves as a learner, both areas of strength and need, and their dyslexia journey is a key part of the integrated framework.

Metacognition requires using reflective processes, executive function skills, planning, and action. These critical skills play a vital role in learning and include monitoring one's understanding, being reflective about what is/is not understood and where the breakdown occurs, and strategizing how to clear up confusion. Without these, our lessons and learning are incomplete. Students must actively engage in this process as "to make an individual metacognitively aware is to ensure that the individual has learned how to learn" (Garner 1988). Metacognitive processes cannot be overlooked in dyslexia education, and they should be explicitly taught and modeled and continually embedded within lessons as metacognitive processes continue to develop into young adulthood. This requires teachers to be hypervigilant of:

1. Student self-talk—(academic and self)
2. Modeling aloud the thinking process (teacher and student)
3. Embedded metacognitive practices into lessons through:
   1. Explicit instruction
   2. Built-in reflective processes
   3. Engaging the learner in the process

Learning requires interaction and engagement. As Anita Archer famously states, "Learning is not a spectator sport," and therefore, students must be engaged in these processes. Students are not passive recipients of knowledge but active participants in their own learning journey. They are expected to use critical thinking in many ways on their educational journey. From analyzing text to forming opinions based on readings and knowledge to answering questions, generating conclusions, and synthesizing information, a lot of active thinking needs to coincide as students read. Students need to be actively engaged in the learning process, with a high success rate, and reflection process and develop a sense of *how* they think and learn and *what* they need to develop as strategies to aid in executive function skills, which act as the bedrock or building blocks for learning. A large and growing body of research has demonstrated that skilled readers are highly active, strategic, and engaged, deploying executive skills to manage the reading process (Duke & Cartwright 2021; Georgiou & Das 2018; Pressley & Afflerbach 1995). Students need to engage actively in the lesson tasks and cognitive processes. Our role as educators is to foster metacognitive processes to support student learning and performance through strategic instruction in metacognitive knowledge and regulation strategies. We want students to engage metacognitive processes beyond interventions and into lifelong learning.

Teaching students to engage in metacognitive processes empowers students with:

- Knowledge about how they learn
- Knowledge about what strategies to use when
- Transferring knowledge beyond interventions
- Thinking deeply about what is read
- Active engagement in learning

While we may think these processes are innate, learning how to learn cannot be left to students. It must be taught (Gall et al. 1990). Learning does not happen in isolation, and as educators and parents, we must weave awareness of executive function skills and metacognition into our lessons, as the examples throughout the book and in the mini-lessons shared thus far (My Reading Brain, My Sea of Strength, etc.) show. We need those baby birds to feel empowered to stretch their wings and fly independently.

Language is the vehicle for learning and has an ongoing and recursive relationship with the executive function skills necessary for learning. In the pillars of reading and the structured literacy elements, we discussed the impact of language on literacy. Now, we bring into the fold the development of executive function strategies and mental models and their impact on reading success. Reading comprehension overlaps with the comprehension of listening language. Students express their learning through oral or written forms (output or expressive language) *and* internalize their own thinking through language. They need to engage in verbal reasoning, or verbalization, as part of their learning process.

The teacher also engages in verbalization and verbal reasoning as they explicitly teach and model the portion of the lesson with their "think aloud" or "chalk talk" approach (where the teacher explicitly verbalizes their thinking process at each step, giving students insights into the teachers' thought processes) as was noted in the chapters on structured literacy and scaffolds. This is critical for helping students understand how to narrate their thinking processes. In the integrated framework image, we see language, engagement, executive function, and metacognition encircling all of our work (see Figure 11.2). Knowledge of the relationship between language, literacy, and Executive Function (EF) processes in literacy development guides our understanding of the learning journey and instructional impacts for those with language-based learning differences such as dyslexia. In other

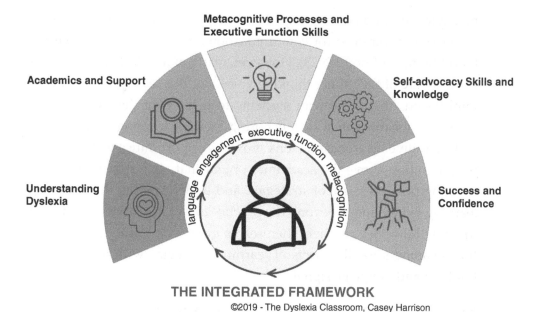

Metacognitive Processes and
Executive Function Skills

Academics and Support

Self-advocacy Skills and
Knowledge

Understanding
Dyslexia

Success and
Confidence

language engagement executive function metacognition

THE INTEGRATED FRAMEWORK
©2019 - The Dyslexia Classroom, Casey Harrison

FIGURE 11.2 Key learning piece.

words, language acts as the in-between for learning academic concepts and the executive function processes necessary for learning to occur.

Verbalization engages words, whether spoken, written, or signed through the use of Sign Language, in processing ideas and is a large part of academic learning through demonstrating knowledge through verbal reasoning.

Building Student Self-talk with Two Mini-Lessons: Academic Focus

Have you ever wondered how you know you are learning? Are there language signals that you tune into? Many people report a form of internal dialogue, or inner speech, in which active communication exists as silent speech directed to the self. The internalization of thinking relies on paying attention to language. This internal language or speech can be retained and retrieved for communication and seen as a cognitive tool (Fernyhough & Borghi 2023). However, many of my students need to be made aware of their inner thinking voice. For this reason, I have several mini-lessons that I use with students to help bring this awareness to light in a meaningful way. Anchoring student learning around these metacognitive awareness lessons provides opportunities to gain a level of recognition above the academic content that allows for reflection of thinking processes, use of strategies, and understanding themselves as learning to help move beyond the practice of isolated strategy and skills to know how they can help themselves grow as a learner and transfer this awareness to all aspects of learning. It begins with awareness of thinking and language signals.

Mini-Lesson: Metacognition and Thinking Language Signals

Purpose: Students will learn about metacognition, language that signals thinking, and how it aids in reading comprehension and learning in all domains. This foundational lesson can be broken up over several days and then continually embedded within lessons to strengthen metacognitive awareness.

1. Ask students to share what they believe occurs when they think about or read something. How do you know that you are thinking? Make note of student responses. Students, especially those struggling, may often generate things like reading the words, reading with fluency, etc., but may need a deeper understanding of what occurs when reading and thinking.
2. Are there different ways in which we think to ourselves throughout the day? When we engage in thinking we may generate mental lists, wonder about things, reflect on things, etc. Model/share a few examples of times when you recognize you are thinking. It is helpful to share or give students a peek into your thinking processes

and model how we often think to ourselves throughout the day in multiple ways and settings. Have students generate or note times in their day when they are actively thinking and the kind of thinking used.

Some examples: What do I need to buy at the grocery store for dinner (mental lists)? What causes magnification to occur? (wonderings about the world around us), ____ part of the lesson today was challenging or confusing (recognition and reflection); before this reading, I thought ____, but now I'm thinking ____ (recognizing changes in thinking); this worked well for me today/this didn't work well. Next time I am going to try ____. (reflection and planning)

3. "When the mind is thinking, it is talking to itself."—Plato.
   1. Introduce the quote from Plato and ask students to share what they think this means. Discuss ways in which students recognize they are thinking. Ask guiding questions such as: What is happening when you are thinking? How can you tell what you are thinking? Discuss that thinking, as Plato stated, is talking to oneself. As readers, it is essential that we monitor when we are thinking or how we are interacting with the text/story. Students can add the quote to a reflection notebook, generate an anchor chart, or discuss.

4. Introduce the term metacognition—or thinking about our thinking—and ask students to link it to the Plato quote. Explain that we will work more on recognizing our thinking patterns and thinking about ourselves as learners.

5. If we pay attention to the thinking voice in our heads, what language signals are used to indicate thinking? How can we pay attention to these language cues? For example, *I think …, I was surprised by …, This makes me think of …, Hmmm, I am not sure about …, Wait, what is happening?, etc.* are all language cues we use when engaging in internal thinking. Generate with students' language that indicates we are thinking. Many students need practice and assistance

How do I know when I am thinking?
What language signals my thinking?

FIGURE 11.3 How do I know when I am thinking?

in recognizing when learning and thinking occur. Help students see that we must also pay attention to our "thinking voice" when reading and learning. Create an anchor chart or download the blank anchor chart and example from the book resources website page www.thedyslexiaclassroom.com/teachingbeyondthediagnosis.

Continue to reference and cycle this understanding of our inner thinking voice and the language that indicates thinking and learning. You may wish to take a "thinking picture" of each student and create a poster (see Figure 11.3). I laminate mine, and we use dry-erase markers to write on them for annotations, to show our thinking, etc.—the kids love them! For my older students, we create an anchor chart.

Mini-Lesson: Connecting Language to Self

The words we say and the language we use when speaking to ourselves matter. Our internalized narrative becomes the world around us. How we talk to ourselves becomes a habit and can become our truth. Our most powerful voice is in our heads; therefore, how students speak about their dyslexia journey matters—helping students understand that owning their story and stepping into the journey is the bravest thing they can do. This inner speech can provide opportunities to reflect on ourselves (Bermúdez 2018) and form a more coherent self-concept (Morin 2018). The mini-lessons on "My Sea of Strengths" and "Only One Me" can support awareness of self. In addition, monitoring how students speak about themselves (I am bad at spelling, a horrible reader, etc.) can provide opportunities to shift language to understanding and grace and lessons about the language we use with ourselves.

While academic success can boost self-esteem, awareness of how we speak about and to ourselves impacts emotional well-being. Simply telling students they are not bad students or readers doesn't help shift the narrative. Instead, we can focus on recognizing the area of challenge and shifting the language used to, "I am still working on developing my spelling, and using ___ strategy to meet my goal of _____" and "I am using my word attack strategies to help me decode larger words when reading, which will increase my reading," etc., moves the focus to the growth. I remind students that if we could erase all our past mistakes, we would also erase all of the wisdom we have gained. This is such an essential concept for us to help our children understand. Mistakes are lessons in our lives as long as we are open to the process of reflection and growth. We are in the process of learning.

Mini-lesson: Identify self-talk chart. (Optional books to read with students: *The Magical Yet* by Angela DiTerlizzi and *Your Thoughts Matter: Growth Mindset* by Ester Pia Cordova, both suitable for younger students; *After the Fall: How Humpty Dumpty Got Back Up Again* by Dan Santat and *Salt in His Shoes: Michael Jordan in Pursuit of a Dream* by Delores Jordan, both good for older students.)

Shifting Our Language

WHAT YOU SAY MATTERS

Tune into your inner voice. What do you notice about your self talk?

WHAT I NOTICE IN MY SELF-TALK	DO I NEED TO SHIFT THIS LANGUAGE TO FOCUS ON LEARNING?			WHAT IS MY GOAL?	STRATEGY TO HELP REACH GOAL	NEW SELF TALK LANGUAGE
I can't read big words.	Yes	No	Maybe	To read new big words in books/passages	Use my syllable division chart and steps	I am using my word attack strategies to help me grow my reading of big words.
	Yes	No	Maybe			
	Yes	No	Maybe			
	Yes	No	Maybe			
	Yes	No	Maybe			

FIGURE 11.4 Shifting self-talk chart.

Materials: Make a chart like the one in Figure 11.4 or download the PDF at www.thedyslexiaclassroom.com/teachingbeyondthediagnosis.

Purpose: We can help children see that failures are learning opportunities. In that case, we can shift their perspective into a more reflective state by looking at what we did well and where we got stuck (failed) and use that knowledge to determine what needs to change, build a plan, and then move forward and try again.

Help students recognize or tune into their inner voice, reflect on the language used, determine if a shift needs to be made, identify the area of challenge, link to their goal (see the next section for more about setting goals), determine what strategies will be used to achieve the goals (see next portion of this chapter), and generate new self-talk language. Guide students in this process through frequent review and modeling.

Executive Function and Metacognitive Processes in Reading Lessons

Integrating critical thinking, EF skills, and metacognitive processes should be done with intention and woven throughout the lesson (see Figure 11.5). Here are seven key pieces to include in the integrated

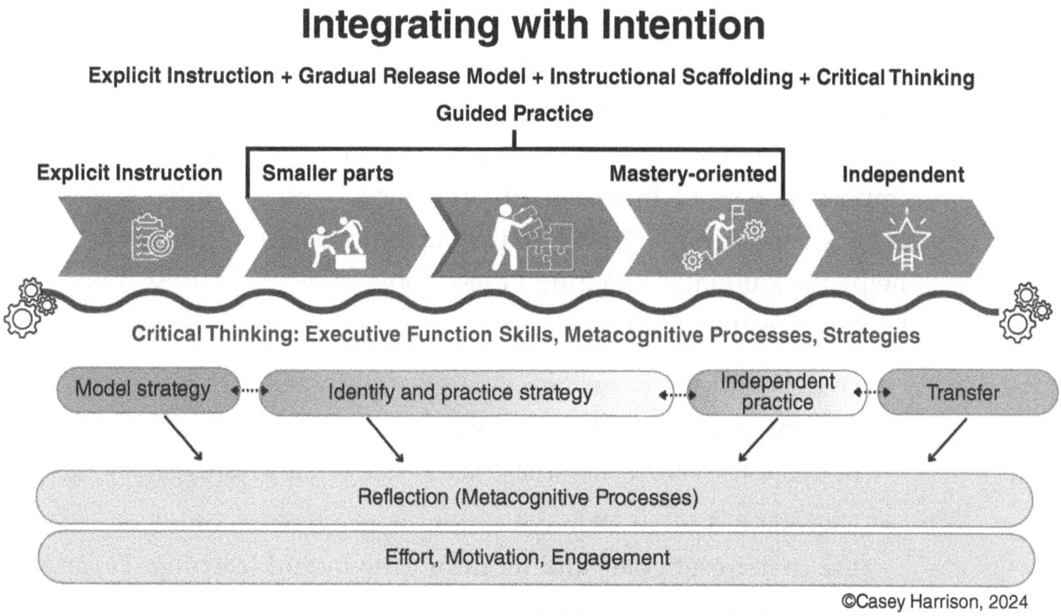

FIGURE 11.5 Integrating with intention.

framework: goal setting, flexible thinking, organizing and prioritizing, working memory, and self-monitoring in connection to metacognitive and reflective practices.

First, teach students that their brains are wired to grow (create new neural pathways). This is a big part of the "Our Reading Brain" mini-lesson and the integrated framework. We can grow our brains through deliberate practice with multimodal lessons in a structured literacy approach to learning.

Second, keep learning at the forefront and set goals with this in mind. **Goal setting** ensures that we are heading *toward* something. Just as teachers set goals for their lessons, students also need to set goals for their learning and growth. This engages the EF skills of self-determination and resiliency in our lessons and brings awareness and ownership to our students. When setting goals, students need to have an understanding of their dyslexia learning journey, including their areas of strength and need, an understanding of the big objective or task along with the value that it holds in attaining their goal, and a plan for achievement. Guiding students in setting individual goals and focusing on the process of learning to achieve those goals is an important part of fostering EF and metacognitive skills. Conversations surrounding "How will they achieve these goals?" and "What helps the student?" can guide these conversations. Setting goals with students requires that they:

- Understand their learning strengths and needs. Think back to the student learning profile, the sea of strength lesson, etc., from previous chapters. How may these set the stage for setting goals?

- Understand what data-collection or progress monitoring we can use to help set goals and monitor growth and learning. For example, a student whose goal is to increase reading fluency may chart on a graph over time their reading rate and accuracy percentage. In addition, they can chart their prosody in the text with a 4-3-2-1 rubric. Bringing metacognitive awareness to the stages of the learning process to achieve the big goal helps students stay motivated and focused on learning.

- Value the strategy, task, and lesson. Students need to "see" how the hard work they are engaged in within dyslexia instruction will serve them beyond the intervention. This requires the teacher to make a clear connection between the how and why of the task and use progress monitoring, keen observations, and feedback to highlight the value of the task. Why do we need to learn this? How will this help me achieve my goals? Dyslexia intervention is not a quick fix, and it is imperative that we help students see the value of the hard work and persistence they are putting forward, even if they don't recognize it themselves.

- Continually check-in with their learning process and reflect on what is working well, what needs to be clarified or tweaked, what needs to be scaled up or down, etc. Beginning the lesson with reflection about the how the use of a strategy or accommodation is going in their classroom, or noting how a strategy was used and aided in learning, etc. can be woven into the lessons. Reflection is a powerful metacognitive tool that we want to instill in our students and use as a tool to guide them in their learning journey.

- Set realistic objectives and goals along the way. Each month, my students and I spend a few moments generating our goals. We chose three goals to target based on our learning needs and personal goals. My students place these on a sticky note on their "Sea of Strengths" page, and we jot down three specific and attainable goals that connect to our learning and heftier goals. For example, a student may set a goal to read two books this month, learn all of the upper-case cursive letters while increasing their writing fluency to 18 letters per minute, and consistently use their word attack strategies to read new unknown words. We can monitor these goals through a reading log/reading check-in (audiobooks count, too!), handwriting fluency checks, and the use of a strategy tracker chart. (Download student strategy tracker at www.thedyslexiaclassroom. com/teachingbeyondthediagnosis) Many of these are designed to bring the student along the monitoring journey—I want them to raise awareness of self-monitoring in connection to their goals. At the end of the month, we revisit our goals and determine if we met them, want to carry them to the next month, or create new ones.

Another key piece to integrating EF skills and metacognition within lessons is to develop a classroom grounded in reflective practices. Creating a culture of learning that supports metacognitive practices includes giving students opportunities to reflect on what strategies they are using and what they are finding difficult or confusing; modeling the thinking processes involved in the strategy, concept, and lesson; and bringing students into active engagement with metacognitive processes to understand themselves as learners. Embed reflection practices such as:

- **The Sandwich Approach**—start and end the lesson with a quick reflection question. Students can give thumbs up/down, answer with an emoji, circle in or check box, verbal responses, etc. The goal is to get them thinking about what they are learning. I use this quick check-in at the beginning and end of the lesson to ask questions like, How did the word attack strategy we used work in your classes today? Or what did you find helpful about the spelling chart I shared with you? Or how did you feel about the strategy we used for ____? Which accommodations are helping you in ____ class? This really sets the stage for thinking about learning and provides me with an understanding of metacognitive areas, strategies, etc., to review or layer into my lessons. When students leave the lesson, I ask similar questions about the concept of the day.

- **Reflect and Connect**—Have students state the links between what they knew and the connection to new learning. Explicitly noting and modeling the connections in the lesson (new learning to previously held knowledge) helps those students who do not independently transfer this knowledge of connections across the learning. Research indicates that setting meaningful processing tasks helps students analyze their thinking and allows the teacher to check for understanding and clarify, scaffold, reteach, or extend learning (Ausubel 1968). Engaging students in the learning process through reflection and connection expands their metacognitive awareness and understanding of content. Using a simple language starter like, "We know____, and now we see how _____ links to this" can help students engage in this reflection. (We know that /s/ can be spelled <s>, but now we see that /s/ can also be spelled with <c> in words like city, center, and cycle where the <c> comes before the letter e, i, or y.)

Providing opportunities for students to deliberately practice strategies while reflecting on their use of these strategies through a focus on academics and well-being, as well as engaging in discussions, oral and written responses, retrieval practices, and monitoring (tracking strategy use, anchor charts, etc.) cannot be overlooked. If students are to move toward independence, they must have opportunities to reflect and consistently put these strategies into practice. (See examples in the lesson breakdown in the following sections.)

Working Memory and Retrieval

Lessons should intentionally embed retrieval practices focusing on low-stakes strategies and high engagement, as well as distributed and interleaved practices. While part of retrieval practices means regular testing, shifting to low-states practices can help alleviate some of the stress associated with testing by normalizing and embedding retrieval quiz or application as part of the lesson, provide feedback, and ample opportunities for fostering student achievement, and removing points or scores shifting the focus to learning and application. For example, daily spelling retrieval within a lesson requires students to recall the learned graphemes for the phoneme given and produce it in written form, teacher provides appropriate feedback, and students reflect on their recall and understanding of phoneme-grapheme correspondences. This type of low-stakes retrieval is especially important when working with students with dyslexia, as Rapid Automatic Naming, the ability to quickly recall or retrieve information, can be challenging for some students. Purposeful planning that ensures retrieval practices are used can strengthen memory retention and boost learning (Jones 2020). Support **Working Memory and Retrieval Practice** by intentionally implementing and focusing on these as learning strategies. When thinking of the role of memory within reading instruction, we may immediately think of how we get the information to the students and the student output through assessments or products, but what if we focus on getting information out of students' heads and the use of strategies to aid in retrieval practices. We want to encourage students to retrieve information *during* learning to improve their understanding and retention of materials.

Working Memory, the student's ability to maintain and manipulate information with active attention, acts as a mental "sketchpad" or "workbench" where thinking occurs when learning new material and, therefore, is limited in terms of how much information can be held in one time. Supports for working memory include visual aids, concise language and cues, smaller chunks of information or chunked tasks, etc and can aid in sustaining and redirecting attention to the expected task.

When a student struggles to sustain attention to an activity or concept before we remind the student to stay on task, we can ask:
Is the student inattentive due to weak working memory?
Are they struggling with holding onto information?
What supports can I include to aid in or strengthen the learning outcome?

The intentional use of a structured approach to literacy instruction, which encompasses explicit instruction and the application of incremental learning, is critical in addressing working memory limitations and building networks of knowledge in a student's long-term memory (Rosenshine 2012; Hollingsworth & Ybarra 2009; Hanham et al. 2017). Getting information into long-term memory is our goal, and research shows that slower, effortful retrieval leads to long-term learning. We want students to store information, be able to retrieve that information, and then apply that knowledge to new learning.

The retrieval of information is an important learning strategy in dyslexia interventions and is intentionally embedded throughout our lessons as students retrieve information for different purposes. When we retrieve information, we must think of something we know that has been stored and organized in our long-term memory. The big question for us as educators is how we most effectively have students access or retrieve knowledge. What are the best practices to focus on within our lessons to engage students in this learning process?

Retrieval practices *within* a lesson are more beneficial than only asking questions after learning, reading, or taking notes. We can intentionally focus on two practices in our lessons to strengthen memory retention and enhance learning: retrieval practices to support learning and distributed practices, which we see as core elements throughout all structured literacy approach lessons. These practices have been shown to benefit students of different ages and abilities in addition to improving student learning performance (Ruiz-Martin et al. 2024; Jones 2020; Bjork 2012).

Retrieval practices for learning should include those that prime students for new learning by retrieving known prerequisite knowledge, as well as distributed or spaced retrieval practice along with interleaving.

Retrieval Practice	Distributed Practice	Interleaving
Purpose—recall information from memory	Purpose—spaced retrieval, or spreading out over time creating an intentional delay increasing the effort to retrieve information (in turn improving learning)	Purpose—mixing up different types of learning; looking at different but related problems combined in a single learning session
Examples within the reading lesson: -alphabet sequence tasks -reading decks (letter cards, sound cards) also called visual drill -auditory drill (recall spelling representation) -referencing syllable division strategy	Examples within the reading lesson: -cycling concepts as students increase difficulty (example, weaving in morphology within the scope and sequence at appropriately spaced lessons, reading a list of words that review a previously taught concept, etc.)	Examples within the reading lesson: -introducing vocabulary through multiple aspects of language (phonology, orthography, morphology, etymology, semantics, pragmatics), connect to text, responses (oral or written) which include concepts
These are not exhaustive examples of retrieval practices with dyslexia interventions. There are many opportunities in a well-designed lesson for intentional application of retrieval practices.		

In addition, we need to highlight flexible thinking for students. **Cognitive Flexibility** is the ability to easily switch between strategies and approaches, and looking at things differently is required when we read. We want students to engage in reading and identify the big idea and smaller details, which requires constantly shifting our thinking, reflecting on our understanding, and teasing out irrelevant information while building understanding and knowledge. Cognitive flexibility can occur at all levels of reading. For example, a student learning to read multisyllabic words needs the cognitive flexibility to shift pronunciation based on the stress of a syllable or the vowel sound in words and have a connection to meaning. For example, we need to apply cognitive flexibility to read the word contest differently as in the sentence: It will do you no good to contest the results of the contest. The sounds shifted, and we need to be flexible with pronunciation to understand the sentence. This is the graphophonological-semantic cognitive flexibility (Duke & Cartwright 2023), or letter-sound-meaning flexibility, that is required of proficient readers. This graphophonological-semantic cognitive flexibility should be part of our scope and sequence and explicitly taught to students as a strategy when reading—be flexible with the sounds in thoughtful ways. Spelling generalizations also connect to cognitive flexibility. Think of the different spelling representations for /k/–cat, kid, truck, traffic, school, antique. In addition to morphophonological-semantic cognitive flexibility, students need to be flexible in their thinking and comprehension during reading. When reading and writing, we need to shift between big ideas and supporting details to help determine irrelevant information, important ideas, and the main idea. The use of graphic organizers, templates, and modeling supports the teaching cognitive of flexibility.

Sequencing or **organizing** information based on relative importance can be challenging for some students with dyslexia. Organizing lessons systematically and sequentially is crucial for students as we move through explicit instruction. In addition, students need to understand how to organize their thinking when reading and sort and categorize information. In connection to reading instruction, carefully choose textbooks and reading materials that are designed with **prioritizing** and organizing the content as the focus (table of contents, vocabulary highlighted, clear chapter stopping points, etc.) to help students understand the organization of text in a straightforward manner. The use of graphic organizers, thinking maps, and note templates benefits students in organizing information and prioritizing the essential parts as they read and write because it involves a visual representation of the relationships between concepts, a strategy used to strengthen memory retention.

Explicitly teach students what graphic organizer to use with a specific genre or task and keep these general and easily accessible for students. In other words, choose clean graphic organizers that provide ample space for writing and, ideally, can be drawn by the students so they can transfer their use beyond the intervention setting.

These skills and strategies can't be left to chance and should be planned purposefully within our lessons from the beginning. Doing so correlates well with the research-based principles of instruction and the role of explicit systematic instruction which includes modeling, thinking aloud, and providing scaffolds and supports. We also engage students in the learning process and critical thinking of their learning to help unfold an understanding of why we are practicing a skill or concept and how that moves our learning forward.

Student Strategy Trackers

As we use an explicit instruction model to move students through the stages of learning (explicit–guided–independent), we weave metacognitive practices into the lesson (Figure 11.5) through the following steps:

1. **Model strategy** (explicit instruction)—here, the teacher models with concise language and steps a strategy for students to use to achieve the target goal (syllable division steps for reading multisyllabic words, decoding/sounding out words with vowel-consonant-e through coding, using phrasing to build reading fluency, etc.) This is aligned with the goal of the lesson.

    Reflect on how this strategy is helping (the teacher thinks aloud and identifies what the strategy is, how it is helping, and when to use the strategy). For example, if teaching syllable division of multisyllabic word reading, the teacher would explicitly teach steps, model, and simultaneously talk it out (think aloud): "When I come to a word that I do not know, I want to first look for any prefixes or suffixes and box those. Then, I can identify and code any special spelling patterns we have learned, like vowel-r and vowel-consonant-e. Now, I can look for syllable division patterns. I know that each syllable has a vowel sound, so we can follow our syllable division chart to help determine where to divide first. I also need to remember to be cognitively flexible with those division patterns. This will help me to read the word."

2. **Identify** and **practice** the strategy (explicit to guided) and get the kids thinking!—explicitly identify the strategy or process being used to achieve the goal and have the student verbalize their thinking as they practice (use a visual chart or intentional support with a multimodal experience to provide ample opportunities to practice the strategy). You may wish to have students keep track of their use of the strategy on a simple chart like those in Figure 11.6. Download these at www.thedyslexiaclassroom.com/teachingbeyondthediagnosis.

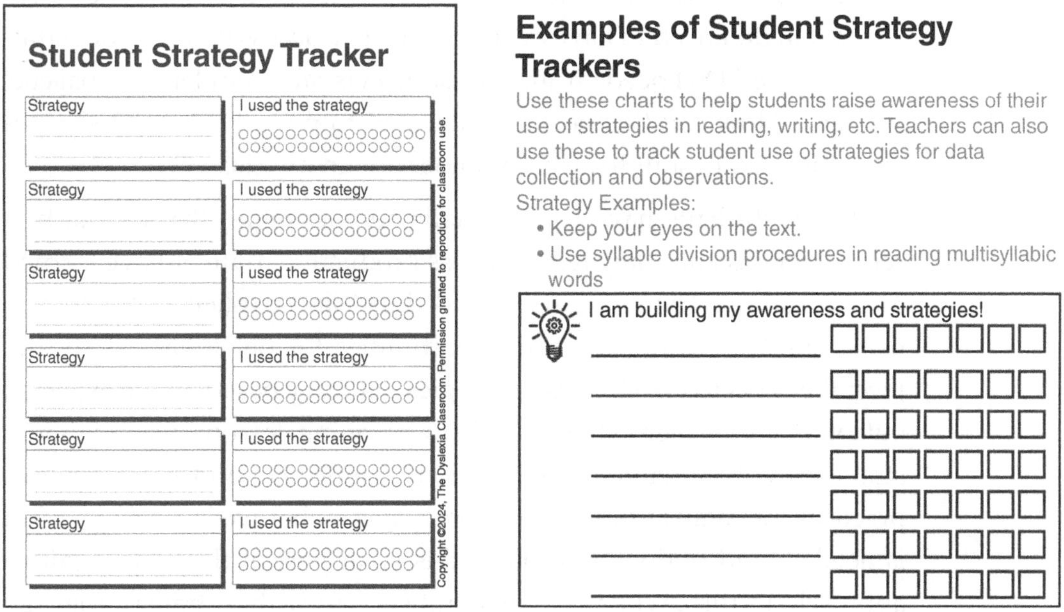

Student Strategy Tracker

Strategy	I used the strategy
Strategy	I used the strategy
Strategy	I used the strategy
Strategy	I used the strategy
Strategy	I used the strategy
Strategy	I used the strategy

Examples of Student Strategy Trackers

Use these charts to help students raise awareness of their use of strategies in reading, writing, etc. Teachers can also use these to track student use of strategies for data collection and observations.
Strategy Examples:
- Keep your eyes on the text.
- Use syllable division procedures in reading multisyllabic words

I am building my awareness and strategies!

FIGURE 11.6 Student strategy tracker.

Together, the student and teacher **reflect** aloud on what the strategy is, how it is helping, what is working or not, and what needs attention (here, immediate corrective feedback, clarifying understanding, possible reteaching, and scaffolding are used based on teacher observation as the teacher fades out support).

3. **Independent** practice—students are gradually moving to the independent application of the strategy taught.

   Reflect—students reflect on their use of the strategy and how and when they will use this in the future.

4. **Transfer** to independent application beyond the intervention setting. The goal is for students to increase their awareness of the strategies they use and apply them in other areas of academics, not just in the intervention setting.

   Reflect—Guide students through the reflection process and questions, such as, How can this strategy help me in my other classes? What do I need to have available to me to access this support, strategy, etc.? Do I need an anchor chart, a visual reminder, a verbal cue, etc.? How can this be communicated to my other teachers? Does this need to shift to an accommodation in my classes?

Many students have learned skills and strategies that do not best serve them because they rely on a less productive route or have learned to compensate. Therefore, they need direct and explicit instruction in using effective strategies with opportunities for deliberate practice to meet the expected goal. These strategies will vary based on the expected outcome, so teachers should look to planning lessons that highlight strategies with intentional integration of reflective and metacognitive practices. Engaging students in reflection on what we have done, what is needed, and options to achieve this is all part of the metacognitive approach. In turn, when students find success with a strategy, they are engaged and motivated, directly impacting their emotional well-being and view of themselves as learners. It is empowering.

Set Students Up for Success—Take a Step Back

At times, taking a step back may be just what we need to move forward. One of my daughters, when set with the task of feeding our horses, repeatedly tried to push the barn door open. I could hear her frustration, and I saw her repeating the same movement of moving the gate forward—when, in fact, she needed to pull the gate back to unlock it. It made me think of our students and classrooms where we are sometimes just pushing forward, hitting a wall, and then just pushing forward again when, in fact, we need to take a step back and make an adjustment to move forward. Taking a step back to reflect requires the student to have enough awareness and regulation to pause and identify the challenge. This ability to learn from our mistakes requires the student to be able to self-evaluate, and self-evaluation comes from self-reflection. In addition, when we self-reflect, we can think backward or travel back to a past event. If we struggle with working memory, this can be challenging and therefore needs instruction and practice. As you see, the complexity of metacognitive processes requires many executive function skills. As educators, we often engage in these cognitive processes to help us best serve students within dyslexia instruction—we actively take a step back to determine where the student is and what we need to do instructionally to help the student make the connections to move forward. We can also challenge ourselves to bring this thought process to the cognitive processes we expect students to use in reading instruction.

Reflection questions:

How can we set this kind of metacognitive reflection up in our classrooms or interventions?

Conclusion

As teachers, we need time to intentionally reflect and analyze where our children are in terms of their knowledge, skills, and cognitive processes and then create plans to help them develop these within our lessons. It can feel overwhelming, but when we utilize direct instruction with appropriate scaffolding that intentionally weaves in metacognitive processes focusing on instructional strategies and EF skills, we set the stage for this kind of learning and awareness.

It is critical that we understand that children are still developing these metacognitive processes. Students are still learning how to manage their attention, communicate their feelings, and recognize themselves as learners, including their strengths and needs, as well as developing reflective practices that focus on learning. Our role is to guide, support, and nurture them through these learning processes.

Key Takeaways

- Metacognitive processes and executive function skills can be intentionally woven into lessons.

- Educators can foster and develop critical thinking, executive function skills, and metacognitive practices before, during, and after the lesson with the goal of fostering self-awareness, reflective practices, deepening comprehension, and lifelong learning.

- Using these cognitive processes to increase student awareness of themselves as learners leads to agency, increases learning outcomes, and leads to self-advocacy skills.

> Simplify your path to practice. What did you put in your pocket?
> What stepping stones, or nuggets of knowledge, are you taking from this chapter?

CHAPTER TWELVE

Accommodation Toolbox

"One of the most common errors of teaching a dyslexic child to read is to withdraw prematurely the instruction that seems to be working."

—Dr. Sally Shaywitz

Integrated Framework Component: Self-Advocacy Skills and Knowledge

In this part of the journey, we delve into how the knowledge and use of accommodations, in tandem with the development of self-advocacy skills and metacognitive practices, bolster learner outcomes and empower teachers and students (see Figure 12.1). When students are armed with the tools, language, and skills that pave the way for success within the classroom and beyond, they can take ownership of their journey. This chapter underscores the importance of understanding accommodations and the shift towards creating an accommodation toolbox, ensuring educators feel knowledgeable and prepared.

As a child, I would spend time helping my father with projects around the house. As a builder and an architect he constantly designed and built things that required many tools. Each tool had a purpose, and one of my favorite things to do was to help find the tools from his toolbox to assist in getting a job done. If I brought the wrong tool, my father would

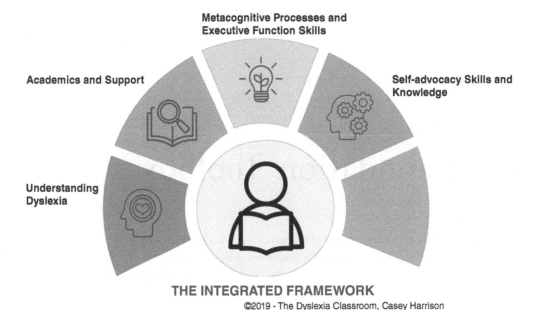

THE INTEGRATED FRAMEWORK
©2019 - The Dyslexia Classroom, Casey Harrison

FIGURE 12.1 The integrated framework—self-advocacy skills.

explain which tool was needed and why. He taught me the importance of using different tools to accomplish various tasks. While we could use some tools to get a job done, if it isn't the best or most efficient tool or if we need help understanding how to use it, our outcome may not show our best work or may take longer than is necessary to complete.

I have carried this idea of having specific tools for a particular role or job into my work with children who have accommodations. Accommodations can change how students access information and demonstrate their knowledge, skills, and abilities while keeping the same academic expectations and standards. They provide a tool to address a specific barrier that their learning difference has created. I encourage the students, families, and educators I work with to shift their thinking of accommodations to the tools that help students access the curriculum, with the understanding that we use the tools when we need assistance and keep access to them within our accommodation toolbox. This directly ties into the importance of helping students develop a metacognitive understanding of themselves as learners, what the accommodation is, why it is required, and when and how to use it. Our accommodations must carry meaning for the student and educator so they understand why they are in place and when and how to use them. An accommodation without this knowledge is useless. The goal is to create efficiency in learning for our students. If you are in the world of dyslexia, understanding and advocating for accommodations is part of the journey.

What Are Accommodations?

Accommodations play a crucial role in providing equal learning access for our children with dyslexia. They are the empowering tools that enable students to demonstrate their learning and knowledge of the content and curriculum, overcoming the barriers directly related to their learning challenges. These tools, such as extra time, tolerance for spelling errors outside of a final draft, and not requiring reading aloud in front of peers, are not a crutch but a means for our students to level the academic playing field. They ensure equal learning access by addressing instruction and assessment needs in various aspects of education. These reasonable adjustments change how a person accesses their learning and allow students to demonstrate their knowledge of the material without changing the performance expectations. Accommodations vary based on individual needs for the instructional task and do not guarantee success but provide the tools for access. Without explicitly teaching students how and when to use the accommodations, they become a meaningless checklist and will only contribute to the student's frustration. While accommodations are not a substitute for appropriate intervention and instruction, they should be used in tandem to provide students with effective and equitable access to the grade-level curriculum in the general education classroom.

Many accommodations are focused on the English Language Arts classes, which makes sense as reading and writing are core elements within these classes and are directly impacted by dyslexia. However, dyslexia and its impacts reach beyond reading and writing courses. When we reflect on the amount of reading and writing students are asked to do throughout the day, we see just how much access to the written word we require. Students are asked to read word problems in math, articles, and textbooks in biology, social studies, chemistry, and world cultures—reading is embedded into all aspects of education. Even something like having students work in groups to create a poster can bring about a need for accommodations. Many of my students will identify their needs and speak up—perhaps asking their peers to write for the group as they generate ideas or showcase their knowledge in another way. But this takes time, acknowledgment, and self-advocacy skills on the part of the students. As noted throughout the book, the impacts of dyslexia expand beyond the reading class, and careful consideration should be made regarding the barriers that dyslexia may pose in other classes.

The Nuts and Bolts of Accommodations

Addressing the "nuts and bolts" of common dyslexia accommodations is helpful in establishing an accommodation toolbox in our classrooms and lessons. Many accommodations are generally used in the classroom, as they are best teaching practices, such as the use of concrete materials, information provided in smaller steps, explicit modeling, and checking for understanding. Other accommodations may be specific to a student's learning profile. Educators, parents, and students can work as a team to determine which accommodations are needed to ensure that the student is on equal footing with those who do not have dyslexia. These accommodations should be an integral part of the normal cycle of teaching and testing and used consistently in classrooms so students can be measured accurately on their abilities without the barrier of their learning difference. Some common areas addressed include how lessons are presented, materials utilized, different student responses, learning environments, time, organizations, and classroom and standardized assessments.

1. Lesson presentation and instruction—What student accommodations are needed to access content, understanding, and instructional materials during the lesson? (verbal directions, repetition of instructions, audio-format, etc.)

2. Student responses and materials—What student accommodations are needed to aid students in their ability to receive and express their understanding of the lesson? Curriculum? Assignment? (alternatives for completion of assignments, verbal responses, etc.)

3. Assessments—What student accommodations are needed on assessments both within the general classroom setting and on standardized tests? (small group, assistive technology, alternative test form, etc.)

4. Learning environment and organization—What student accommodations are needed for organizing and navigating assignments, studies, and assessments? Does the student need a different learning environment for testing or assignments?

5. Assistive technology—What student accommodations are needed to provide access to expected learning materials and tests addressing the reading and writing barriers due to the learning disability while facilitating access to curriculum expectations?

While this is not an exhaustive list, it includes some key accommodations to implement within lessons. A great deal of metacognition goes into teaching and applying accommodations properly. Practice is the key to the effective use of accommodations in the classroom and on assessments. These should be explicitly taught, practiced, and used within our lessons. Reflect on the following questions as you think about implementing accommodations:

Reflection Questions:

Are we providing enough opportunities to explicitly teach and use accommodations to build our students' toolboxes? Are we including the use of the accommodation within our lessons? Have we built in reflection time and conversations to determine how the accommodation has helped or needs refinement?

As we've emphasized throughout this book, explicit instruction is the cornerstone of effective teaching, and this thread continues into accommodations. When planning, teachers should think about how they can explicitly teach and include accommodations for students with diverse learning needs. These accommodations could include providing additional resources, modifying the pace of the lesson, or adjusting the complexity of the tasks with additional supports.

When determining accommodations for a student, we need to reflect on the current barrier that dyslexia is posing for the student, and how the accommodation is linked to the student's learning. This may vary from instruction to assessment. Mindful and intentional implementation should begin with the student and their instructional needs in mind, purposefully planning for accommodations to address those needs, intentionally integrating into lessons with ample opportunities for practice, reflection on the implementation of the accommodations, and working as a team across the disciplines to ensure equal access to learning.

Accommodations in Action

When planning lessons, careful consideration must be taken regarding lesson presentation, instruction delivery, and use of materials. This includes changing the way that instruction, directions, and information is presented to the student. For example, students may need the directions to be repeated, intentional and purposeful use of visual prompts of cues, graphic organizers to aid learning, providing a copy of lesson notes, etc. For a student with dyslexia who is still decoding text and not yet independently reading grade level text, this barrier can be addressed with the accommodation of audiobooks, text-to-speech software, and clarifying or simplifying written instructions. In addition, students may experience laborious reading or reading fatigue, especially as they progress through the grades and the reading workload increases across the disciplines, resulting in a barrier and a call for audiobooks, frequent breaks, and extended time may be appropriate accommodations-highlighting the need for accommodations to be viewed as tools which are accessible to students.

Teacher Tip: Plan ahead for materials students are required to read and those that can be read aloud or accessed on audiobooks.

The instructional practices covered in this book, such as the Gradual Release of Responsibility model (GRR) where the teacher explicitly models, directly teaches, provides guided practice and scaffolds, then fades as students gain independence should also be applied to the teaching and embedding of accommodations within the lesson including the use of clear and concise language to reduce confusion and presenting information in small sequential steps. The elements of structured literacy set the stage for accommodations to seamlessly become part of the lesson. Other examples of accommodations may include clarifying understanding, frontloading vocabulary and providing a word bank or glossary with a focus on the use and pronunciation of words to build oral language and spelling knowledge. Emphasizing daily review helps students link previous learning to new concepts, and providing a visual schedule or outline as an accommodation helps students stay organized and focused in the lesson, both proven to enhance learning.

Some accommodations that I find especially beneficial to students where dyslexia is causing difficulty in written expression and comprehension are the use of graphic organizers and instructional aids such as graphic organizers, speech-to-text software, checklists and templates implemented within lessons. The use of these tools, when explicitly taught and used within the GRR model, empowers students and gives them an easy application to use and transfer beyond the intervention classroom or lesson. I focus on two to four organizers based on the text features and keep them very simple. I want students to be able to draw or create these independently and understand how to use them across disciplines.

Notetaking is another powerful accommodation when done well. When not implemented with the student's learning needs in mind, it can be cumbersome and frustrating. Often, requesting a copy of teacher notes is appropriate. By providing students with notes or partial notes, you can reduce the amount of copying required by a student with dyslexia or dysgraphia. This allows the focus to be on the information in the lesson and creates a bridge to the expectations by removing the challenges with writing and spelling caused by the learning difference. This is not to say that our students will not be expected to take notes, but rather that this skill builds with the student as they gain proficiency in reading and writing. Notetaking can be scaffolded as well based on the needs of the student. For example, some students benefit from having a complete copy of the teacher's notes for the lesson, in which they can highlight important pieces. Other students may benefit from partial notes, or cloze notes, where they need to fill in or complete the information from the lesson. As students progress in their writing, or for those who need less support, a note-taking template like Cornell Notes may be beneficial.

Highlighting or noting important information in lessons and readings is another key teaching and accommodation for students. It helps them identify and connect important information. Have students highlight important information or answers within the notes or text instead of writing them out. Highlighting is also a helpful tool in identifying the important information, main idea, details, etc., but it needs to be explicitly taught and practiced to be effective. Anyone who has purchased a used college book and opens the chapter only to see every line highlighted realizes that teaching how to identify the critical information needs to be practiced.

Reading guides are another great tool to use with students to check for understanding and engage students in the reading process. A reading guide provides students with a roadmap of the assignment and builds in stopping points to check for understanding. This can be developed to address specific needs and include scaffolds particular to the student, such as "stop and check" after a paragraph, page, or section. I will place an "x" or a sticky note at the critical junctures where I want students to stop, reflect, respond, annotate, etc.

Sometimes, students need an accommodation to address their response or how they receive and express their understanding of lessons and curriculum. This may include alternatives for completing assignments, lessons, assessments, and materials to enhance students' performance.

Oftentimes, our lessons provide alternative ways for students to show understanding. This may include but isn't limited to, video/audio presentations, visual presentations, oral administration of assessments, and use of speech-to-print technology, in addition to individual, small group, and large group work. Allowing for changes in response mode provides the student with an opportunity to demonstrate their knowledge differently, in a way that doesn't highlight their areas of need in language or motor difficulties. For example, a student with dysgraphia or dyslexia may use typing or underline the answer in the text. A student with fine motor difficulties may be given a paper with larger spacing or highlighted lines. In addition, the use of graph paper or calculators for math may be an accommodation provided. Some students may have difficulty transferring information from one place to another, causing the errors such as bubbling in the wrong place, writing a scaled-down sentence due to small spatial availability, etc. Alternative answer sheets focus on content and decrease formatting challenges.

Along those same lines, at times, an accommodation of reducing the amount of text or breaking it into smaller pieces may be appropriate. I often cut apart or fold assignments to minimize the overwhelm and help my students focus on the task—mindful preparation of materials that cut out inessential information, which can hinder learning and add extra load to student working memory (Sweller et al. 1980) is another appropriate accommodation. Chunking information into meaningful parts, using readable sans-serif fonts, such as Arial, which provide better spacing (British Dyslexia Association 2023), and removing irrelevant images can help students focus on the vital information.

Instructional teaching aids or materials are a common practice across classrooms, but determining what is specifically needed to meet the needs of each student with dyslexia highlights the necessity of knowing each student's learning profile and the integration required in honoring their learning journey. Things like letter strips, cursive/print cues, number strips, mouth picture cards, manipulatives, and calculators are examples of instructional aids. In addition, providing a clear rubric that describes the assignment's expectations, broken into smaller chunks, can act as a support for students, along with examples of successfully completed work to serve as a model.

To support students in written responses, provide sentence starters, transition words, and anchor charts, even in the upper grades, to set students up for success. Sequencing and organizing ideas can often be difficult for students with dyslexia and ADHD, so providing these tools shows a student what language can assist with transitioning and organizing their thoughts onto paper.

Many students with dyslexia need extended time for assignments and assessments to allow them to process the information and give extra time for reading and writing. Within the lesson, we can be mindful of the pacing of the lesson and the reading and writing expectations. Many of my middle and high school students will use their phone or computer cameras to capture the notes on the board in order to keep up with the pacing of the class lecture. Even something like copying down the assignment as the bell rings to move to another class is stressful for students and should cause educators to reflect on what writing is required by students regarding the time allotted.

Practice, practice, practice. Depending on the skill and the student, providing students with additional practice of the accommodation allows for the transfer of knowledge. With correct skill repetition, we create new neural pathways in the brain. This may include hierarchal worksheets and assignments that begin with simpler problems, weaving in retrieval practices to lead to more challenging applications, and setting students up for success. Accommodations without implementation, practice, and reflections/evaluation are meaningless. Students must be provided time to implement, practice with intention, and reflect on the effectiveness of the accommodation.

Assistive Technology

In the world of dyslexia and education, the term Assistive Technology is used often and found on many IEP and 504 plans. The goal of assistive technology is to provide tools that ease reading and writing demands due to the learning disability and facilitate access to curriculum expectations. These can be **low-tech** or **high-tech** tools that help students with dyslexia save time and overcome challenges as they provide access to learning and assistance in the output of knowledge. At the core, assistive technology refers to tools that support students in accessing the curriculum and demonstrating their understanding. These tools are specifically chosen to aid the student's learning profile and should be explicitly taught and used within lessons. When planning and determining appropriate accommodation tools, we must remember the tasks that we are asking students to do, as well as the student profile, which can determine what type of assistive technology will benefit the student.

Types of Assistive Technology

Assistive technology can be broken into two large categories.

- **Low-tech assistive technology**—use of tools such as highlighters, graphic organizers, reading strips, reading guides, etc., that provide access to the curriculum.

- **High-tech assistive technology**—digital highlighters, audiobooks, speech-to-text, text-to-speech, etc.

Access to speech-to-text software can aid in bridging the gap between oral language and motor output. Speech-to-text may allow a student to more easily transfer their ideas to paper and then go back in and revise and edit. Assistive technology within speech-to-text software can aid in grammar, spelling, and sentence structure elements. Communicating ideas and seeing them come to life on the page eases some of the stress of writing. It is recommended that explicit instruction in the efficient use of speech-to-text software in conjunction with the writing process and skills be embedded into lessons. The use of assistive technology can (and should) be discussed and used across disciplines and with all members who work with the student. In turn, students need ample opportunities to learn and practice applying assistive technology within their lessons.

Testing Accommodations

Student accommodations involving standardized assessments and tests within the classroom setting, should also be established and integrated into classroom practice before expected use in assessment situations. Providing opportunities for students to practice with the accommodations before state standardized tests is important, as classroom accommodations should mirror state assessment accommodations when applicable. Many states include universal accessibility features within their provision of accommodations, such as magnified text, spell-check software, repetition of instructions, digital notepads, highlighters, etc. It is always recommended that teachers and parents review their state's current published guidelines indicating specific permitted assessment accommodations. Currently, in the United States, all 50 states have published guidelines. These may vary from state to state, so it is necessary to know what is approved for your state. In addition, there are accommodation guidelines available in other countries pertaining to dyslexia.

Building the Toolbox—What Teachers, Parents, and Students Need to Know

"Failing to prepare is preparing to fail."

—Anonymous

The Teacher's Role in Accommodations

Teachers are the gatekeepers for accommodations in the classroom. How we plan our lessons and provide accommodations to address a barrier due to a learning difference sets the stage for equitable learning. Depending on how accommodations are used or viewed in a class, they can empower students or create a negative stigma and make a child feel that their learning difference has been pointed out to everyone. Many of my students, especially my older students, comment about how the access to accommodations directly impacted their self-esteem and emotional wellness within a class. Year after year, students share that a teacher in a middle school makes them walk to the back of the room during class time to get their accommodation notes and materials. Middle school is a time of uncertainty for students, and they are hyperaware of their status with peers. Highlighting a learning difference in front of the class made my students shy away from using their accommodations, resulting in learning failure and negatively impacting self-esteem. I share this not to shame the teacher, who most likely believes they are doing a good job providing the accommodation, but to highlight the importance of bringing compassionate empathy and awareness into our classrooms. How teachers set up their classroom accessibility to accommodations matters and should be part of the classroom preparation at the beginning of the year and revisited throughout.

The introduction of accommodations to our students and access and application within our classrooms is key for building and preserving self-esteem and self-advocacy skills. If we place accommodations on a "list" but don't teach those tools or provide practice, it is not beneficial to our children. An important part of our role as educators and interventionists is to teach students how to use their accommodations effectively.

Here are some ways to help remove the stigma or shame that may accompany using accommodations.

Tips for Classroom and Intervention Application of Accommodations

Consider a student's learning profile when planning lessons and assignments to understand and identify areas of strength and need. *How will this student's learning profile impact their access to the lesson? Are there ways to incorporate different options for students to access the curriculum? Can they show their knowledge in another way such as PowerPoint, presentation, video, etc.?*

Determine what accommodations to include in a student's toolbox and how those will be included within the classroom setting (assignments, instruction, environment, assessments). Work with the student team (teachers, parents/caregivers, student, etc.) to establish appropriate accommodations.

Create opportunities for reflection, teaching, and reteaching of accommodations. Every dyslexia therapy and reading intervention lesson provides an opportunity for a "check-in" to discuss and reflect on accommodations used in the classroom and establish a plan that leads us to our set goals. In an intervention or small group setting, beginning lessons with a quick reflection on what accommodations were used, why and how they benefited learning, and what could be altered, helps bring students into the learning process. Doing this well requires ongoing conversations with the student about their role in learning and developing their mindset and metacognitive skills so they are actively participating in reflection and their education plan.

Introduce the accommodation tool to the child or class. Often, we think that accommodations should only be provided to students with 504/IEPs, and yet, as we saw in the list above, many items identified as accommodations are good teaching practices. Many students, whether identified as dyslexic or not, benefit from using different tools to aid learning. A child with ADHD or anxiety may benefit from access to audiobooks or speech-to-text tools, many of which are standard within computer systems and, with the development of technology, becoming more mainstream in availability. We should teach the majority of these learning tools (accommodations) to all students in the classroom for many reasons. By bringing awareness of different tools available to students and teaching them how and when to access them, we are addressing the metacognitive skills needed in planning, reflecting, and creating a plan—skills we want all students to have! In addition, this eliminates singling out students for using accommodations. Many accommodation tools, such as graphic organizers and clarifying understanding, are considered best practices for all students and warrant explicit teaching and availability for all.

We want students to have multiple ways to solve problems and access learning. Letting all students practice using the accommodation tool and make it accessible for all is a great way to scaffold instruction and support every student! Tools provide this for all learners.

Model when, how, and why to use each accommodation. By showing students what tools to use and when, we are giving them the necessary skills to guide their learning, become reflective about their learning process, and dive into metacognitive skills. Win-win!

Practice, reflect, practice. We know that without practice, we don't learn things well. Practice makes permanent academic outcomes, and this is true for reflecting on how we use our tools to aid in learning. We need to be mindful of helping students bridge their knowledge to practice.

> *Are we providing enough opportunities to use an accommodation? Are we including the use of the accommodation within our lessons? Have we built in reflection time and conversations to determine how the accommodation has helped or needs to be refined?*

Document accommodations and outcomes. The IEP/504 plan is a living document designed to aid students in achieving academic success. Keeping documentation of applied accommodations and their outcomes provides qualitative data for review during IEP/504 meetings and deepens our understanding of intangible factors like behaviors, habits, and experiences.

Bring students into the learning and reflective process. The goal for our children is to have developed the self-advocacy skills and awareness of themselves as learners to take control of their learning needs and educational path. For this to happen, we must help students develop academic skills alongside those connected to their self-awareness and social-emotional growth. This includes reflecting on what accommodations are needed and speaking up and asking for accommodations. The development of this skill is not something that comes naturally but must be fostered and practiced over time. Early on in a child's journey with dyslexia, the adults are their voice and strongly advocate for the child's needs. This includes educators, parents, family members, tutors, therapists, and anyone who knows the child. Over time, we want to begin to release the advocacy work to the child as they gain confidence in their voice and understanding of their needs as a learner. Achieving this level of self-advocacy includes careful planning and embedded components that go into conversations and lessons over time.

The Parent's Role in Accommodations

Creating a team approach to helping students with dyslexia includes connecting and communicating with teachers, parents, tutors, and students. Communication between parents and educators is crucial for our dyslexic learners. Parents play an essential role in bridging the work from the classroom to home and providing accommodations for homework. When students are given homework or long assignments, parents can provide accommodations at home when applicable. For this successful partnership, parents need support and awareness of what accommodations to offer and how to support their child. For example, I have my parents read the question-and-answer choices on homework assignments and scribe for their child if the paper does not provide adequate spacing or if the child is fatigued and has this as an accommodation. I also have parents document the time needed for an assignment to be completed, what accommodations were provided, and if the work requires extended time or is broken into smaller chunks or assignments. This documentation and observation is encouraged to be shared with educators who work with their child and included in the notes for the IEP/504 meeting. Parents are also the advocates for their child in their learning journey and may need guidance in how to release or gradually shift that advocacy work to the student.

The Student's Role in Accommodations

Students should take an active role in their understanding of accommodations within the classroom. When students understand their learning journey and what they need to help them achieve their goals, they step into the beginning stages of the role of self-advocacy. Part of developing this self-awareness, knowledge, and self-advocacy is through the development of the accommodation toolbox. Students should be aware of what accommodations they have, when and how to use them, how to ask for application of those accommodations, and know that they will be supported in their journey. The attributes of self-awareness, emotional stability, goal setting and perseverance are powerful predictors of success (Raskind et al. 1999; Reiff, Gerber, & Ginsberg 1997; Wehmeyer 1996; Werner and Smith 1992; Duke 2021). There are many skills, from academic to metacognitive to executive function skills, and beyond that, develop over time and lead to self-advocacy.

Examples of Planning for Accommodations

A simple chart like this one can ensure that clear communication about accommodations, those responsible for implementing them, and frequency of use is established. Download this editable document at www.thedyslexiaclassroom.com/teachingbeyondthediagnosis.

Accommodation Plan Student: John	Year: 2022–2023		Grade: 7
Area of educational need	Accommodation or Service	Person(s) responsible for implementing	Frequency of accommodation or service
Organization of assignments	Use iPad to take picture of assignment listed on board	-Student -Teacher posting assignments -Parent	-Daily: at the end of each class -check-in with Mr. Smith weekly -parent check weekly
Note taking assistance	Partial notes (with fill in the blank)	-Student -Teacher (ELA, Science, World Culture)	-as needed
Reflection/Observation of accommodation use:			

One of the biggest things that I see occurring in the academic setting is the removal of accommodations much too soon. A student is performing well, at or above grade level, with their accommodations in place and then because they are doing so well, their accommodations are removed. This is incredibly frustrating and speaks to the necessary shift in how we view accommodations.

"One of the most common errors of teaching a dyslexic child to read is to withdraw prematurely the instruction that seems to be working." (Shaywitz)

When students are using their tools or accommodations and the student is performing well, we need to determine how they are accessing their accommodations and ensure that we are not pulling these from their toolbox. We keep tools; we place them in the toolbox and know when and where to pull them out for use. Often, in school settings, when students are performing well, accommodations may be pulled because the student is "doing well," but this is something I caution against. Instead, keep the tools in the toolbox and aid students in understanding when to access and self-advocate for the use of those tools.

Conclusion

When it comes to accommodations, we must be the stewards for our children. We must see the benefits of taking the time to weave these accommodations tools into our lessons, bring awareness to how they are helping and why, and then guide students in this reflective process of thinking about what tools helped and why. All of this is part of the journey for those with learning differences, and we can guide students to know themselves as learners and begin to self-advocate for the tools that best assist them.

Key Takeaways

- Accommodations are not a substitute for appropriate intervention or instruction.

- Accommodations should be viewed as tools to access the curriculum, which level the playing field. They are not cheating or giving an unfair advantage.

- Accommodations must be taught, practiced, and reviewed with the goal in mind.

- A team approach to accommodations shifts the focus to learning, not a checklist.

> Simplify your path to practice. What did you put in your pocket?
> What stepping stones, or nuggets of knowledge, are you taking from this chapter?

CHAPTER THIRTEEN

Classroom Environment

"My needs aren't special. How my needs are met may be different, but they are the same needs as anyone else's."

—Unknown author

Integrated Framework Component: Self-Advocacy Skills and Knowledge

In this part of the journey, we look at how educators can foster and develop an environment within our classrooms and school communities that represents those with dyslexia through understanding and support.

Like many teachers, I was excited each year, and I would look for ways to decorate my classroom and create systems for all of the requirements and things I wanted to implement with my students. There is no end to teacher decorations, posters, or designs one can find for their classrooms. Our students spend a lot of time in our buildings and rooms, and we want the spaces to be inviting and comfortable. A delicate balance also exists in ensuring that we are setting students up for success through the intentional design of equity-based environments within our classrooms to meet needs.

At the beginning of my teaching career, I had a student who required some sizeable medical equipment to remain in the classroom and constant access for mobility with the equipment to all classroom areas. This accessibility completely shifted how I set up my room and changed how I viewed my classroom environment from that point forward. It took me some time to realize and reflect on what my students really needed from the physical environment and how the intentional design of this allowed me to better set them up for success.

Creating and Fostering a Dyslexia-Friendly Classroom/School

Classrooms set the stage for learning. Every teacher, at some point, has had a student with dyslexia in their class. Creating a dyslexia-friendly classroom is not just a support system, it's a game-changer for students. It establishes an environment that supports every student, ensuring they have access to resources that address academic needs while remaining emotionally sound, which is essential for all students to thrive.

The right kind of support enables individuals to thrive, and designing a dyslexia-friendly environment helps learners feel understood and encouraged by the proper instruction and environment. For teachers to have the fullest impact on their students, they must connect with students on two separate but overlapping levels—academic and emotional—as seen in the warm demander/champion approach. In order for students to be able to learn new educational content, their emotional brain must tell them that it is both safe and essential to learn the material (Hardiman 2003). Part of addressing academic needs is establishing a community and environment conducive to learning. Fostering a dyslexia-friendly community means bringing together the elements of the integrated framework and using our understanding to speak to and connect with learners on a journey with dyslexia. As a teacher or parent of a child with dyslexia, learning all they can about dyslexia and how it impacts learning significantly impacts how students feel about themselves as they navigate their school years. Building a classroom and home environment with an intention that honors the learning differences and needs in our world is important for nurturing understanding and empathy.

As we plan for our classrooms and school settings, we put in place some things up front that set students up for success such as desk placement, visual schedules, routines, checklists, etc. Bringing these to the forefront of our planning and classroom design sets the tone for our lessons and environment and reminds us as educators of the value of establishing structure, routines, and predictability within the school environment. Just as reading strategies for dyslexic learners benefit all students, so do intentionally designed classroom environments and learning strategies designed with the neurodivergent learner in mind. At the core, high expectations need to be paired with high levels of intentional support. This means explicitly teaching students both academic and behavioral expectations, providing support throughout the lesson and classroom environment with intention.

Environment and Classroom Design

Effective classrooms foster the conditions of a learning-focused environment through teaching practices aligned with how students learn. High expectations paired with high levels of intentional support within the dyslexia intervention and classroom bring together the elements of the integrated framework into the classroom. This chapter shows these elements coming together as we purposefully design dyslexia-friendly classrooms.

Some strategies and intentional designs we can include in our classrooms include teaching and communicating **clear expectations** for the lesson and environment. We set the stage for success by establishing and explicitly teaching expectations for lessons and classroom community that support students' focus on learning. These teachings include demonstrating respectful interactions to foster a positive learning environment, visible cues for expectations, and a clear understanding of the teacher and student role within the classroom. It is also important to set the stage for success even when meeting in small groups for intervention or one-to-one sessions. Communicating clear expectations establishes a learning-focused environment. Students can be engaged in this process and develop visual support such as an "Active learning looks like—and sounds like" chart for learning expectations or the reading brain activity.

Our dyslexia instruction is grounded in a structured approach and anchored in a clear structure and routine, offering predictability within the lesson. This helps establish classroom predictability and prepares students for learning success. Explicit instruction, practice, and application of the structure and routine of the lesson is practiced across all learning settings (whole class, small group, one-to-one). The teacher provides clear and consistent approaches with high expectations to support student learning, responsive teaching, and the development of metacognitive skills.

Visual supports are a powerful tool for helping students gain metacognitive awareness of their learning process, completion of tasks, and movement toward goals. These intentional tools offer support for the child, such as a visual schedule, expectations, multistep directions chart, anchor chart, list of homework assignments, etc. Many students struggle with understanding elapsed time, and timers can aid in supporting awareness of this. Visual supports do not have to be complicated to be effective. Some of my most effective visual supports are generated when meeting with students, and we often create them together on an index card.

When setting up the classroom, we can reflect on the impact of visual supports through these reflection questions:

- What are those supports that set students up for success? (those things that students refer to as tools, use within the lesson)
- Do my students know the visual supports and how to use them?
- Did I explicitly teach students to use those tools independently and the process of doing so?

As we've explored in previous chapters, executive function skills foster self-regulated learning and task awareness and remain integral to the dyslexia-friendly classroom. Learning necessitates that students maintain focus and attention, comprehend the expectations and intended goals of their learning, and develop awareness and regulation of their engagement in the lesson, thereby aiding them in self-regulation and learning. This underscores the pivotal role of metacognitive processes in learning.

As educators, one of our primary responsibilities is to ensure high student engagement in lessons, particularly within interventions. This involves providing ample opportunities for high levels of practice, as the **amount of practice** needed to solidify a concept can vary from student to student. Our role is to create an intentional routine that elicits the most student responses throughout the lessons and lessons should look more like a game of tennis where the engagement and responses bounce back and forth between the teacher and the student throughout the lesson. With the correct repetition and application of a skill, we create a new pathway in the brain. This intentional repetition, is not drill, but purposeful application of a target skill or concept to create change at the synaptic level where the neurons meet. The more correct repetition or practice we include in our reading instruction, the stronger and faster the connection between the neurons becomes. Students with dyslexia will need more intensity and ample opportunities to turn practice into permanence in reading and writing. They may vary in the ease with which concepts are solidified, but all students should be actively engaged in the lesson. This can be achieved through choral responses in small groups, responses on whiteboards, thumbs up/down, individual responses, etc.

Questions to reflect on often include:

- Am I providing enough opportunities for my students to practice the skill or concept in meaningful and intentional application?

(Continued)

(Continued)

- How have I woven in intentional application throughout the lesson? For instance, have I provided opportunities for students to apply the concept in multiple ways, or have I designed activities that require them to use the skill in different contexts? What student responses have I woven into the lesson? (choral response, peer reading, whiteboard, etc.)
- Games can serve as a powerful tool to increase practice opportunities if they are intentionally planned with a high ratio of repetition or application. Activities such as Spin and Read, Spin and Spell (The Dyslexia Classroom), or repeated reading of decodable sentences within a game format are excellent examples of ways to engage students in a high number of practice opportunities. Teachers must be cautious that the game or activity chosen: (1) addresses the level of need for student learning; (2) is completed within the allotted timeframe of the lesson for that component; and (3) provides a high level of practice with corrective feedback (see Figure 13.1).

Develop a keen eye for **objective performance cues.** Teachers need to develop a keen eye and ability to observe and note student performance on concept knowledge, skills, and tasks to address learning needs at the moment as we noted in earlier chapters. This is a more reliable indicator of learning than looking at student engagement, perceived

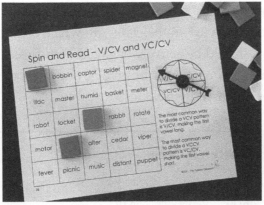

FIGURE 13.1 Application of practice. Retrieved with permission from The Dyslexia Classroom.

student interest, or enthusiasm, as these can often be misleading about what the students have learned. So, while we want to provide intentional opportunities for high levels of engagement with students, teacher knowledge, and the ability to observe and adapt their teaching, providing the necessary support and scaffolds at the moment is vital.

Develop **awareness of dyslexia** to meet students' learning, emotional, and aspirational needs. This includes not just anticipating students' individual learning needs and planning to anticipate possible barriers, but also understanding and anticipating the impacts of dyslexia beyond academics. For example, a student may benefit from explicit frontloading instruction in targeted vocabulary, including an analysis of the words at the phonological (sounds), morphological (meaning), orthographic (spelling), and syntactic awareness (grammar and sentence knowledge) levels in preparation for text reading. In addition to meeting academic needs within the classroom, this understanding brings a sense of responsibility to ensure the accessibility and implementation of accommodations and representation.

Accessibility Within the Classroom

One of my seventh grade students explained in our session that he wasn't utilizing his accommodations within his math or science courses as the accessibility to the note assistance accommodation, which he vitally needed, was located in the back of the room. When instructed to get their notes out during the lesson, he was supposed to stand up and walk to the back of the room to get the specialized note paper. The teacher would remind him in front of his peers to get the notes, which was traumatizing to a middle schooler as it highlighted his need for something different to access learning. Instead, he opted not to get the tool he needed and, in turn, was doing poorly in class. It was a terrible cascade of events rooted in not understanding or empathizing with the student (perhaps an oversight by the teacher), which had devastating results, including a disconnect in trust in the teacher and his desire to advocate for himself.

Students with accommodations may feel like a nuisance in classrooms where accessibility is not a part of the environment. Suppose access to accommodation tools or resources is something students have to request in front of their peers or is projected as something special or a burden. In that case, this brings a great deal of shame to the student, and in turn, they will often forgo the use of the accommodation to the detriment of their own learning. To mitigate this, we can be mindful of setting up the classroom so student learning is the focus and access to learning is the heartbeat of the environment. Intentional, proactive planning with the use of accommodations embedded within the lesson and thoughtfulness of how these will be accessible promotes a classroom environment that is welcoming for students with dyslexia.

Things to consider in accessibility within the classroom:

- What systems do I have for introducing students to tools and accommodations within my classroom? Within the school?

- Am I embedding the use of the accommodation tool within my lesson? How are these application opportunities continued?

- Do students have open access to the tools needed? If not, how will access work in my classroom that honors their learning needs without shame?

Representation

Representation matters for all students, including those with learning differences. One way to bring representation, empathy, and understanding of dyslexia into the learning environment is through books. By carefully selecting books, we can provide opportunities for students to see themselves in the pages. This can lead to open discussions among students and teachers and can encourage peer empathy and understanding. (*Note, it is a student's personal decision if they wish to share their learning difference with classmates and should not be openly noted in class.)

Books on this subject matter have benefited students in many ways. Pictures and chapter books highlighting dyslexia and a growth mindset have provided opportunities to discuss differences and ways to overcome challenges. Books allow students to connect with a character they can relate to and build empathetic reasoning. They provide engaging ways for teachers to share learning differences with their students and honor the various ways people learn. They also support social-emotional learning and provide opportunities for a powerful springboard to discussions and mini-lessons showing how we can all overcome challenges, developing the theory of mind. These shared reading experiences can foster a sense of community and understanding among students and educators.

Books that highlight different learning experiences also create the possibility to remove existing or lingering stigmas of dyslexia that may exist. The more students see themselves in books, the less they feel alone. We are now in a place where others are sharing their journey with dyslexia, and through their voices and stories, our students can see dyslexia and all its facets. Using books is a great way to align with content expectations in theme, character and story development, literary devices, etc., and can be woven into the curriculum expectations and lessons. They are great for classroom meetings, character education, teaching character traits, and learning differences. See the list below for some books many from dyslexic authors which are noted—this isn't an exhaustive list, and I will continue to add books to the website page along with lesson plans and ideas. Never underestimate the power of a book!

Some Student Friendly Books About Dyslexia

- *Dyslexia Explained: Without the Need for Too Many Words*—Mike Jones (dyslexic author)
- *It's Called Dyslexia (Live and Learn)*—Jennifer Moore-Mallinos

(Continued)

(Continued)

- *Can I Tell You About Dyslexia?: A Guide for Friends, Family and Professionals*—Alan M. Hultquist

- *My Gift of Difference: 7 Steps to Embracing Your Learning Difference*—Jordan Ashley Greene (dyslexic author)

- *Tom's Special Talent*—Kate Gaynor

- *The Alphabet War*—Diane Burton Robb

- *Thank You, Mr. Falker*—Patricia Polacco (dyslexic author)

- Hank Zipzer Series—Henry Winkler (dyslexic author)

- *Two-Minute Drill*—Mike Lupica

- *My Name is Brain Brian*—Jeanne Betancourt (dyslexic author)

- *Fish in a Tree*—Lunda Mullaly Hunt

- Percy Jackson Series—Rick Riordan

- *Looking for Heroes: One Boy, One Year, 100 Letters*—Aidan A. Colvin (dyslexic author)

- *A Walk in the Words*—Hudson Talbot (dyslexic author)

- *The Wild Book*—Margarita Engle

- *Dr. Dyslexia Dude*—Dr. Shawn Robinson (dyslexic author) and Inshirah Robinson

- *Hacking the Code: The Ziggety Zaggety Road of a Dyslexic Kid*—Gea Meijering

- *The Hoopstar*—Chavon D. White

- *I Define Me*—Kyler Eric Smith (dyslexic author)

- *Cartwheels: Finding Your Special Kind of Smart*—Tracy S. Peterson

- *Magnificent Meg: A Read-Aloud to Encourage Children with Dyslexia*—Andra Harris

- *Did You Say Pasghetti?: Dusty and Danny Tackle Dyslexia*—Tammy Fortune
- *The Junkyard Wonders*—Patricia Polacco (dyslexic author)
- The Lark Series—Natasha Deen
- *The Dyslexia Legends Alphabet Book*—Alphabet legends
- *Aaron Slater, Illustrator: A Picture Book*—Andrea Beaty
- *Brilliant Bea: A Story for Kids With Dyslexia and Learning Differences*—Shaina Rudolph
- *A Kids Book About Dyslexia*—Sarah Travers (dyslexic author)
- *Molly Tells the World: A Book About Dyslexia and Self-esteem*— Krista Weltner (dyslexic author)
- *Finding My Superpower*—Sarah Prestidge
- *Wonderfully Wired Brains: An Introduction to the World of Neurodiversity*—Louise Goodling
- *D is for Darcy: Not Dyslexia*—Abigail C. Griebelbauer
- *All the Way to the Top: How One Girl's Fight for Americans with Disabilities Changed Everything*—Annette Bay Pimentel

Highlight authors with dyslexia. Many well-known authors have dyslexia, and highlighting these within the lesson can be empowering for students with dyslexia while also demystifying the idea that those with dyslexia can't write well.

Some Dyslexic Authors

- Dav Pilkey
- Patricia Polacco
- Agatha Christie (note in the front of *And Then There Were None*)

(Continued)

(Continued)

- Henry Winkler
- Octavia Spencer
- Carmen Agra Deedy
- Sally Gardner
- Jeanne Betancourt
- Joe Griffith
- Avi (Edward Wortis)
- Ahmet Zappa
- Tom McLaughlin
- Stacey R. Campbell
- Jerry Pinkney
- Anne Rice
- Max Brooks
- Octavia Butler
- Garth Cook
- John Irving
- Philip Schultz, Pulitzer Prize–Winning Poet
- Victor Villanseñor
- Benjamin Zephaniah
- Brad Falchuk
- Wendy Wasserstein, Pulitzer Prize–Winning Playwright and Author

Bring awareness of this to your classroom as you learn about the author or during author studies. Even just a quick mention that the author is dyslexic can empower students and ease stigmas that they may carry. The stories of these authors can inspire and motivate both students and educators.

Dyslexia doesn't need to hold someone back from their dreams. We can weave dyslexia awareness through all content areas by highlighting scientists, mathematicians, entrepreneurs, actors, artists, etc. who have dyslexia. A bulletin board or mini book highlighting others who share their dyslexia journey allows students to see possibilities in their academics, career choices, and beyond.

Teacher Tip: Reach out to the community and see if adults in the students' lives would like to share their journey with dyslexia.

Just some of the famous people who have shared their journey with dyslexia:

Artists, Architects, Designers—Jerry Pinkney

Math/Scientists/Inventors—Beryl Benacerraf, Brian Meersma, Dr. Carol Greider, Catherine Drennan, Dr. Maggie Aderin-Pocock

Astronauts/NASA—Charles Conrad

Chefs—Jamie Oliver

Musicians—Carly Simon, Cher

Business/Entrepreneurs—Ben Foss, Barbara Corcoran, Daymond John, Kate Griggs, Richard Branson, Charles Schwab

Athletes—Malcom Mitchell, Alex Green, Tim Tebow, Brent Sopel, Carrie Lofgren, Meryl Davis, Magic Johnson, Sir Jackie Stewart, Joe Whitt, Jr.

Actors/Performers—Tom Holland, Keira Knightly, Orlando Bloom, Octavia Spencer, Anthony Hopkins, Tom Cruise, Channing Tatum, Jennifer Anniston, Salma Hayek

Reflecting for Personal Growth

If you were to shadow a student for a day, what experiences would you have? While this may vary based on the grade, some common threads across our current educational settings deserve reflection as we seek to create dyslexia and neurodivergent-friendly classrooms and learning-based environments. One key reflection is that students tend to sit all day, which is exhausting. Can you recall a time that you attended a conference or daylong professional development session in which you were sitting and actively taking notes and listening to the presenters? By the end of the day, you were most likely exhausted. The amount of mental focus students need to maintain throughout the day is a lot—as teachers, we may forget as we are moving from student to student as we provide assistance or standing as we teach the lessons—but for the students, they are often provided with limited opportunities for movement and meaningful multimodal experiences within their classrooms. Intentional planning of meaningful multimodal experiences should be woven into the structured literacy lesson to engage students in active learning and practice.

Embrace reflective practices as a means of professional growth. Establish **reflective practices** to review the critical areas of your classroom design for students with learning differences and use this as an opportunity for growth. Asking reflective questions and identifying the areas of strengths and need for growth is part of the metacognitive processes we want students to engage in, and we can model this in our practices to continue to grow as educators as we think about our classroom environment for those with dyslexia. Take some time each quarter to reflect on the areas you feel are going well (glows) and the areas you would like to revamp or refine (grows). Allowing students to reflect on the environment can help establish a team approach, empower them to advocate for themselves, and reflect on what they need to succeed in the classroom (see the "Reflection of Dyslexia-Friendly Classroom" chart).

Download this in PDF form at www.thedyslexiaclassroom.com/teachingbeyond thediagnosis

Reflection of Dyslexia-Friendly Classroom		
Area	Glows	Grows
Dyslexia-friendly environment		
Classroom routines and procedures		
Teaching strategies and supports		
Accessibility of accommodations		
High levels of practice with meaningful multimodal experiences		
Executive function skills		
Objective performance cues		
Dyslexia awareness and representation in the classroom		

Conclusion

Students spend a great deal of their day within schools, and for those with dyslexia, this can be challenging; however, when students are placed in an environment that sets the stage for success, understands dyslexia, holds high standards with the proper support in place, focuses on a strength-based model, and honors the journey of each student, individuals with dyslexia can find success and reach their potential.

Key Takeaways

- The intentional design of the classroom environment sets the stage for success.

- Careful planning of how the lesson can incorporate accommodations and setting the stage and accessibility creates opportunities for success and minimizes shame.

- Bring representation of dyslexia into the classroom, in different forms, and across disciplines by noting those with dyslexia that students may study in literature, science, math, etc.

- Reflect on accessibility and a dyslexia-friendly environment throughout the year. Do this as a teacher and provide students with an opportunity to share their perspectives as well.

- Create a culture of understanding that we all have strengths and areas to grow.

> Simplify your path to practice. What did you put in your pocket?
> What stepping stones, or nuggets of knowledge, are you taking from this chapter?

Self-Advocacy, Success, and Confidence

"Success is the result of small efforts, repeated day in and day out."
—Robert Collier

Integrated Framework Component: Self-Advocacy, Success, and Confidence

In this part of the journey, where the pieces of the integrated framework come together for students, teachers, and parents, we see a shift or a transfer to self-advocacy as students gain confidence and skills to speak to their strengths and needs (see Figure 14.1).

Observing my students find success and confidence in their reading and writing abilities with empowerment, knowledge, and confidence in self-advocacy skills, is one of the best parts of this journey. However, the journey can't be overlooked or rushed - all of the elements of the integrated framework need to be developed and fostered as we move to this point. A middle school student was late to receive a diagnosis of dyslexia and spent years of feeling like a fraud because she was compensating and flying under the radar of teachers, hiding her frustration and struggles in reading, instead spending hours after school trying to keep up with her peers.

Metacognitive Processes and
Executive Function Skills

Academics and Support

Self-advocacy Skills and
Knowledge

Understanding
Dyslexia

Success and
Confidence

THE INTEGRATED FRAMEWORK
©2019 - The Dyslexia Classroom, Casey Harrison

FIGURE 14.1 The integrated framework—success and confidence.

Finally, upon the request of the student and the family, she was tested at her school and identified with dyslexia. At this point the family had lost faith in the school, as mom had been asking about dyslexia since kindergarten, and brought the child to work with me at my clinic. Upon this diagnosis, she opened up about how, for so long, there was a disconnect between what she was being told by teachers, who saw how bright she was, and her struggles, leading to negative impacts on her self-esteem. With the diagnosis of dyslexia, her thirst for understanding dyslexia and herself as a learner grew, and her willingness to separate who she was from the struggles allowed her to breathe, shed the shame, and see how her brain worked and the strengths she possessed. Through our work, she began making academic connections, deepened her understanding of dyslexia, and began to know herself as a learner. With the integrated framework, we created a path for learning and growing sans shame or negative self-talk and began to step into a place of self-advocacy. Her journey to self-advocacy was a powerful one, paved in success and confidence, empowering not only herself but also those around her. One day, about six months into our dyslexia intervention sessions, she told me she started a lunch bunch with her friends at school. They asked her how she knew about so many reading spelling concepts and if she could teach them, and she replied, "Oh, I'm dyslexic. I learn well when things are broken down and connected. I can teach you. It's really the best way for everyone to learn." And so she did.

Witnessing someone step into feelings of confidence after years of struggle is a powerful thing. It is also something that is a result of small, consistent steps and intentional conversations over time. For students with dyslexia, the ability to advocate for themselves in the academic setting is paramount, and yet it should be developed over time, with intention and utilizing a gradual release of responsibility to the student.

For many of my students, once they leave elementary school, they are often expected to advocate for themselves from that point on, and many just aren't equipped to do so.

Stepping into a place where you willingly disclose something about yourself that is often misunderstood requires vulnerability and strength. To prepare my students for this part of their journey, we practice in "stages and ages" of development with a gradual shift of responsibility over time and through the grades. Much like the Gradual Release of Responsibility model for academic components, we can adopt the same approach for advocacy—gradually fading out and passing the baton to the student. For students in the early grades or early stages of self-advocacy skills, the adult acts as the advocate for the student, and as students gain a better understanding of dyslexia and their learning, they begin to take part in conversations, perhaps IEP/504 meetings, and eventually are empowered with advocacy, often leading to self-efficacy. These stages of developing self-advocacy skills are woven within the integrated framework as we build awareness of dyslexia, personal "glows and grows," academic success, application of accommodations, and metacognition (see Figure 14.2).

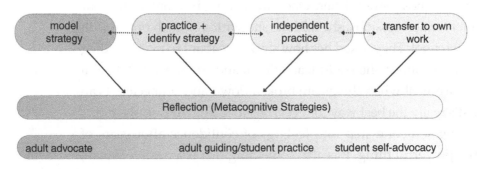

FIGURE 14.2 Stages for developing self-advocacy.

Perception of Dyslexia

First, students need to understand dyslexia and what it means for them as learners—saying "dyslexia" and being able to tell others what dyslexia is and is not. The adult advocate models language surrounding dyslexia and the student-friendly definition of dyslexia.

Strengths and Needs

Students begin to understand that we all hold areas of strength and areas of need. These differ from person to person, highlighting the importance of focusing on the idea that everyone's growth looks different. Therefore, as we continue to grow, we compare our growth with what we did yesterday and not those around us.

Academics and Supports + EF Skills and Metacognition

As students receive appropriate academic support, they find success in the strategies and approaches used. Success helps bring awareness to what is working and knowledge of why a strategy works draws on executive function skills and the metacognitive awareness addressed. Once students understand what helps them learn, they can reflect on what strategies and approaches are working for them and begin to analyze what accommodations or supports can help them in the classroom.

Self-Advocacy and Knowledge

As students begin to strengthen their understanding of their learning journey and processes, they should keep the focus on their abilities and not their difficulties when advocating. For example, using statements like, "I do well with a graphic organizer to help me get started on my essay writing" is a proactive statement for advocating needs.

Through all these stages or parts of the framework, the teacher or adult should explicitly model, provide the language, share their thinking and observations surrounding learning specific to the student, and gradually release the responsibility to the student. This is an essential transition as students must possess the skills to self-advocate in secondary school and even in the workplace when applicable.

Create a Script

To help prepare the student, ongoing dialogue rehearsal should be included in lessons. From early on, when students say the word "dyslexia," to explaining dyslexia, to speaking about their strengths and needs, to the language needed to advocate, rehearsal of this kind of dialogue is encouraged. This is something that I do with all of my students as part of our ongoing conversations. In addition to oral dialogue rehearsal, my older students practice writing emails requesting accommodations, which provides powerful opportunities for discussions using a format that will carry over into their daily lives.

Create a bank of appropriate communication guidelines for students, including a lesson on tone, body language, verbal and nonverbal communication, eye contact (when appropriate for student), how to express feelings, discuss challenges, be proactive, etc. Students also need practice navigating how to respectfully respond to a multitude of reactions, including a negative or perceived negative response to a request, an indifferent response, and even a positive one. As language can, at times, be challenging for some students with dyslexia, practicing ongoing dialogue is beneficial.

Students need to be part of their learning journey, including being aware of their IEP or 504. Creating a student-friendly plan and reviewing their IEP/504 is an excellent way for them to share their strengths, identify their needs and tools, and showcase their uniqueness.

Students can actively engage in this by creating an "all about me" bio sheet for teachers that highlights strengths/needs/likes. Providing an opportunity for students to control the narrative about how they are perceived is powerful. Students can use a sheet of paper, create a video or PowerPoint, or another response to highlight who they are and what they need to achieve their goals. This activity takes time to teach, but as students gain awareness, self-recognition, and cognitive skills to reflect on their learning journey, it can boost self-esteem and awareness.

At some point in their journey, students should attend academic meetings, often beginning in upper elementary or middle school. We want students to take an active role in their learning journey, and part of this is attending IEP/504 meetings when ready. Preparing a student for a meeting that centers around their learning goals can be intimidating. It should be determined where the student is on the stages toward self-advocacy and move to this next step as students gain confidence in their journey with dyslexia. Preparing for a meeting, what to expect, the language that will be used, and what message the student wants to express are all necessary for developing self-advocacy skills. As a dyslexia therapist, teacher, specialist, or tutor, walking alongside your student and facilitating or guiding this path is essential. We cannot assume that students know how to step into this role, and we should offer guidance, support, encouragement, and grace by gradually releasing that responsibility.

Create a "toolbox" of accommodations that is a living document and is part of their daily reflective process to learning (knowing when/how to use their accommodations, when to change them, etc.) For educators, keeping notes of what is working in the classroom, having conversations with the student, and providing opportunities for reflection on the accommodation benefits all parties.

Follow Up Often

Learning how to advocate for oneself takes time and is a process. Students will need adults to follow up with them as they gain confidence in these skills and begin to actively advocate for themselves.

Conclusion

Self-advocacy is an essential skill for students with dyslexia. The ability to speak up for what they need to access learning takes great confidence, practice, guidance and support. We can support students on the next phase of their journey with dyslexia and provide opportunities to speak up and ask for help through explicit instruction and opportunities for application embedded within our lessons.

Key Takeaways

- Building to self-advocacy occurs over time with strategic lessons, reflections, and conversations.
- The integrated framework helps lay the path to self-advocacy.
- Provide support to students as they gradually move toward self-advocacy following the stages for developing self-advocacy (Fig. 14.2).
- Celebrate successes and confidence.

> Simplify your path to practice. What did you put in your pocket?
> What stepping stones, or nuggets of knowledge, are you taking from this chapter?

Conclusion

Throughout this book, the integrated framework represents the complexities surrounding the journey with dyslexia and how we can empower students, educators, and parents beyond the diagnosis. Flip back to the very first words of this book and the question of why the little boy was left behind on the beach and how, through this framework, the student is supported, allowing the individual to move forward in their journey. Let's review the big ideas of the integrated framework:

1. Understanding dyslexia ensures that those working with students and the students themselves hold a deeper understanding of dyslexia and can recognize their strengths and needs to keep learning at the forefront.
2. Academics and supports must be grounded in a structured literacy approach that utilizes systematic and explicit instruction and evidence-based practices.
3. Metacognitive processes and executive function skills empower and support students through awareness, reflective practices, and critical thinking within and beyond reading and writing.
4. Self-advocacy and knowledge of one's learning needs lead to empowerment, self-efficacy, and agency.
5. Success and confidence, both academically and personally, are what we seek for students to hold throughout their lives.

Over these chapters, I have tried to unpack what this looks like in practice. Whether you teach kindergarten or high school students, the integrated framework supports learners and is necessary to honor the students before us. It is a process. A path. A journey. Along the way, I asked you to pick out those small stones or nuggets of knowledge to take with you, and I ask that as you continue to step forward in your implementation of the integrated framework, you reflect on and commit to standing with our students with dyslexia on this journey as we see them take flight.

I will be there with you. Let's get to it!

Resources

Introduction

Moats, L. (2011). Knowledge and practice standards for teachers of reading: A new initiative by the International Reading Association. *Perspectives on Language and Literacy*, 37 (2): 51.

National Reading Panel (US) and National Institute of Child Health and Human Development (US). (2000). *Report of the National Reading Panel: Teaching children to read: an evidence-based assessment of the scientific research literature on reading and its implications for reading instruction*. US Dept. of Health and Human Services, Public Health Service, National Institutes of Health, National Institute of Child Health and Human Development.

Piasta, S.B., Connor, C.M., Fishman, B.J., & Morrison, F.J. (2009). Teachers' knowledge of literacy concepts, classroom practices, and student reading growth. *Scientific Studies of Reading* 13, 224–248.

The Reading League. (2023, June 1). *Science of Reading: Defining Guide*. https://www.thereadingleague.org/what-is-the- science-of-reading/.

Sohn, E. (2024, September 1). Untangling dyslexia myths and misconceptions. *Monitor on Psychology* 55 (6). https://www.apa.org/monitor/2024/09/dyslexia-myths.

Stanovich, K.E. (1986). Matthew effects in reading: Some consequences of individual differences in the acquisition of literacy. *Reading Research Quarterly* 21: 360–406.

Stanovich, K.E. (2009). Matthew effects in reading: Some consequences of individual differences in the acquisition of literacy. *Journal of Education* 189 (1–2): 23–55.

Stanovich, P.J. & Stanovich, K.E. (2003). Using research and reason in education: How can teachers use scientifically based research to make curricular and instructional decisions? National Institute of Child Health and Human Development; Department of Education; and Department of Health and Human Services.

Chapter 1

Al Otaiba, S., Connor, C.M., Foorman, B., Schatschneider, C., Greulich, L., & Sidler, J.F. (2009). Identifying and intervening with beginning readers who are at-risk for dyslexia. *Perspectives on Language and Literacy* 35 (4): 13–19.

Al Otaiba, S., Puranik, C.S., Ziolkowski, R.A., & Montgomery, T.M. (2009). Effectiveness of early phonological awareness interventions for students with speech or language impairments. *The Journal of Special Education* 43 (2): 107–128. https://doi.org/10.1177/0022466908314869.

Alabbad, M., Khan, M.A., Siddique, N., Hassan, J.A., Bashir, S., & Abualait, T. (2023). Early predictors in language-based learning disabilities: A bibliometric analysis. *Front Psychiatry* 4 (14): 1229580. doi: 10.3389/fpsyt.2023.1229580;

Allor, J.H., Mathes, P.G., Roberts, J.K., Cheatham, J.P., & Al Otaiba, S. (2014). Is scientifically based reading instruction effective for students with below-average IQs? *Exceptional Children* 80 (3): 287–306.

American Psychiatric Association. (2013). *Diagnostic and Statistical Manual of Mental Disorders* (5th ed., text revision) (DSM-5-TR). American Psychiatric Association Publishing.

American Psychiatry Association. (2024). What is specific learning disorder? https://www.psychiatry.org/patients-families/specific-learning-disorder/what-is-specific-learning-disorder.

Australian Dyslexia Association. (n.d.). What is dyslexia? https://dyslexiaassociation.org.au/what-is-dyslexia/.

British Dyslexia Association (BDA). (2010). What is dyslexia? https://www.bdadyslexia.org.uk/dyslexia/about-dyslexia/what-is-dyslexia.

Dehaene, S. (2009). *Reading in the Brain: The Science and Evolution of a Human Invention*. New York: Viking.

Dyslexia Association of Hong Kong. https://www.dyslexiahk.com/#:~:text=Dyslexia%20Association%20of%20Hong%20Kong&text=We%2.

Dyslexia Association of Ireland. (2022). What is dyslexia? https://dyslexia.ie/info-hub/about-dyslexia/what-is-dyslexia/.

Dyslexia Association of Singapore. (2019). What is dyslexia? https://das.org.sg/learning_differently/understanding-dyslexia/#:~:text=It%20is%20a%20learning%20difficulty, fluent%20word%20reading%20and%20spelling.

Erbeli, F., Rice, M., & Paracchini, S. (2021). Insights into dyslexia genetics research from the last two decades. *Brain Sciences* 12 (1): 27. doi: 10.3390/brainsci12010027.

European Dyslexia Association. (2020). What is dyslexia? https://eda-info.eu/what-is-dyslexia/.

Fletcher, J.M., Lyon, G.R., Fuchs, L.S., & Barnes, M.A. (2019). Learning disabilities: From identification to intervention (2nd ed.). Guilford Press.

Foorman, B., & Al Otaiba, S. (2009). Reading remediation: State of the art. In: *How Children Learn to Read: Current Issues and New Directions in the Integration of Cognition, Neurobiology and Genetics of Reading and Dyslexia Research and Practice* (ed. K. Pugh & P. McCardle), 257–274. New York: Psychology Press.

Francis, D.J., Shaywitz, S.E., Stuebing, K.K., Shaywitz, B.A., & Fletcher, J.M. (1996). Developmental lag versus deficit models of reading disability: A longitudinal, individual growth curves analysis. *Journal of Educational Psychology* 88 (1): 3.

Gaab, N. (2017, March). It's a myth that young children cannot be screened for dyslexia! *The IDA Examiner*. International Dyslexia Association.

Goldberg, R.J., Higgins, E.L., Raskind, M.H., & Herman, K.L. (2003). Predictors of success in individuals with learning disabilities: A qualitative analysis of a 20-year longitudinal study. *Learning Disabilities Research & Practice* 18 (4): 222–236. https://doi.org/10.1111/1540-5826.00077.

Goldberg, M., Goldenberg, C. (2020). Lessons learned? Reading wars, reading first, and a way forward. *The Reading Teacher* 75 (5): 621–630.

Goswami, U., Wang, H.L., Cruz, A., Fosker, T., Mead, N., & Huss, M. (2011). Language-universal sensory deficits in developmental dyslexia: English, Spanish, and Chinese. *Journal of Cognitive Neuroscience* 23 (2): 325–337. doi: 10.1162/jocn.2010.21453. Epub 2010 Feb 10.

Goswami, U. (2010). Phonology, reading and reading difficulties. In: *Interdisciplinary Perspectives on Learning to Read* (ed. K. Hall, U. Goswami, C. Harrison, S. Ellis, & J. Soler), 103–116 (Chapter 8).

Hasbrouck, J. (2020). Conquering dyslexia: A Guide to Early Detection and Intervention for Teachers and Families. Benchmark Education.

Hasbrouck, J. (2022). My conclusions for reading research. https://www.dropbox.com/sh/sj4whyl9x2upqbz/AAAVkwuKyU1Q-KF4Qzw6vrsva?dl=0&preview=ALL+Kids+Can+Read+Hasbrouck.pdf.

International Dyslexia Association (2002). Definition of dyslexia. https://dyslexiaida.org/definition-of-dyslexia/.

International Dyslexia Association. (2024). *Perspectives on Language and Literacy 75th Anniversary Edition*.

Juel, C. (1988). Learning to read and write: A longitudinal study of 54 children from first through fourth grades. *Journal of Educational Psychology* 80 (4): 437.

Justino, J., & Kolinsky, R. (2023). Eye movements during reading in beginning and skilled readers: Impact of reading level or physiological maturation?, Acta Psychologica 236: 103927. ISSN 0001-6918.

Kalashnikova, M., Goswami, U., & Burnham, D. (2019). Delayed development of phonological constancy in toddlers at family risk for dyslexia. *Infant Behavior and Development* 57: 101327. https://doi.org/10.1016/S0042-6989(00)00310-2.

Kilpatrick, D.A. (2015). *Essentials of Assessing, Preventing, and Overcoming Reading Difficulties*. Hoboken, NJ: Wiley.

Lim, L. et al. (2019). Using the MULTILIT literacy instruction program with children who have down syndrome. *Reading and Writing* 32: 2179–2200.

Lyon, G.R., & Goldberg, M. (2023). Scientific research and structured literacy. *Perspectives*.

Maharashtra Dyslexia Association (Mumbai). https://mdamumbai.com/.

Mather, N., & Schneider, D. The use of cognitive tests in the assessment of dyslexia. *Journal of Intelligence* 11 (5): 79. doi: 10.3390/jintelligence11050079.

Mathes, P.G. et al. (2005). The effects of theoretically different instruction and student characteristics on the skills of struggling readers. *Reading Research Quarterly* 40: 148–182.

Miller, C. (2024). What is neurodiversity? https://childmind.org/article/what-is-neurodiversity/.

Moats, L. (2011). Knowledge and practice standards for Teachers of Reading—A new initiative by the International Reading Association. *Perspectives on Language and Literacy* 37 (2): 51–52.

Moats, L.C. (2020). *Teaching Reading Is Rocket Science: What Expert Teachers of Reading Should Know and Be Able to Do*. American Federation of Teachers, 1–29.

Montgomery, J.L. (2013). A case study of the preventing academic failure Orton-Gillingham approach with five students who are deaf or hard of hearing: Using the mediating tool of cued speech. PhD thesis. Columbia University. https://doi.org/10.7916/D8QV3TQN.

Mugnaini, D., Lassi, S., La Malfa, G., & Albertini, G. (2009). Internalizing correlates of dyslexia. *World Journal of Pediatrics* 5: 255–264.

National Reading Panel. (2004). A closer look at the five essential components of effective reading instruction: A review of scientifically based reading research for teachers. US Department of Education. Learning Point Associates. https://files.eric.ed.gov/fulltext/ED512569.pdf.

Norton E.S., Beach, S.D., & Gabrieli, J.D. (2015). Neurobiology of dyslexia. *Current Opinion in Neurobiology* 30: 73–78. doi: 10.1016/j.conb.2014.09.007. Epub 2014 Oct 4.

Norton, E.S., & Wolf, M. (2012). Rapid Automatized Naming (RAN) and reading fluency: Implications for understanding and treatment of reading disabilities. *Annual Review of Psychology* 63 (1): 427–452. https://doi.org/10.1146/annurev-psych-120710-100431.

Pugh, K.R., Mencl, W.E., Shaywitz, B.A., Shaywitz, S.E., Fulbright, R.K., Constable, R.T., Skudlarski, P., Marchione, K.E., Jenner, A.R., Fletcher, J.M., Liberman, A.M., Shankweiler, D.P., Katz, L., Lacadie, C., & Gore, J.C. (2000). The angular gyrus in developmental dyslexia: Task specific differences in functional connectivity in posterior cortex. *Psychological Science* 11 (1): 51–59. https://doi.org/10.1111/1467-9280.00214.

Rashotte, C.A., MacPhee, K., & Torgeson, J.K. (2001). The effectiveness of a group reading instruction program with poor readers in multiple grades. *Learning Disability Quarterly* 24: 119–134.

Rayner, K. (2009). Eye movements and attention in reading, scene perception, and visual search. *Quarterly Journal of Experimental Psychology* 62 (8): 1457–1506. doi: 10.1080/17470 210902816461. Epub 2009 May 14.

Rayner, K., Binder, K.S., Ashby, J., & Pollatsek, A. (2001). Eye movement control in reading: word Word predictability has little influence on initial landing positions in words., *Vision Research*, Volume 41 (7): 943–954.

Rayner, K., Yang, J., Castelhano, M.S., & Liversedge, S.P. (2011). Eye movements of older and younger readers when reading disappearing text. *Psychology and Aging* 26 (1): 214–223. doi: 10.1037/a0021279.

Shaywitz, S. (2005). *Overcoming Dyslexia, Yale Center for Dyslexia and Creativity*. Random House.

Shaywitz, S. (2020). *Overcoming Dyslexia* (2nd ed., completely revised and updated). Knopf Doubleday Publishing Group.

Shaywitz, S.E. (1998). Dyslexia. *New England Journal of Medicine* 338 (5): 307–312.

Shaywitz, S.E. (2003). *Overcoming Dyslexia: A New and Complete Science-Based Program for Overcoming Reading Problems at Any Level*. New York: Knopf.

Shaywitz, S.E., Shaywitz, J.E., & Shaywitz, B.A. (2021). Dyslexia in the 21st century. *Current Opinion in Psychiatry*. 34 (2): 80–86.

Simos, P.G., Fletcher, J.M., Bergman, E., Breier, J.I., Foorman, B.R., Castillo, E.M., et al. (2002). Dyslexia-specific brain activation profile becomes normal following successful remedial training. *Neurology* 58: 1203–1213.

Stanovich, K.E. (1986). Matthew effects in reading: Some consequences of individual differences in the acquisition of literacy. *Reading Research Quarterly* 21: 360–407.

Together in Literacy. (n.d.). 10 ways you can combat the Matthew effect in your classroom. https://www.togetherinliteracy.com/blog/10-ways-you-can-combat-the-matthew-effect-in-your-classroom.

Torgesen, J.K., & Burgess, S.R. (1998). Consistency of reading-related phonological processes throughout early childhood: Evidence from longitudinal-correlational and instructional studies. In: *Word Recognition in Beginning Literacy* (ed. J.L. Metsala & L.C. Ehri), 161–188. Lawrence Erlbaum Associates Publishers.

Torgesen, J.K. (2004). Avoiding the devastating downward spiral: The evidence that early intervention prevents reading failure. *American Educator* 28 (3): 6–9, 12–13, 17–19, 45–47.

US Department of Education, Office for Civil Rights. (2010). *Free Appropriate Public Education for Students With Disabilities: Requirements Under Section 504 of the Rehabilitation Act of 1973*. Washington, D.C.

US Department of Education. Letter. https://sites.ed.gov/idea/idea-files/osep-dear-colleague-letter-on-ideaiep-terms/.

Vaughn, S., & Fletcher, J. (2020). Identifying and teaching students with significant reading problems. *American Educator* 44 (4).

Vaughn, S., & Fletcher, J.M. (2023). Helping Children with Significant Reading Problems. https://www.aft.org/ae/fall2023/vaughn_fletcher.

Vaughn, S., & Wanzek, J. (2014). Intensive interventions in reading for students with reading disabilities: Meaningful impacts. *Learning Disabilities Research & Practice* 29 (2): 46–53.

Vellutino, F.R., Fletcher, J.M., Snowling, M.J., & Scanlon, D.M. (2004). Specific reading disability (dyslexia): What have we learned in the past four decades? *Journal of Child Psychology and Psychiatry.* 45 (1): 2–40.

Vellutino, F.R., & Fletcher, J.M. (2007). Developmental dyslexia. In: *The Science of Reading: A Handbook* (ed. M.J. Snowling & C. Hulme), 362–278. Malden, MA: Blackwell Publishing.

Wanzek, J., & Vaughn, S (2007). Research-based implications from extensive early reading interventions. *School of Psychology Review* 36 (4): 541–561.

Ziegler, J.C., & Goswami, U. (2005). Reading acquisition, developmental dyslexia, and skilled reading across languages: A psycholinguistic grain size theory. *Psychological Bulletin* 131 (1): 3–29. https://doi.org/10.1037/0033-2909.131.1.3.

Chapter 2

American Speech-Language-Hearing Association (ASHA). (n.d.). Domains of Language, from Clinical Topics, Spoken Language Disorders, Language in Brief. https://www.asha.org/.

American Speech-Language-Hearing Association. (1993). Definitions of communication disorders and variations (relevant paper). https://www.asha.org/policy/rp1993-00208/.

American Speech-Language-Hearing Association. (2003). American English dialects (technical report). https://www.asha.org/policy/tr2003-00044/.

Berko Gleason, J. (2005). *The Development of Language* (6th ed.). Pearson Education.

Bishop, D.V., & Adams, C. (1990). A prospective study of the relationship between specific language impairment, phonological disorders and reading retardation. *Journal of Child Psychology and Psychiatry* 31: 1027–1050.

Bishop, D.V., McDonald, D., Bird, S., & Hayiou-Thomas, M.E. (2009). Children who read words accurately despite language impairment: Who are they and how do they do it? *Child Development* 80: 593–605.

Bishop, D.V., & Snowling, M.J. (2004). Developmental dyslexia and specific language impairment: Same or different? *Psychological Bulletin* 130: 858.

Brady, S.A., & Shankweiler, D.P. (Eds.). (1991). *Phonological Processes in Literacy: A Tribute to Isabelle Y. Liberman.* Lawrence Erlbaum Associates, Inc.

Burns, M., Griffin, P., & Snow, C. (Eds.). (1999). *Starting Out Right: A Guide to Promoting Children's Reading Success*. National Academy Press. Retrieved from http://www.nap.edu/download/6014 .

Colorado Department of Education. (2020). The role of co-morbidity in the identification and treatment of dyslexia. *Colorado Department of Education Dyslexia Handbook*. https://www.cde.state.co.us/node/43723.

Darweesh, A.M., Elserogy, Y.M., Khalifa, H. et al. (2020). Psychiatric comorbidity among children and adolescents with dyslexia. *Middle East Curr Psychiatry* 27: 28. https://doi.org/10.1186/s43045-020-00035-y.

Eunice Kennedy Shriver National Institute of Child Health and Human Development, NIH, DHHS. (2010). *Developing Early Literacy: Report of the National Early Literacy Panel* (NA). Washington, DC: US Government Printing Office.

Goldfeld, S., Snow, P., Eadie, P., Munro, J., Gold, L., Orsini, F., Connell, J., Stark, H., Watts, A., & Shingles B. (2020). Teacher knowledge of oral language and literacy constructs: Results of a randomized controlled trial evaluating the effectiveness of a professional learning intervention. *Scientific Studies of Reading* 25 (1): 1–30. https://doi.org/10.1080/10888438.2020.1714629.

Goswami, U., & Bryant, P. (1990). *Phonological Skills and Learning to Read*. Lawrence Erlbaum Associates, Inc.

International Dyslexia Association. (2002). Adopted by the IDA Board of Directors, Nov. 12, 2002. Many state education codes, including New Jersey, Ohio, and Utah, have adopted this definition. Learn more about how consensus was reached on this definition: Definition Consensus Project. https://dyslexiaida.org/definition-of-dyslexia/.

Laasonen, M., Smolander, S., Lahti-Nuuttila, P., Leminen, M., Lajunen, H.R., Heinonen, K., Pesonen, A.K., Bailey, T.M., Pothos, E.M., Kujala, T., Leppänen, P., Bartlett, C.W., Geneid, A., Lauronen, L., Service, E., Kunnari, S., & Arkkila, E. (2018). Understanding developmental language disorder—the Helsinki longitudinal SLI study (HelSLI): A study protocol. *BMC Psychology*. https://doi.org/10.1186/s40359-018-0222-7.

Liberman, I.Y., & Shankweiler, D. (1985). Phonology and the problems of learning to read and write. *Remedial and Special Education* 6 (6): 8–17. https://doi.org/10.1177/074193258500600604.

Logan, J. (2009). Dyslexic entrepreneurs: The incidence; their coping strategies and their business skills. *Dyslexia* 15 (4): 328–346. https:// doi. org/ 10.1002/dys.388.

McGrath, L.M., & Stoodley, C.J. (2019). Are there shared neural correlates between dyslexia and ADHD? A meta-analysis of voxel-based morphometry studies. *Journal of Neurodevelopmental Disorders* 11: 31. https://doi.org/10.1186/s11689-019-9287-8.

Mehta, P.D., Foorman, B.R., Martin, L., & Taylor, W.P. (2005). Literacy as a unidimensional multilevel construct: Validation sources of influence and implications in a longitudinal study in grades 1 to 4. *Scientific Studies of Reading* 9 (2): 85–116.

Moll, K., Snowling, M.J., & Hulme, C. (2020). Introduction to the special issue: Comorbidities between reading disorders and other developmental disorders. *Scientific Studies of Reading* 24 (1): 1–6. https://doi.org/10.1080/10888438.2019.1702045.

National Center for Family Literacy. (2009). *Developing Early Literacy: Report of the National Early Literacy Panel*. Washington, DC: National Institute for Literacy.

Navarrete-Arroyo, S., Virtala, P., Nie, P., Kailaheimo-Lönnqvist, L., Salonen, S., & Kujala, T. (2024). Infant mismatch responses to speech-sound changes predict language development in preschoolers at risk for dyslexia. *Clinical Neurophysiology* 162: 248–261 https://doi.org/10.1016/j.clinph.2024.02.032.

Nelson, N.W. (2014, November). Raising awareness among school professionals and school-age students. Paper presentation at the American Speech-Language-Hearing Association Convention, Orlando, FL.

Nelson, N.W., & Crumpton, T. (2015). Reading, writing, and spoken language assessment profiles for students who are deaf and hard of hearing compared with students with language learning disabilities. *Topics in Language Disorders* 35 (2): 157–179. https://doi.org/10.1097/TLD.0000000000000055.

Pennington, B.F., McGrath, L.M., & Peterson, R.L. (2019). *Diagnosing Learning Disorders: From Science to Practice* (3rd ed.). New York: The Guilford Press.

Rojas, N. (2024, April 4). Getting ahead of dyslexia. *Harvard Gazette*. https://news.harvard.edu/gazette/story/2024/04/when-does-dyslexia-develop/.

Scott, C. & Windsor, J. (2000). General language performance measures in spoken and written narrative and expository discourse of school-age children with language learning disabilities. *Journal of Speech, Language, and Hearing Research* 43: 324–339. 10.1044/jslhr.4302.324.

Shaywitz, S. (2005). *Overcoming Dyslexia, Yale Center for Dyslexia and Creativity*. Random House.

Shaywitz, S.E. (1998). Dyslexia. *New England Journal of Medicine* 338 (5): 307–312.

Shaywitz, S.E. (2003). *Overcoming Dyslexia: A New and Complete Science-Based Program for Overcoming Reading Problems at Any Level*. New York: Knopf.

Shaywitz, S.E., Shaywitz, J.E., & Shaywitz, B.A. (2021). Dyslexia in the 21st century. *Current Opinion in Psychiatry* 34 (2): 80–86.

Snow, P.C. (2024). Oral language competence is necessary but not sufficient for reading success. PowerPoint presentation at Plain Talk About Literacy and Learning Conference. New Orleans (31 January–2 February).

Snowling, M.J., Hayiou-Thomas, M.E., Nash, H.M. & Hulme, C. (2020). Dyslexia and developmental language disorder: Comorbid disorders with distinct effects on reading comprehension. *Journal of Child Psychology and Psychiatry* 61: 672–680. https://doi.org/10.1111/jcpp.13140.

Wagner, R.K., & Torgesen, J.K. (1987). The nature of phonological processing and its causal role in the acquisition of reading skills. *Psychological Bulletin* 101 (2): 192–212. https://doi.org/10.1037/0033-2909.101.2.192.

Chapter 3

Ahmed, Y., Francis, D.J., York, M., Fletcher, J.M., Barnes, M., & Kulesz, P. (2016). Validation of the direct and inferential mediation (DIME) model of reading comprehension in grades 7 through 12. *Contemporary Educational Psychology* 44: 68–82.

Bazen, L., Bree, E., Boer, M., & Jong, P. (2022). Perceived negative consequences of dyslexia: the influence of person and environmental factors. *Annals of Dyslexia* 73 (2): 214–234. doi: 10.1007/s11881-022-00274-0.

Cromley, J.G., & Azevedo, R. (2007). Testing and refining the direct and inferential mediation model of reading comprehension. *Journal of Educational Psychology* 99 (2): 311.

Francis, D.A., Caruana, N., Hudson, J.L., McArthur, G.M. (2019). The association between poor reading and internalising problems: A systematic review and meta-analysis. *Clinical Psychology Review* 67: 45–60. doi: 10.1016/j.cpr.2018.09.002. Epub 2018 Sep 15.

Lyon, G.R., Shaywitz, S.E., & Shaywitz, B.A. (2003). A definition of dyslexia. *Annals of Dyslexia* 53 (1): 1–14.

Pei, X. et al. (2023). Associations between dyslexia and children's mental health: Findings from a follow-up study in China. *Psychiatry Research* 324 (3): 115188.

Stevens, E.A., Hall, C. & Vaughn, S. (2022). Language and reading comprehension for students with dyslexia: An introduction to the special issue. *Annals of Dyslexia* 72: 197–203. https://doi.org/10.1007/s11881-022-00260-6.

Chapter 4

Andersen, S.C., & Nielsen, H.S. (2016). Reading intervention with a growth mindset approach improves children's skills. *Proceedings of the National Academy of Sciences of the United States of America* 113 (43): 12111–12113.

Becker, S., & Wong, N. (2006). *Maxwell's Mountain*. Charlesbridge.

Burns, M.K., Duke, N.K., & Cartwright, K.B. (2023). Evaluating components of the Active View of Reading as intervention targets: Implications for social justice. *School Psychology* 38 (1): 30–41. https://doi.org/10.1037/spq0000519.

Byers, G. & Bobo, K.A. (2018). *I Am Enough* (1st ed.). New York: Balzer + Bray, an imprint of HarperCollins Publishers.

Cornwall, G. (2017). *Jabari Jumps*. Somerville, MA: Candlewick Press.

Duke, N.K., & Cartwright, K.B. (2021). The science of reading progresses: Communicating advances beyond the Simple View of Reading. *Reading Research Quarterly* 56 (S1): S25–S44. https://ila.onlinelibrary.wiley.com/doi/full/10.1002/rrq.411.

Goldberg, B., & Brintnell, S. & Goldberg, J. (2002). The relationship between engagement in meaningful activities and quality of life in persons disabled by mental illness. *Occupational Therapy in Mental Health* 18 (2): 17-44. 10.1300/J004v18n02_03.

Haft, S.L., Chen, T., Leblanc, C., Tencza, F., & Hoeft, F. (2019). Impact of mentoring on socio-emotional and mental health outcomes of youth with learning disabilities and attention-deficit hyperactivity disorder. *Child and Adolescent Mental Health* 24, 318–328. doi: 10.1111/camh.12331.

Haft, S.L., Myers, C.A., & Hoeft, F. (2016). Socio-emotional and cognitive resilience in children with reading disabilities. *Current Opinion in Behavioral Sciences* 10, 133–141. 10.1016/j/cobeha.2016.06.005.

Hedenius, M., Ullman, M.T., Alm, P., Jennische, M., & Persson, J. (2013). Enhanced recognition memory after incidental encoding in children with developmental dyslexia. *PLOS One* 8 (5): e63998. https://doi.org/ 10.1371/journal.pone.0063998.

Hossain, B., Chen, Y., Bent, S., Parenteau, C., Widjaja, F., Haft, S., Hoeft, F., & Hendren, R. (2021). The role of grit and resilience in children with reading disorder: A longitudinal cohort study. *Annals of Dyslexia* 72: 1–27. 10.1007/s11881-021-00238-w.

International Dyslexia Association (2002); Adopted by the IDA Board of Directors, Nov. 12, 2002. Many state education codes, including New Jersey, Ohio, and Utah, have adopted this definition. Learn more about how consensus was reached on this definition: *Definition Consensus Project*. https://dyslexiaida.org/definition-of-dyslexia/.

John, J., & Oswald, P. (2021). *The Smart Cookie* (1st ed.). New York: Harper, an imprint of HarperCollins Publishers.

Kranz, L. (2006). *Only One You*. Cooper Square Publishing. ISBN-10. 0873589017; ISBN-13. 978-0873589017.

Llistosella, M., Torné, C., García-Ortiz, M., López-Hita, G., Ortiz, R., Herández-Montero, L., Guallart, E., Uña-Solbas, E., & Miranda-Mendizabal, A. (2023). Fostering resilience in adolescents at risk: Study protocol for a cluster randomized controlled trial within the resilience school-based intervention. *Frontiers in Psychology* 13. https://doi.org/10.3389/fpsyg.2022.1066874.

Lovett, M.W., Frijters, J.C., Steinbach, K A., Sevcik, R.A., & Morris, R.D. (2021). Effective intervention for adolescents with reading disabilities: Combining reading and motivational remediation to improve outcomes. *Journal of Educational Psychology* 113 (4): 656–689. https://doi.org/10.1037/edu0000639.

Marks, R.A., Norton, R.T., Mesite, L., Fox, A.B., & Christodoulou, J.A. (2023). Risk and resilience correlates of reading among adolescents with language-based learning disabilities during COVID-19. *Reading and Writing* 36 (2):401–428. doi: 10.1007/s11145-022-10361-8. Epub 2022 Nov 11.

Ofiesh, N.S., & Mather, N. (2023). Resilience and the child with learning disabilities. In: *Handbook of Resilience in Children* (3rd ed.) (ed. S. Goldstein & R. B. Brooks), 469–494. Springer Nature Switzerland AG. https://doi.org/10.1007/978-3-031-14728-9_25.

Orkin, M., Vanacore, K., Rhinehart, L., Gotlieb, R., & Wolf, M. (2022). The importance of being fluent: A comprehensive approach. *The Reading League* 3 (2): 4–13.

Orton, S.T. (1928). Specific reading disability—strephosymbolia. *Journal of the American Medical Association* 90 (14): 1095–1099.

Palacio, R.J. (2017). *We're All Wonders*. Puffin.

Palser, E.R. et al. (2021). Children with developmental dyslexia show elevated parasympathetic nervous system activity at rest and greater cardiac deceleration during an empathy task. *Biological Psychology* 166 (108203): 1–12. https://doi.org/10.1016/j.biopsycho.2021.108203.

Saltzberg, B. (2010). *Beautiful Oops!* New York: Workman Publishing.

Schneps, M. H., Brockmole, J. R., Sonnert, G., & Pomplun, M. (2012). History of reading struggles linked to enhanced learning in low spatial frequency scenes. *PLOS One* 7 (4): e35724. https:// doi.org/10.1371 journalpone.0035724.

Shaywitz, S. (2005). *Overcoming Dyslexia*. Random House.

Shaywitz, S.E. (1998). Dyslexia. *New England Journal of Medicine* 338 (5): 307–312.

Shaywitz, S.E., Shaywitz, J.E., & Shaywitz, B.A. (2021). Dyslexia in the 21st century. *Current Opinion in Psychiatry* 34 (2): 80–86.

Shaywitz, S.E. (2003). *Overcoming Dyslexia: A New and Complete Science-Based Program for Overcoming Reading Problems at Any Level*. New York: Knopf.

Spires, Ashley. (2023). *The Most Magnificent Maker's A to Z*. Toronto: Kids Can Press.

Sturm, V.E., et al. (2021). Enhanced visceromotor emotional reactivity in dyslexia and its relation to salience network connectivity. *Cortex* 134 (278): 295. https://doi.org/10.1016/j.cortex.2020.10.022.

Von Karolyi, C., Winner, E., Gray, W., & Sherman, G.F. (2003). Dyslexia linked to talent: Global visual-spatial ability. *Brain and Language* 85 (3): 427–431. https://doi.org/10.1016/S0093-934X(03)00052-X.

Williams, C.J., Chen, J.M., Quirion, A., & Hoeft, F. (2024). Peer mentoring for students with learning disabilities: The importance of shared experience on students' social and emotional development. *Frontiers in Education* 9: 1292717. https://doi.org/10.3389/feduc.2024.1292717.

Wolf, M., Gotlieb, R.J.M., Kim, S.A. et al. (2024). Towards a dynamic, comprehensive conceptualization of dyslexia. *Annals of Dyslexia* 74: 303–324. https://doi.org/10.1007/s11881-023-00297-1.

Wolff, U., & Lundberg, I. (2002). The prevalence of dyslexia among art students. *Dyslexia* 8 (1): 34–42. https://doi.org/10.1002/dys.211.

Zheng, C., Erickson, A.G., Kingston, N.M., Noonan, P.M. (2014). The relationship among self-determination, self-concept, and academic achievement for students with learning disabilities. *Journal of Learning Disabilities* 47: 462–474. doi:10.1177/0022219412469688.

Chapter 5

American Federation of Teachers. (1999). Teaching reading is rocket science. https://www.louisamoats.com/Assets/Reading.is.Rocket.Science.pdf.

Birsh, J.R. (2005). *Multisensory Teaching of Basic Language Skills: Research and Reading Disability*. Brooks Publishing.

Duke, N.K., & Cartwright, K.B. (2021). The science of reading progresses: Communicating advances beyond the simple view of reading. *Reading Research Quarterly* 56 (S1): S25–S44. https://doi.org/10.1002/rrq.411.

Gough, P.B., & Tunmer, W.E. (1986). Decoding, reading, and reading disability. *Remedial and Special Education* 7 (1): 6–10. https://doi. org/10.1177/074193258600700104.

Hardiman, M. (2003). *Connecting Brain Research with Effective Teaching: The Brain-Targeted Teaching Model*. Lanham, MD: Scarecrow Press.

Hardiman, M., Rinne, L., Gregory, E., & Yarmolinskaya, J. (2012). Neuroethics, neuroeducation, and classroom teaching: Where the brain sciences meet pedagogy. *Neuroethics* 5 (2): 135–143. https://doi.org/10.1007/s12152-011-9116-6.

Harris, K.R., & Graham, S. (1996). *Making the Writing Process Work: Strategies for Composition and Self-regulation*. Cambridge, MA: Brookline Books.

Hoover, W.A., & Gough, P.B. (1990). The simple view of reading. *Reading and Writing* 2 (2): 127–160. https://link.springer.com/article/10.1007/BF00401799.

Hoover, W.A., & Tunmer, W.E. (2018). The simple view of reading: Three assessments of its adequacy. *Remedial and Special Education* 39 (5): 304–312. https://journals.sagepub. com/doi/10.1177/0741932518773154.

Hoover, W.A., & Tunmer, W.E. (2020). The Cognitive Foundations of Reading and its Acquisition. Dordrecht, Netherlands: Springer.

Hudson, R.F., High, L., & Al Otaiba, S. (2011). Dyslexia and the brain: What does current research tell us? *The Reading Teacher* 60 (6): 506–515.

Jensen, E. (2000). *Brain-based Learning: The New Science of Teaching and Training*, 3–4. San Diego: The Brain Store.

Maughan, B., & Carroll, J. (2006). Literacy and mental disorders. *Current Opinion in Psychiatry* 19 (4): 35 0–354. https://doi.org/10.1097/01.yco.0000228752.79990.41.

Moats, L.C. (2020). Teaching reading is rocket science, 2020. https://www.aft.org/sites/ default/files/moats.pdf.

National Reading Panel. (2004). A closer look at the five essential components of effective reading instruction: A review of scientifically based reading research for teachers. US Dept of Education, Learning Point Associates. https://files.eric.ed.gov/fulltext/ED51 2569.pdf.

Saralegui, I., Ontañón, J.M., Fernandez-Ruanova, B., Garcia-Zapirain, B., Basterra, A., & Sanz-Arigita, E.J. (2014). Reading networks in children with dyslexia compared to children with ocular motility disturbances revealed by fMRI. *Frontiers in Human Neuroscience* 8. https://doi.org/10.3389/fnhum.2014.00936.

Scaborough, H.S. (2001). Connecting early language and literacy to later reading (dis) abilities: Evidence, theory, and practice. In: *Handbook for Research in Early Literacy* (ed. S. Neuman & D. Dickinson), 97–110. New York: Guilford Press.

Seidenberg, M. (2017). Language at the Speech of Sight: How We Read, Why So Many Can't, and What Can Be Done About It. New York: Basic Books.

Shaywitz, B.A., Shaywitz, S.E., Blachman, B.A., Pugh, K.R., Fulbright, R.K., Skudlarski, P., et al. (2004). Development of left occipitotemporal systems for skilled reading in children after a phonologically-based intervention. *Biological Psychiatry* 55: 926–933.

Shaywitz, B.A., Shaywitz, S.E., Pugh, K.R., Mencl, W.E., Fulbright, R.K., Skudlarksi, P., et al. (2002). Disruption of posterior brain systems for reading in children with developmental dyslexia. *Biological Psychiatry* 52: 101–110.

Shaywitz, S.E. (1996). Dyslexia. *Scientific American* 275 (5): 98–104.

Shaywitz, S.E., Fletcher, J.M., Holahan, J.M., Shneider, A.E., Marchione, K.E., Stuebing, K.K., et al. (1999). Persistence of dyslexia: The Connecticut Longitudinal Study at adolescence. *Pediatrics* 104: 1351–1359.

Shaywitz, S.E., Shaywitz, B.A., Fletcher, J.M., & Escobar, M.D. (1990). Prevalence of reading disability in boys and girls: Results of the Connecticut Longitudinal Study. *Journal of the American Medical Association* 264: 998–1002.

Shaywitz, S.E., Shaywitz, B.A., Fulbright, R.K., Skudlarski, P., Mencl, W.E., Constable, R.T., et al. (2003). Neural systems for compensation and persistence: Young adult outcome of childhood reading disability. *Biological Psychiatry* 54: 25–33.

Shaywitz, S.E., Shaywitz, B.A., Pugh, K.R., Fulbright, R.K., Constable, R.T., Mencl, W.E., et al. (1998). Functional disruption in the organization of the brain for reading in dyslexia. *Proceedings of the National Academy of Sciences* 95: 2636–2641.

Sohn, E. (2024). Untangling dyslexia myths and misconceptions. *Monitor on Psychology* 55 (6): 40. https://www.apa.org/monitor/2024/09/dyslexia-myths.

Sturm, V.E. et al. (2021). Enhanced visceromotor emotional reactivity in dyslexia and its relation to salience network connectivity. *Cortex* 134 (278): 295. https://doi.org/10.1016/j.cortex.2020.10.022.

US Department of Education, Institute of Education Sciences, National Center for Education Statistics, National Assessment of Educational Progress (NAEP). (2002). NAEP report card: 2022 NAEP reading assessment. *The Nation's Report Card*. https://www.nationsreportcard.gov/highlights/reading/2022/.

US Department of Education, National Center for Education Statistics, Program for the International Assessment of Adult Competencies (PIAAC). (2019). Adult literacy in the United States. https://nces.ed.gov/pubs2019/2019179/index.asp#:~:text=This%20tran slates%20into%2043.0%20million%20U.S.%20adults,cognitive%20or%20physical%20in ability%20to%20be%20interviewed.

Wolf, M., Gotlieb, R. Kim, S., Pedrova, V., Rhinehart, L., Gorno-Tempini, M.L., & Sears, S. (2024). Towards a dynamic, comprehensive conceptualization of dyslexia. *Annals of Dyslexia* 74: 1–22. 10.1007/s11881-023-00297-1.

Chapter 6

Archer, A., & Hughes, C.A. (2011). *Explicit Instruction: Effective and Efficient Teaching*. New York: Guilford Press.

Birsh, J. (ed.) (2011). *Multisensory Teaching of Basic Language Skills* (3rd ed.). Baltimore: Brookes Publishing.

Caravolas, M., Hulme, C., & Snowling, M.J. (2001). The foundations of spelling ability: Evidence from a 3-year longitudinal study. *Journal of Memory and Language* 45 (4): 751–774. https://doi.org/10.1006/jmla.2000.2785.

Catts, H.W., Nielsen, D.C., Bridges, M.S., Liu, Y. & Bontempo, D. (2015). Early identification of reading disabilities within a RTI framework. *Journal of Learning Disabilities* 48: 281–297.

Cowen. C. (2016). What is structured literacy? *International Dyslexia Association*. https://dyslexiaida.org/what-is-structured-literacy/.

Ehri, L.C. (2005). Learning to read words: Theory, findings and issues. *Scientific Studies of Reading* 9: 167–188.

Ehri, L.C., Dreyer, L.G., Flugman, B., & Gross, A. (2007). Reading rescue: An effective tutoring intervention model for language-minority students who are struggling readers in first grade. *American Educational Research Journal* 44 (2): 414–448.

Eunice Kennedy Shriver National Institute of Child Health and Human Development, NIH, DHHS. (2000). Report of the National Reading Panel: Teaching children to read: reports of the subgroups (00-4754). Washington, DC: US Government Printing Office.

Flynn, L.J., Zheng, X., & Swanson, H.L. (2012). Instructing struggling older readers: A selective meta-analysis of intervention research. *Learning Disabilities Research & Practice* 27 (1): 21–32. https://doi.org/10.111/j.1540-5826.2011.00347.x.

Foulin, J.N. (2005). Why is letter-name knowledge such a good predictor of learning to read? *Reading and Writing: An Interdisciplinary Journal* 18 (2): 129–155. https://doi.org/10.1007/s11145-004-5892-2.

Gallagher, A., Frith, U., & Snowling, M.J. (2000). Precursors of literacy delay among children at genetic risk of dyslexia. *Journal of Child Psychology and Psychiatry* 41 (2): 202–213. https://doi.org/10.1017/S0021963099005284.

Gersten, R., Haymond., K. Newman-Gonchar, R., Dimino, J., & Jayanthi, M. (2020). Meta-analysis of the impact of reading interventions for students in the primary grades. *Journal of Research on Educational Effectiveness* 13 (2): 401–427. https://doi.org/10.1080/19345747.2019.1689591.

Giant Leaps Speech Therapy. (2020). Structured literacy: Effective instruction for students with dyslexia and related reading difficulties. https://www.giantleaps.nz/blog/structured-literacy-for-reading-success.

Gough, P.B., Hoover, W.A., & Peterson, C.L. (1996). Some observations on a simple view of reading. In: *Reading Comprehension Difficulties: Processes and Intervention* (ed. C. Cornoldi & J. Oakhill), 1–13. Mahwah, NJ: Erlbaum.

Guajardo, N.R., & Cartwright, K.B. (2024). Structured literacy: Grounded in the science of reading. *Perspectives on Language and Literacy* 50 (1): 14–15.

Herrera, S., Truckenmiller, A.J., & Foorman, B.R. (2016). *Summary of 20 years of research on the effectiveness of adolescent literacy programs and practices (REL 2016-178)*. U.S. Department of Education, Institute of Education Sciences, National Center for Education Evaluation and Regional Assistance, Regional Educational Laboratory Southeast.

International Dyslexia Association (2024). *Perspectives on Language and Literacy* 50 (1). International Dyslexia Association, Inc. DyslexiaIDA.org. Used with permission.

International Reading Association and National Association for the Education of Young Children. (1998). Learning to read and write: Developmentally appropriate practices for young children. A joint position statement of the International Reading Association and the National Association for the Education of Young Children. Retrieved from www.naeyc.org/files/naeyc/file/positions/PSREAD98.PDF.

Leppänen, U., Aunola, K., Niemi, P., & Nurmi, J.-E. (2008). Letter knowledge predicts grade 4 reading fluency and reading comprehension. *Learning and Instruction* 18 (6): 548–564. https://doi.org/10.1016/j.learninstruc.2007.11.004.

Moats, L. (2016, January). Allegiance to the facts: A better approach for dyslexic students. IDA Examiner. https://dyslexiaida.org/allegiance-to-thefacts-best-approach-for-students-with-dyslexia/.

Moats, L. (2020). Structured literacy: Effective instruction for students with dyslexia. *International Dyslexia Association*. https://dyslexiaida.org/structured-literacy-effective-instruction-for-students-with-dyslexia-and-related-reading-difficulties/.

Moats, L.C. (2017). Can prevailing approaches to reading instruction accomplish the goals of RTI? *Perspectives on Language and Literacy* 43: 15–22.

Moats, L.C., Dakin, K., & Joshi, M. (eds.) (2012). *Expert Perspectives on Interventions for Reading*. Baltimore, MD: International Dyslexia Association.

Moats, L.C. (2020). Teaching reading is rocket science, 2020. https://www.aft.org/sites/default/files/moats.pdf.

National Early Literacy Panel (2008). *Developing Early Literacy*. Washington, DC: National Institute for Literacy.

National Reading Panel, *Teaching Children to Read*. https://www.nichd.nih.gov/sites/default/files/publications/pubs/nrp/Documents/report.pdf.

O'Malley, K., Francis, D.J., Foorman, B.R., Fletcher, J.M., & Swank, P.R. (2002). Growth in precursor and reading-related skills: Do low-achieving and IQ-discrepant readers develop differently? *Learning Disabilities Research and Practice* 17 (1): 19–34. doi:10.1111/1540-5826.00029.

Reading League. (n.d.). The science of reading. https://www.thereadingleague.org/what-is-the-science-of-reading/.

Rivera, M.O., Moughamian, A.C., Lesaux, N.K., & Francis, D.J. (2008). *Language and Reading Interventions for English Language Learners and English Language Learners with Disabilities*. Portsmouth, NH: RMC Research Corporation, Center on Instruction.

Schatschneider, C., Fletcher, J.M., Francis, D.J., Carlson, C.D., & Foorman, B.R. (2004). Kindergarten prediction of reading skills: A longitudinal comparative analysis. *Journal of Educational Psychology* 96 (2): 265–282.

Spear-Swerling, L. (2018). Structured literacy and typical literacy practices: Understanding differences to create instructional opportunities. *Teaching Exceptional Children* 51 (3): 201–211. https://doi.org/10.1177/0040059917750160.

Where Learning Takes Flight. https://www.thedyslexiaclassroom.com/blog?tag=phonemic+awareness.

Chapter 7

Adams, M.J. (1990). *Beginning to read: Thinking and learning about print*. Cambridge: The MIT Press.

Birsh, J. (ed.) (2011). *Multisensory Teaching of Basic Language Skills* (3rd ed.) Baltimore: Brookes Publishing.

Castiglioni-Spalten, M.L., & Ehri, L.C. (2003). Phonemic awareness instruction: Contribution of articulatory segmentation to novice beginners' reading and spelling. *Scientific Studies of Reading* 7 (1): 25–52. https://doi.org/10.1207/S1532799XSSR0701_03.

Esplendori, G.F., Kobayashi, R.M., & Püschel, V.A.A. (2022). Multisensory integration approach, cognitive domains, meaningful learning: Reflections for undergraduate nursing education. Revista da Escola de Enfermagem da USP. 2022 11;56:e20210381. doi: 10.1590/1980-220X-REEUSP-2021-0381.

Farrell, M., Pickering, J., North, N., & Schavio, C. (2004). What is multisensory instruction? *The IMSLEC Record* 8 (3).

Ferreira, F.M., & Vasconcelos, C. (2020). The impact of multisensory instruction on geosciences learning and students' motivation. *Geosciences* 10 (11): 467. https://doi.org/10.3390/geosciences10110467.

International Dyslexia Association (2002); Adopted by the IDA Board of Directors, Nov. 12, 2002. Many state education codes, including New Jersey, Ohio and Utah, have adopted this definition. Learn more about how consensus was reached on this definition: *Definition Consensus Project*. https://dyslexiaida.org/definition-of-dyslexia/.

Lovell, O. (2021). *Sweller's cognitive load theory in action*. John Catt Educational.

Okray, Z., Jacob, P.F., Stern, C. et al. Multisensory learning binds neurons into a cross-modal memory engram. *Nature* 617, 777–784 (2023). https://doi.org/10.1038/s41586-023-06013-8.

Perspectives on Language and Literacy 75th Anniversary Edition (2024). International Dyslexia Association.

Shimojo, S., & Shams, L. (2001). Sensory modalities are not separate modalities: plasticity and interactions. *Current Opinion in Neurobiology* 11 (4): 505–509. ISSN 0959-4388, https://doi.org/10.1016/S0959-4388(00)00241-5.

Thorpe, H.W., & Borden, K.S. (1985). The effect of multisensory instruction upon the on-task behaviors and word reading accuracy of learning disabled children. *Journal of Learning Disabilities* 18 (5): 279–286. https://doi.org/10.1177/002221948501800507.

Willingham, D.T. (2009). *Why Don't Students Like School?: A Cognitive Scientist Answers Questions About How the Mind Works and What It Means for the Classroom*. Jossey-Bass.

Chapter 8

Alberto, P.A., Troutman, A.C. (2005). *Applied Behavior Analysis for Teachers*. Upper Saddle River, NJ: Prentice-Hall.

Benson, B. (1997). Scaffolding (coming to terms). *English Journal* 86 (7): 126–127.

Collins, A., Brown, J.S., & Holum, A. (1991). Cognitive apprenticeship: making thinking visible. *American Educator* 15 (3): 6–11, 38–39.

Durkin, D. (1979). What classroom observations reveal about reading comprehension. *Reading Research Quarterly* 14: 581–544.

Elliot, K., Frey, N. & Fisher, D. (2019), Leading learning through a gradual release of responsibility instructional framework. In: *The Gradual Release of Responsibility in Literacy Research and Practice* (ed. M.B. McVee, E. Ortlieb, J.S. Reichenberg, & P.D. Pearson), 91–102. Literacy Research, Practice and Evaluation 10. Leeds: Emerald Publishing Limited.

Engelmann, S. (1992). *War Against the Schools' Academic Child Abuse*. Portland: Halcyon House.

Engelmann, S. (1998). *Vita*. Eugene, OR: College of Education, University of Oregon.

Engelmann, S. & Carnine, D. (1991). *Theory of Instruction: Principles and Applications.* Eugene, OR: ADI Press.

Fisher, D. (2008). *Effective Use of the Gradual Release of Responsibility Model.* New York: Macmillan/McGraw-Hill.   https://www.mheonline.com/treasures/pdf/douglas_fisher.pdf.

Fisher, D. & Frey, N. (2008). Releasing responsibility: Giving students ownership of learning. *Educational Leadership* 66 (3).

Fisher, D. & Frey, N. (2013). *Gradual Release of Responsibility Instructional Framework*. IRA E-ssentials 1–8. 10.1598/e-ssentials.8037.

Frey, N., Fisher, D., & Almarode, J. (2023). *How Scaffolding Works: A Playbook for Supporting and Releasing Responsibility to Students.* Corwin.

Fuchs, L. S., Fuchs, D., & Malone A.S. (2017). The taxonomy of intervention intensity. *Teaching Exceptional Children* 50 (1): 35–43.

Kame'enui, E.J., Carnine, D.W., Dixon, R.C., Simmons, D.C., & Coyne, M.D. (2002). *Effective Teaching Strategies That Accommodate Diverse Learners* (2nd ed.). Upper Saddle River, NJ: Merrill Prentice Hall.

Larkin, M. (2002). Using scaffolded instruction to optimize learning. *ERIC Digest*. ERIC Clearinghouse on Disabilities and Gifted Education. Arlington, VA.

Lin, N.C., & Cheng, H. (2010). Effects of gradual release of responsibility model on language learning. *Procedia—Social and Behavioral Sciences* 2 (2): 1866–1870. https://doi.org/10.1016/j.sbspro.2010.03.1000.

Maurice, C., Green, G., & Foxx, R.M. (2001). *Making a Difference: Behavioral Intervention for Autism*. Austin, TX: Pro-Ed.

Pearson, P.D., & Gallagher, M.C. (1983). The instruction of reading comprehension. *Contemporary Educational Psychology* 8 (3): 317–344. https://doi.org/10.1016/0361-476X(83)90019-X.

Rosenshine, B. & Meister, C. (1992). The use of scaffolds for teaching higher-level cognitive strategies. *Educational Leadership* 49 (7): 26–33.

Tajeddin, Z., Alemi, M., & Kamrani, Z. (2020). Functions and strategies of teachers' discursive scaffolding in English-medium content-based instruction. *Iranian Journal of Language Teaching Research* 8 (3): 1–24.

Wood, D., Bruner, J.S., & Ross, G. (1976). The role of tutoring in problem solving. *Journal of Child Psychology and Psychiatry* 17: 89–100.

Chapter 9

Acadience site. https://acadiencelearning.org/.

Arnbak, E. & Elbro, C. (2000). The effects of morphological awareness training on the reading and spelling skills of young dyslexics. *Scandinavian Journal of Educational Research* 44: 229–251. 10.1080/00313830050154485.

Berninger, V.W., Abbott, R.D., Jones, J., Wolf, B.J., Gould, L., Anderson-Youngstrom, M., Shimada, S., & Apel, K. (2006). Early development of language by hand: Composing, reading, listening, and speaking connections; three letter-writing modes; and fast mapping in spelling. *Developmental Neuropsychology* 29 (1): 61–92. doi: 10.1207/s15326942dn2901_5.

Berninger, V. W., & Wolf, B. J. (2009). Teaching students with dyslexia and dysgraphia: Lessons from teaching and science. Paul H. Brookes Publishing Co.

Bloom, B.S. (1968). Learning for mastery. Instruction and curriculum. Regional Education Laboratory for the Carolinas and Virginia, Topical Papers and Reprints, no. 1.

Boyer, N. & Ehri, L.C. (2011). Contribution of phonemic segmentation instruction with letters and articulation pictures to word reading and spelling in beginners. *Scientific Studies of Reading* 15 (5): 440–470.

Brady, S., Shankweiler, D., & Mann, V. (1983). Speech perception and memory coding in relation to reading ability. *Journal of Experimental Child Psychology* 35 (2): 345–367. http://dx.doi.org/10.1016/0022-0965(83)90087-5.

Castiglioni-Spalten, M. & Ehri L.C. (2003). Phonemic awareness instruction: Contribution of articulatory segmentation to novice beginners' reading and spelling. *Scientific Studies of Reading* 7 (1): 25.

Catts H.W. (1986). Speech production/phonological deficits in reading-disordered children. *Journal of Learning Disabilities* 19 (8): 504–508. http://dx.doi.org/10.1177/002221948601900813.

Cox, A.R. (1967, 1992). *Structures and Techniques—Multisensory Teaching of Basic Language Skills*. Educators Publishing Service.

Ehri, L.C. (2005). Learning to read words: Theory, findings and issues. *Scientific Studies of Reading* 9: 167–188.

Ehri, L.C. (2014). Orthographic mapping in the acquisition of sight word reading: Spelling, memory, and vocabulary learning. *Scientific Studies of Reading* 18 (1): 5–21. https://doi.10.1080/10888438.2013.819356.

Elbro, C., & Arnbak, E. (1996). The role of morpheme recognition and morphological awareness in dyslexia. *Annals of Dyslexia*. 46 (1): 209–240. doi: 10.1007/BF02648177.

Eunice Kennedy Shriver National Institute of Child Health and Human Development, NIH, DHHS. (2000). Report of the National Reading Panel: Teaching children to read: Reports of the subgroups (00-4754). Washington, DC: US Government Printing Office.

Farquharson, K., Centanni, T.M., Franzluebbers, C.E., & Hogan, T.P. (2014). Phonological and lexical influences on phonological awareness in children with specific language impairment and dyslexia. *Frontiers in Psychology* 5. http://dx.doi.org/10.3389/fpsyg.2014.00838.

Foulin, J. N. (2005). Why is letter-name knowledge such a good predictor of learning to read? *Reading and Writing: An Interdisciplinary Journal* 18 (2): 129–155. https://doi.org/10.1007/s11145-004-5892-2.

Gillingham, A., & Stillman, B.W. (1960). *Remedial Training for Children with Specific Disability In Reading, Spelling, and Penmanship*. Cambridge, MA: Educators Publishing Service.

Gillingham, A., & Stillman, B. W. (1997). *The Gillingham Manual: Remedial Training for Children with Specific Disability in Reading, Spelling, and Penmanship* (8th ed.). Cambridge, MA: Educators Publishing Service.

Gillon, G.T., (2003). *Phonological Awareness: From Research to Practice*. Guilford Press.

Hasbrouck & Glaser (2018). Reading fluently does not mean reading fast (literacy leadership brief). International Literacy Association.

Kamhi, A G., Catts, H.W., & Mauer D. (1990). Explaining speech production deficits in poor readers. *Journal of Learning Disabilities* 23: 631–636. http://dx.doi.org/10.1177/002221949002301012.

National Reading Panel. (2000). Teaching children to read: An evidence-based assessment of the scientific research literature on reading and its implications for reading instruction. NIH Pub. No. 00-4769.

National Reading Panel. (2004). A closer look at the five essential components of effective reading instruction: A review of scientifically based reading research for teachers. US Department of Education. Learning Point Associates. https://files.eric.ed.gov/fulltext/ED512569.pdf.

O'Shea, L., & Sindelar, P. (1983). The effects of segmenting written discourse on the reading comprehension of low- and high-performance readers. *Reading Research Quarterly* 18 (4): 458–465.

Togesen, J.K. (1996). A model of memory from an information processing perspective: The special case of phonological memory. In: *Attention, Memory, and Executive Function* (ed. G.R. Lyon & N.A. Krasnegor), 157–184. Paul H. Brookes Publishing Co.

Chapter 10

Casale, C., et al. Developing empathetic learners. *Journal of Thought* 52 (3–4): 3–18. https://www.jstor.org/stable/90026734.

Cushman, K. (1995). Less is more: The secret of being essential. *Horace* 11 (2).

Cushman, K. (2005). *Fires in the Bathroom: Advice for Teachers from High School Students*. New York: New Press.

Cushman, K. (2006). Help us make the 9th grade transition. *Educational Leadership* 63 (7): 47–52.

Dore, R.A., Amendum, S.J., Golinkoff, R.M., et al. Theory of mind: A hidden factor in reading comprehension? *Educational Psychology Review* 30: 1067–1089 (2018). https://doi.org/10.1007/s10648-018-9443-9.

Hammond, Z. (2014). *Culturally Responsive Teaching and the Brain*. Corwin.

Healey, M.L., & Grossman, M. (2018). Cognitive and affective perspective-taking: Evidence for shared and dissociable anatomical substrates. *Frontiers in Psychology* 9: 491. doi:10.3389/fneur.2018.00491.

Hoffman, E. (1988). *The Right to Be Human: A Biography of Abraham Maslow*. Los Angeles: Jeremy P. Tarcher.

Hoffman, M. (2018). Culturally responsive teaching—Part 2: Pedagogical considerations and teacher–student relationships. National Association of School Psychologists. *Communique*, 47 (3): 12–15.

Kenrick, D.T., Neuberg, S.L., Griskevicius, V., Becker, D.V., & Schaller, M. (2010). Goal-driven cognition and functional behavior: The fundamental-motives framework. *Current Directions in Psychological Science* 19 (1): 63–67.

Kleinfeld, J. (1975). Effective teachers of Eskimo and Indian students. *School Review* 83: 301–344.

Laird, L. (2015). Empathy in the Classroom: Can music bring us more in tune with one another? *Music Educators Journal* 101 (4): 56–61. http://www.jstor.org/stable/24755601.

Maslow, A.H. (1943). A theory of human motivation. *Psychological Review* 50 (4): 370–396.

Maslow, A.H. (1954). *Motivation and Personality*. New York: Harper and Row.

Maxwell, B. (2017). Pursuing the aim of compassionate empathy in higher education. In: *The Pedagogy of Compassion at the Heart of Higher Education* (ed. P. Gibbs), 33–48. doi:10.1007/978-3-319-57783-8_3.

McLeod, S. (2024). Maslow's hierarchy of needs. *Simply Psychology*. https://simplypsychology.org/maslow.html.

Ratka, A. (2018). Empathy and the development of affective skills. *American Journal of Pharmaceutical Education* 82 (10): 7192. doi:10.5688/ajpe7192.

Safir, S. (2019). Becoming a warm demander. *ASCD* 76 (6). https://ascd.org/el/articles/becoming-a-warm-demander.

Tamkeen, Z. (2023). The importance of incorporating holistic and invitational approaches in an elementary school in Karnataka, India. Master thesis. Brock University. https://core.ac.uk/download/564023268.pdf.

Wahba, M.A., & Bridwell, L.G. (1976). Maslow reconsidered: A review of research on the need hierarchy theory. *Organizational Behavior and Human Performance* 15 (2): 212–240.

Wellman, H. M., D. Cross, & J. Watson. 2001. Meta-analysis of theory-of-mind development: The truth about false belief. *Child Development* 72: 655–684.

Chapter 11

Altemeier, L.E., Abbott, R.D., & Berninger, V.W. (2008). Executive functions for reading and writing in typical literacy development and dyslexia. *Journal of Clinical and Experimental Neuropsychology* 30 (5): 588–606. doi: 10.1080/13803390701562818.

Baddeley, A.D., & Andrade, J. (2000). Working memory and the vividness of imagery. *Journal of Experimental Psychology: General*, 129 (1): 126–145.

Barkley, R.A. (2012). Executive Functions: What they are, how they work, and why they evolved. New York: The Guilford Press.

Bermúdez, J. (2018). Inner speech, determinacy, and thinking consciously about thoughts. In: *Inner Speech: New Voices* (ed. P. Langland-Hassan, & A. Vicente), 199–220. Oxford. https://doi.org/10.1093/oso/9780198796640.003.0008.

Bjork, R.A., Dunlosky, J., & Kornell, N. (2013). Self-regulated learning: Beliefs, techniques, and illusions. *Annual Review of Psychology* 64: 417–444. doi: 10.1146/annurev-psych-1130 11-143823. Epub 2012 Sep 27.

Blankenship, T.L., Slough, M.A., Calkins, S.D., Deater-Deckard, K., Kim-Spoon, J., & Bell, M.A. (2019). Attention and executive functioning in infancy: Links to childhood executive function and reading achievement. *Developmental Science* 22 (5): e12824.

Borkowski, J.G., Carr, M., Rellinger, E., & Pressley, M. (1990). Self-regulated cognition: Interdependence of metacognition, attributions, and self–esteem. In: *Dimensions of Thinking and Cognitive Instruction* (ed. B.F. Jones & L. Idol), 53–92. Hillsdale, NJ: Lawrence Erlbaum.

Brunstein, J.C., Schultheiss, O.C., & Grässmann, R. (1998). Personal goals and emotional well-being: The moderating role of motive dispositions. *Journal of Personality and Social Psychology* 75 (2): 494–508. doi: 10.1037//0022-3514.75.2.494.

Chapman, J.W., & Tunmer W.E. (2003). Reading difficulties, reading-related self-perceptions, and strategies for overcoming negative self–beliefs. *Reading and Writing Quarterly* 19 (1): 5–24.

Chu Ho, E.S. (2018). Reading engagement and reading literacy performance: Effective policy and practices at home and in school. *Journal of Research in Reading* 41 (4): 657–679. https://doi.org/10.1111/1467-9817.12246.

Conklin, H.M., Luciana, M., Hooper, C.J., & Yarger, R.S. (2007). Working memory performance in typically developing children and adolescents: Behavioral evidence of protracted frontal lobe development. *Developmental Neuropsychology* 31: 103–128.

Cordova, E.P., & Elizarova, M. Your Thoughts Matter: Negative Self-Talk, Growth Mindset. Power of Yet, 2019.

DiTerlizzi, A., and Lorena, A. (2020). *The Magical Yet* (1st ed.). Los Angeles: Disney-Hyperion, 2020.

Duke, N.K., & Cartwright, K.B. (2021). The science of reading progresses: Communicating advances beyond the simple view of reading. *Reading Research Quarterly* 56 S25–S44. https://doi.org/10.1002/rrq.41.

Evans, V. (2015). The Crucible of Language: *How Language and Mind Create Meaning*. Cambridge University Press.

Fernyhough, C. & Borghi, A. (2023) Inner speech as language process and cognitive tool. *Trends in Cognitive Sciences* 27 (12): 1180–1193.

Feurer, E., Saussu, R., Cimeli, P., & Roebers, C. (2015). Development of meta-representations: procedural metacognition and the relationship to theory of mind. *Journal of Educational and Developmental Psychology* 5 (1).

Gall, M.D., Gall, J.P., Jacobsen, D.R., & Bullock, T.L. (1990). *Tools for Learning: A Guide to Teaching Study Skills*. Association for Supervision and Curriculum Development.

Garner, R. (1988). *Metacognition and Reading Comprehension*. Norwood, NJ: Ablex.

Georgiou, G K., & Das, J.P. (2018). Direct and indirect effects of executive function on reading comprehension in young adults. *Journal of Research in Reading* 41 (2): 243–258. https://doi.org/10.1111/1467-9817.12091.

Goldstein, S., & Naglieri (eds.) (2014). *Executive Functioning Handbook*. New York: Springer.

Green, B.C., Johnson, K.A., Bretherton, L. (2014). Pragmatic language difficulties in children with hyperactivity and attention problems: An integrated view. International Journal of Language and Community Disorders 49 (1): 15–29.

Hammond, L., & Moore, W.M. (2018). Teachers taking up explicit instruction: The impact of a professional development and directive instructional coaching model. *Australian Journal of Teacher Education* 43 (7). http://dx.doi.org/10.14221/ajte.2018v43n7.7.

Hanham, J., Leahy, W., & Sweller, J. (2017). Cognitive load theory, element interactivity, and the testing and reverse testing effects. *Applied Cognitive Psychology* 31 (3): 265–280. https://doi.org/10.1002/acp.3324.

Helliwell, J.F. (2003). How's life? Combining individual and national variables to explain subjective well-being. *Economic Modelling* 20 (2): 331–360, ISSN 0264-9993, https://doi.org/10.1016/S0264-9993(02)00057-3.

Hollingsworth, J. & Ybarra, S. (2009). *Explicit Direct Instruction: The Power of the Well-Crafted, Well-Taught Lesson*. Corwin Press. doi: 10.4135/9781452218977.

Jones, K. (2020). *Retrieval Practice: Resources and Research for Every Classroom*. United Kingdom: John Catt Educational Limited.

Jordan, D., Jordan, R.M., & Nelson, K. (2000). *Salt in His Shoes: Michael Jordan in Pursuit of a Dream*. New York: Simon & Schuster Books for Young Readers.

Kapa, L.L., & Plante, E. (2015). Executive function in SLI: Recent advances and future directions. *Current Developmental Disorders Report* 2 (3): 245–252.

Kasser, T., & Ryan, R.M. (1996). Further examining the American dream: Differential correlates of intrinsic and extrinsic goals. *Personality and Social Psychology Bulletin* 22 (3): 280–287. https://doi.org/10.1177/0146167296223006.

McCloskey, G., Perkins, L.A., & VanDivner, B. (2009). *Assessment and Intervention for Executive Function Difficulties*. New York: Routledge Press.

Meltzer, L., Reddy, R., Pollica, L.S., Roditi, B., Sayer, J., & Theokas, C. (2004). Positive and negative self–Perceptions: Is there a cyclical relationship between teachers' and students' perceptions of effort, strategy use, and academic performance? *Learning Disabilities Research and Practice* 19 (1): 33–44. https://doi.org/10.1111/j.1540-5826.2004.00087.x.

Morin, A. (2018). The self-reflective functions of inner speech: Thirteen years later. In: *Inner Speech: New Voices* (ed. P. Langland-Hassan and A. Vicente), 276–298, Oxford University Press.

Pajares, F., & Schunk, D. (2001). Self-beliefs and school success: Self-efficacy, self-concept, and school achievement. In: *International Perspectives on Individual Differences: Self-Perception* (vol. 2) (ed. R.J. Riding, & S.G. Rayner), 239–265. Westport, CT: Ablex.

Pressley, M., & Afflerbach, P. (1995). *Verbal Protocols of Reading: The Nature of Constructively Responsive Reading*. Lawrence Erlbaum Associates, Inc.

Rosenshine, B. (2010). *Principles of Instruction*. Educational Practices Series 21. The International Academy of Education.

Rosenshine, B. (2012) Principles of instruction: Research-based strategies that all teachers should know. *American Educator* 36 (1): 12–39.

Rosenshine, B., & Stevens, R. (1986). Teaching functions. In *Handbook of Research on Teaching* (3rd ed) (ed. M.C. Wittrock), 376–391. New York: Macmillan.

Ruiz-Martin, H., Blanco, F., Ferrero, M. (2024). Which learning techniques supported by cognitive research do students use at secondary school? Prevalence and associations with students' belief and achievement. *Cognitive Research: Principles and Implications* 9 (1): article 44.

Santat, D. *After the Fall: How Humpty Dumpty Got Back Up Again* (1st ed.). New York: Roaring Brook Press, 2017.

Schroder, S.E., & Yu, C. (2022). Looking is not enough: Multimodal attention supports the real time learning of new words. *Developmental Science* 26 (2): article e13290.

Sheldon, K.M., & Elliot, A.J. (1999). Goal striving, need satisfaction, and longitudinal well-being: The self-concordance model. *Journal of Personality and Social Psychology* 76 (3): 482–497. doi: 10.1037//0022-3514.76.3.482.

Spencer, M., Richmond, M.C., & Cutting, L.E. (2020). Considering the role of executive function in reading comprehension: a structural equation modeling approach. *Scientific Studies of Reading* 24 (3): 179–199.

Steinberg, L. (2014). *Age of Opportunity: Lessons from the New Science of Adolescence*. New York: First Mariner Books.

Spencer, M., & Cutting, L.E. (2021). Relations among executive function, decoding, and reading comprehension: An investigation of sex differences. *Discourse Processes* 58 (1): 42–59.

Talbani, S. (2023). Fostering active learning and metacognitive skills in a cognitive-science-based math course. *International Journal of Teaching and Learning in Higher Education* 35 (2): 209–218. http://www.isetl.org/ijtlhe/.

Tanner, K. (2012). Promoting student metacognition. *CBE Life Sciences Education* 11 (2): 113–120. https://www.scienceopen.com/document?vid=cfeee266-a97a-4a9a-a73d-aae1 84172fbe.

Chapter 12

Americans with Disabilities Act—Testing Accommodations. https://www.ada.gov/regs2014/testing_accommodations.pdf.

Americans with Disabilities Act 1990 (PL-101-336).

British Dyslexia Association. (2023). Dyslexia style guide. https://cdn.bdadyslexia.org.uk/uploads/documents/Advice/style-guide/BDA-Style-Guide-2023.pdf?v=1680514568.

Cartwright, K.B., Lee, S.A., Taboada Barber, A., DeWyngaert, L.U., Lane, A.B., & Singleton, T. (2020). Contribution of executive function and intrinsic motivation to university students' reading comprehension. *Reading Research Quarterly* 55 (3): 345–369. https://doi.org/10.1002/rrq.273.

Center for Parent Information and Resources. https://www.parentcenterhub.org.

Council of Parent Attorneys and Advocates. https://www.copaa.org.

Decoding Dyslexia. https://www.decodingdyslexia.net.

Duke, N.K., & Carwright, K.B. (2021). The science of reading progresses: Communicating advances beyond the simple view of reading. *Reading Research Quarterly* 56 (S1): S25–S44. https://ila.onlinelibrary.wiley.com/doi/full/10.1002/rrq.411.

Fletcher, J.M., Coulter, W.A., Reschly, D.J., & Vaughn, S. (2004). Alternative approaches to the definition and identification of learning disabilities: Some questions and answers. *Annals of Dyslexia* 52 (2): 304–331.

Gerber, P.J., Reiff, H.B., Ginsberg, R. (1996). Reframing the learning disabilities experience. *Journal of Learning Disabilities* 29 (1): 98–101. doi: 10.1177/002221949602900112.

High-Stakes Assessment (Teaching LD). https://www.ldonline.org/ld-topics/teaching-instruction/helping-students-ld-pass-high-stakes-tests.

Individual with Disabilities Education Improvement Act (IDEA). (2004). (PL 108-446); Section 504 of the Rehabilitation Act Amendments of 1998 Act Amendments of 1998.

International Dyslexia Association. (2020). Accommodations for students with dyslexia. https://dyslexiaida.org/accommodations-for-students-with-dyslexia.

Lee, A. (2024). Accommodations, modifications, and alternative assessments: How they affect instruction and assessment. https://www.greatschools.org/gk/articles/accommodations-iep/.

Lee, A.M.I. (n.d.). Accommodations: What they are and how they work. *Understood for All*. https://www.understood.org/en/articles/accommodations-what-they-are-and-how-they-work.

Lyon, G.R., Shaywitz, S.E., Shaywitz, B.A. (2003). A definition of dyslexia. *Annals of Dyslexia* 53: 1–14.

Mercer, C. (2002). Accommodating students with dyslexia in all classroom settings. *International Dyslexia Association*. https://www.readingrockets.org/topics/dyslexia/articles/accommodating-students-dyslexia-all-classroom-settings.

National Center on Educational Outcomes. (2011). Forum on Accommodations in the 21st Century: Critical Considerations for Students with Disabilities. https://nceo.umn.edu/docs/OnlinePubs/AccommodationsForumReport2011.pdf.

National Center on Improving Literacy. https://improvingliteracy.org.

National Center for Learning Disabilities. http://www.ncld.org.

Raskind, M.H., Gerber, P.J., Goldberg, R.J., Higgins, E.L., & Herman, K.L. (1998). Longitudinal research in learning disabilities: Report on an international symposium. *Journal of Learning Disabilities* 31: 266–278.

Raskind, M.H., Goldberg, R.J., Higgins, E.L., & Herman, K.L. (1999). Patterns of change and predictors of success in individuals with learning disabilities: Results from a twenty-year longitudinal study. *Learning Disabilities Research & Practice* 14 (1): 35–49.

Reiff, H.B., Gerber, P.J., & Ginsberg, R. (1997). *Exceeding Expectations: Successful Adults with Learning Disabilities*. Pro-Ed.

Shaywitz, S. (2020). *Overcoming Dyslexia: A New and Complete Science-Based Program for Reading Problems at Any Level* (2nd ed.). New York: Alfred A. Knopf.

Sweller, J. (1980). Hypothesis salience, task difficulty, and sequential effects on problem solving. *The American Journal of Psychology* 93 (1): 135–145. https://doi.org/10.2307/1422109.

Sweller, J. (1994). Cognitive load theory, learning difficulty, and instructional design, *Learning and Instruction* 4 (4): 295–312. https://doi.org/10.1016/0959-4752(94)90003-5.

Wehmeyer, M.L. (1996). Self-determination as an educational outcome: Why is it important to children, youth, and adults with disabilities? In: *Self-Determination Across the Lifespan: Independence and Choice for People with Disabilities* (ed. D.J. Sands & M.L. Wehmeyer), 17–36. Baltimore: Paul H. Brookes Publishing Co.

Werner, E.E., & Smith, R.S. (1992). *Overcoming the Odds: High Risk Children from Birth to Adulthood*. Ithaca, NY: Cornell University Press.

Chapter 13

Beaty, A. (2021). *Aaron Slater, Illustrator: A Picture Book*. Harry N. Abrams.

Betancourt, J. (1995). *My Name is Brain Brian* (reprint ed.). Scholastic Paperbacks.

Brissett-Bailey, M. (2023). *Black, Brilliant and Dyslexic*. Jessica Kingsley Publishers.

Chew, S. (2024). Establishing class norms that promote learning. https://www.teachingprofessor.com/topics/student-learning/establishing-class-norms-that-promote-learning/.

Colvin. A. (2016). *Looking for Heroes: One Boy, One Year, 100 Letters* (2nd ed.) CreateSpace Independent Publishing Platform.

Deen, N. (2016). *Lark Holds the Key* (series) (high readability ed.). Orca Book Publishers.

Dyslexia Help. https://dyslexiahelp.umich.edu/successful-dyslexics.

Engle, M. (2014). *The Wild Book* (reprint ed.). Clarion Books.

Feiner, B. (2019). *Dyslexic Legends Alphabet*. Alphabet Legends.

Fortune, T. *Did You Say Pasghetti?: Dusty and Danny Tackle Dyslexia*. Tammy Fortune.

Gaynor, K. (2013). *Tom's Special Talent* (1st ed.) Special Stories Publishing.

Goodling, L. (2023). *Wonderfully Wired Brains: An Introduction to the World of Neurodiversity*. DK Children.

Greene, J. (2016). *My Gift of Difference: 7 Steps to Embracing Your Learning Difference*. CreateSpace Independent Publishing Platform.

Greibelbauer, A. (2020). *D is for Darcy: Not Dyslexia* (2nd ed.) Passage Press.

Hardiman, M. (2003). Connecting Brain Research with Effective Teaching: The Brain-Targeted Teaching Model. Lanham, MD: Rowman & Littlefield Education.

Harris, A. (2020). *Magnificent Meg: A Read-Aloud to Encourage Children with Dyslexia.* Garden Bench Publications.

Helland, S.S., Roysamb, E., Brandlistuen, R.E., Melby-Lervag, M., & Gustavson, K. (2020). A common family factor underlying language difficulties and internalizing problems: Findings from a population-based sibling study. *Journal of Learning Disabilities* 53 (5):399–409. https://doi.org/10.1177/0022219420911634.

Horbach, J., Mayer, A., Scharke, W., Heim, S., & Gunther, T. (2020). Development of behavior problems in children with and without specific learning disorders in reading and spelling from kindergarten to fifth grade. *Scientific Studies of Reading* 24 (1):57–71. https://doi.org/10.1080/10888438.2019.1641504.

Hultquist, A.M. (2013). *Can I Tell You About Dyslexia?: A Guide for Friends, Family and Professionals.* Jessica Kingsley Publishers.

Hunt, L. (2017). *Fish in a Tree* (reprint ed.). Nancy Paulsen Books.

Jones, M. (2015). *Dyslexia Explained: Without the Need for Too Many Words.* Nessy Learning. ISBN 10: 0956004229 ISBN 13: 9780956004222.

Lupica, M. (2009). *Two-Minute Drill (Comeback Kids)* (reprint ed.). Viking Books for Young Readers.

Meijering, G. (2011). *Hacking the Code: The Ziggety Zaggety Road of a Dyslexic Kid.* iCare Press.

Moore-Mallinos, J. (2007). *It's Called Dyslexia.* B.E.S. Publishing.

Peterson, T. (2021). *Cartwheels: Finding Your Special Kind of Smart.* Et Alia Press.

Pimentel, A. (2020). *All the Way to the Top: How One Girl's Fight for Americans with Disabilities Changed Everything.* Sourcebooks Explore.

Polacco, P. (2010). *Junkyard Wonders.* Philomel Books.

Polacco, P. (2012). *Thank You, Mr. Falker.* Philomel Books.

Prestidge, S. (2021). *Finding My Superpower: A Book for Dyslexic Thinkers.* The National Library of New Zealand.

Riordan, R. (2006). *Percy Jackson and the Olympians* (series). Miramax.

Robb, D.B. (2004). *The Alphabet War.* Albert Whitman & Co.

Robinson, S., & Robinson, I. (2023). *Dr. Dyslexia Dude.* Independently published.

Rudolph, S. (2021). *Brilliant Bea: A Story for Kids With Dyslexia and Learning Differences* (1st ed.) Magination Press.

Smith, K. (2019). *I Define Me.* Independently published.

Talbot, H. (2021). *A Walk in the Words*. Nancy Paulsen Books.

Travers, S. (2025). *A Kids Book About Dyslexia*. DK Children.

Weltner, K. (2024). *Molly Tells the World: A Book About Dyslexia and Self-Esteem* (1st ed.). Free Spirit Publishing.

White, C. (2019). *The Hoopstar*. Authorhouse.

Winkler, H. (2019). *Hank Zipzer: The World's Greatest Underachiever* (series) Walker Books.

Yale Center for Dyslexia and Creativity. https://dyslexia.yale.edu/success-stories/?sscat=artists-architects-designers.

Acknowledgments

So many people have contributed to bringing this book to life, each contributing to the direction of my path in education and beyond, and for that, I am grateful for each experience, which provided me with insights, reflection, and opportunities for growth as an educator and human.

I owe a debt of gratitude to the mentors and colleagues who have been my pillars of support throughout my educational journey. Your wisdom, patience, and encouragement have not only guided my professional growth but also shaped me as a person. Your insights have not just enriched my understanding but also bolstered my confidence to take on new challenges. I am deeply appreciative of your role in my life.

To my numerous colleagues, I am continually inspired by your unwavering passion, collaborative spirit, and dedication to our shared mission of fostering growth and advocating for those with dyslexia. Your commitment is a constant source of motivation for me, and I am grateful for the opportunity to work alongside such dedicated individuals.

A special thanks to Emily Gibbons, with whom I have shared endless text messages and passionate conversations both on our podcast and over the phone. I am forever grateful for the world bringing us together in the name of dyslexia and literacy.

A sincere thank you to Katy Vassar, my trusted partner in many endeavors and sounding board. Your knowledge and dedication to dyslexia education and evaluations are invaluable. Our shared vision has enriched my experience and created a community where ideas thrive.

My editor and team at Jossey-Bass—Pete Gaughan, Amy Fandrei, and Sophie Thompson—were supportive, patient, and gracious with this new author, and I am grateful for that. Thanks to editors Danielle Noble and Mike Isralewitz for your thoughtful and helpful suggestions.

Thank you to you, reader, for you all have contributed to a foundation of support and inspiration that I will forever carry with me. Thank you for your guidance, encouragement, and belief in me.

To the students I've had the privilege to serve, I owe a debt of gratitude. You've taught me more about dyslexia and the profound connections between the heart and mind than I could have ever imagined. Your courage, perseverance, and unique perspectives have been my greatest lessons, shaping not only my understanding but also my purpose in this field.

To the families who have entrusted me and walked alongside me on this journey, I want to express my deep appreciation. Your partnership and belief in the power of growth and understanding have been invaluable. Together, we share a mission to nurture potential and celebrate every milestone along the way.

Finally, I would like to thank my family, who endured countless late nights and sacrificed personal time to allow me to complete this project. My husband, Justin, thank you for encouraging me to take this leap and share my passions with the world. I am grateful to my three girls, Harper, Tatum, and Hunter, for your unwavering support and for constantly reminding me of the beauty of learning from one another. Your curiosity, resilience, and encouragement inspire me daily to grow and bring out the best in myself and those around me. You are my greatest teachers, and I am endlessly grateful for the lessons of love, patience, and perspective you bring into my life.

About the Author

Casey Harrison, founder of The Dyslexia Classroom and Wimberley Dyslexia & Learning Center, is a Certified Academic Language Therapist (Academic Language Therapy Association, ALTA), Licensed Dyslexia Therapist (LDT-TX), Certified Structured Literacy Dyslexia Specialist (International Dyslexia Association), and a qualified teacher with nearly three decades of teaching experience. She works with parents, teachers, and pre-K–12 students at her private practice, providing dyslexia therapy, literacy instruction, consultation, resources, and training. She also sits on the National Board of the Academic Language Therapy Association. In addition to her private practice, she co-hosts a podcast, Together in Literacy, which focuses on dyslexia, literacy instruction, and the whole child. She is a national presenter, author, and course creator. Her dedication to advocating for all students, especially those with dyslexia, and highlighting the connection between academics and the social-emotional well-being of students with learning differences is evidenced in her work. She lives in Texas with her husband, their three daughters, and many animals in their little slice of the country.

Index

Page numbers followed by *f* refer to figures.